Wells, Evelyn
Hatshepsut. Doubleday, c1969.
287p. il. Photos.

T

1. Hatshepsut, d. 1468 B.C. 2. Egypt--History.

Books by Evelyn Wells

HATSHEPSUT

A CITY FOR ST. FRANCIS

NEFERTITI

THE GENTLE KINGDOM OF GIACOMO

JED BLAINE'S WOMAN

WHAT TO NAME THE BABY

THE FORTY NINERS (with Harry Peterson)

LIFE STARTS TODAY

MEN AT THEIR WORST (with Dr. Leo Stanley)

FREMONT OLDER, A BIOGRAPHY

CHAMPAGNE DAYS OF SAN FRANCISCO

HATSHEPSUT

by

EVELYN WELLS

1969

DOUBLEDAY & COMPANY, INC.

GARDEN CITY, NEW YORK

Library of Congress Catalog Card Number 69–10980

Printed in the United States of America
First Edition

To
Darcy Anne Stevens
with my love

ILLUSTRATIONS

[Following page 192]

ACKNOWLEDGMENTS

I wish to express my thanks to those heads of Egyptian ministries who invited me to research the history of Hatshepsut in Egypt and who assisted and befriended me while there. Foremost among these is His Excellency Sarwat Okasha, who has given such generous representation of Egypt's treasures to other countries, including his sponsoring of the Tutankhamon exhibit that toured the United States.

For kindnesses shown and interest displayed I am grateful to the Honorable Abdel Moneim El Sawi, Under Secretary of State for the Ministry of Cultural and National Guidance; General Anwar El Asar, in charge of antiquities for all Egypt, and Dr. A. Shoukry, Director General of the Antiquities Service.

Others remembered with gratitude are Dr. H. S. K. Bakry, Director of Inspectates and Excavations at the Museum of Cairo, for research advice and the pleasure of reading his invaluable contributions to Egyptian history; Miss Abou-Ghazi Dia, Curator of the Library of the Museum of Cairo for her comprehensive study of the royal mummies and her knowledge of all writings concerning Hatshepsut; Mohammed Selah, the delightful and dedicated young Inspector General of the Inspectorate and Antiquities Department at Western Thebes with whom I had the pleasure of visiting the excavations there and the tombs and shrines of Hatshepsut's time and her temple at Deir el-Bahari.

I cherish invaluble memories of friends who introduced me to an Egypt old and new; Adel Ahmed Sabet, General Director of Scientific Relations with the Higher Council of Scientific Research and his wife Gazbia Sirry, the foremost woman artist of

Egypt, with whom I saw the pyramids at Giza; the family of General and Mrs. Abdel-Fattah A. Ismail whose lovely daughter Afaf, married to Dr. Samy Shafick of the Cairo Hospital, showed me the unbelievable monuments at Saqqara; Abdel Fattah Eid, whose photographs of Egypt will some day dazzle countries outside his own.

I am indebted to conversations with archaeologists of many lands I met on the sites, the best remembered being an interview at Karnak with Professor Charles Nims, Field Director of Epigraphic Survey of the Oriental Institute of the University of Chicago, who has written so much and so brilliantly of his discoveries in ancient Thebes and whose Hatshepsut findings may be considered the last word on that great lady.

In the United States overdue thanks go to those who gave their kindly interest and introductions to friends in Egypt, Miss Betty Izant formerly of the Huntington Hartford Foundation, and Albert and Pamela Moore of Seattle.

The spelling of ancient Egyptian names are in conflict so I have used the versions that please me, and the dates used are taken from the writings of Professor Nims and Dr. Bakry's New Kingdom list.

I find myself unable to express the gratitude owed to a great man gone, James Henry Breasted, from whose Ancient Records much of Hatshepsut's story has been reconstructed, and which remain the source and inspiration of anyone attempting to write about early Egypt.

HATSHEPSUT

CHAPTER 1

She was a woman of great force of character; and if her portraits speak true, she was endowed with beauty and charm as well.
—Dr. M. A. Murray

On the right as you enter the Metropolitan Museum in New York a large, crouching Sphinx guards the entrance to the Egyptian wing. The lion shape is that which the kings of ancient Egypt assumed to symbolize their royal power.

The stone face is that of Queen Hatshepsut.

It is the face of a strong and beautiful woman. The stone eyes, intelligent and set far apart, meet yours with serenity. The expression is calm and imperious. The beautifully cut mouth is that of a voluptuous woman. This feature, as in all Hatshepsut's portraits, testifies that she was spared the protruding upper teeth that were a family characteristic during her Eighteenth Dynasty.

This statue once stood guard before her memorial chapel at Deir el-Bahari in Western Thebes. It is one of the many Hatshepsut had carved of herself in the image of the Sphinx, the god that was always male and whose shape she as a woman had no right to assume. But she claimed that right, as she did the right to wear male clothing from her childhood, and with it another symbol of divine masculine power, the unbecoming gold beard that is often shown strapped to her delicately rounded chin.

Still she remains to us feminine and appealing. Her wisdom and charm are stressed by the ancient records and by all authorities of Egyptiana. Her beauty is preserved in the many statues, paintings, and stelae Hatshepsut posed for during her lifetime. The sculptors and artists of her time were skilled in portraiture. Reproductions of her face with the good strong features and Platonic eyes are in all the great museums. We know she posed for the greatest artists of her time, ordered and approved the portraits, and doubtless smoothed with a jeweled hand this stone image of herself that is now at the door of the Metropolitan.

One cannot meet the great inquiring eyes without wonder. Who was this woman who made herself the most powerful leader of her world and time and dared to crown herself not queen, but *king* of the two Egypts?

My search to find the answers started with the Sphinx statue one afternoon in the Museum. Through the thick walls, the sound of traffic came snow-muffled from outer Fifth Avenue, The stone face with the great unwinking eyes held a silence as antique as her own Egypt. What could I learn about Hatshepsut? How much is known of her?

She lived three and a half thousand years ago, but her personality is vivid to all interested in Egypt, where both the savant and the man of the street speak of Hatshepsut as if she lived yesterday. Her wisdom and political acumen, her good deeds and sensational achievements, her early loves, and, above all, her beauty, are endlessly discussed.

It is often observed that Egypt is the best documented of all the ancient lands. The Eighteenth is its most carefully recorded dynasty. We have more intimate knowledge of Hatshepsut than of our great-grandmothers. Preserved for us on stone are the details of her career as royal heiress (or crown prince) as queen (or king), her patriotic and religious motivations, her face and form, strength and weaknesses, petty vanities and noble pride. In many places her name has been hacked away and that of a later monarch substituted. But that was ever the way with kings, and always, by error or design, a clue was left so that we may know, this was Hatshepsut!

She was an outstanding regent early in the Eighteenth Dynasty, which was the richest and most powerful of the Egyptian dynasties. She became supreme ruler circa 1490 B.C. This was long before the appearance of two of her famous descendants, King Akhenaton and his beautiful Nefertiti, whose story I had written. Hatshepsut preceded them by centuries, still we know as much about her as we do about these later dark-starred members of her family line.

To trace her life story would mean the searching of many records. The hunt would be careful and long. It would take me into libraries and archives and museums in many countries, up rocky hillsides and over desert sand, through the ruins of temples and shrines and tombs—in all, a detective search of more than thirty thousand miles.

There would be the fitting together of notes made of hieroglyphic translations taken from papyrus scrolls, clay tablets and monuments, from the walls of temples, chapels, public and private buildings, and the walls of tombs, from stelae, statues, wine jugs, vases, boxes, jewelry, and amulets. There would be a remembered montage of people and places and objects she once knew, and many photographs and paintings. Fitted into her history must be Egypt's, gleaned during years of absorbed study in the country's art and architecture and literature. Fascinated attention would be given to the portraits of Hatshepsut in the art galleries of the principal cities of the United States and Europe, and, notably, Egypt.

We are assured of the pictures' accuracy. Egyptian art reached its highest peak during her dynasty. A photographic study of the face of the mummy of Thothmes III placed against the carved face of one of his statues in the Cairo Museum showed the proportions to be exact. So we can put our faith in the art studies of Hatshepsut.

What more do we know of her?

Of utmost importance are the writings and translations of the great authorities who went before us along Hatshepsut's way. Their opinions fitted together form a composite portrait of a delightful child, a charmingly active adolescent, and a woman deep in ambition and love. There emerges the moving semblance of a queen who, in the words of her Theban epitaph, was "more beautiful than anything."

This appraisal was probably dictated and certainly approved by Hatshepsut herself. Egyptian royalty was never modest. Some ancient monarchs went overboard in self-approval. Hatshepsut's own accounts of herself and activities were colorful, but they tell the truth. Her accomplishments were remarkable, and she described them as they were. Her admitted good looks were recorded with equal simplicity. All we observe and read agrees to her being one of the great beauties and leaders of her world and time.

Christiane Desroches-Noblecourt refers to her as "the world's first great queen," while Breasted, the most revered of all Egyptologists, immortalized her in a single line:

"The first great woman in history, Queen Hatshepsut."

His appraisal taunted me as I studied the impassive stone face in the Metropolitan Museum. That serene expression had perplexed the world for centuries. The source of its serenity, and the elements that had gone into the making of this woman, were mysteries I was determined to solve.

When I left the building, the snow had thickened on Fifth Avenue, and traffic had all but come to a standstill. The obelisk of her arch enemy Thothmes III, brought from Thebes to stand behind the Metropolitan Museum in Central Park, was veiled in falling snow.

That evening, my plane lurched up from the International Airport into a cosmic flurry of white waste. It was the worst blizzard of the year.

With a celerity that would have seemed pure magic to a Hatshepsut whose ships and chariots were the fleetest vehicles of her time, I found myself on the following night looking down from the window of a Cairo hotel onto a dark block of a building outlined against a moon-glimmering Nile. Within those massive walls were the opening clues to the mystery of Egypt's strongest-minded queen.

In the morning, having survived a dazzle of Egyptian sunlight and frantic city traffic, I entered the Cairo Museum and began my search for the intimate story of Queen Hatshepsut.

Room Fifty-two on the upper floor of the Cairo Museum has been called "the most personality-haunted room in the world." A plain, too well-lighted room, it is completely filled with glass cases. In these, row on row, are aligned the collection of royal mummies that is considered Egypt's greatest archaeological find.

This is the world-famous depository of royal death.

The cases are narrow as coffins and rest on standards so low that we look directly down into the mummified faces of twenty-nine men and women who were the leading kings and queens of ancient Egypt.

The personalities of the dried and withered forms permeate the vast interior of the Museum. The history of Egypt is crowded into this great, shadowy building. Out of the gloom emerge the images and possessions of those who exulted in life many centuries gone. Here are the statues, often disconcertingly lifelike, of those who were great and near-great before the birth of Christ. Around them, crowding the halls and rooms and corridors, are articles they once cherished: furnishings of the home or grave, clothing, footgear, funerary articles, bibelot, dishes, jewelry, weapons, and tools. The mummified pets they loved are here. A hound preserved in his own tawny hide seems preparing to spring from his glass cage to a master's whistle stilled for thousands of years. Each artifact adds to our knowledge of personalities who shared a supreme civilization long before Europe or America began.

Among these, the powerful personality of Hatshepsut appears in many ways. Her Sphinx statues crouch with masterful force. Other statues, paintings, and bas relief show her slender feminine body in male attire or in the garb of a god. The lovely, thoughtful features are usually marred by the royal male beard. Members of her family are represented. There are inscriptions concerning her, and articles she once touched, and even the handsome sarcophagi she ordered prepared for herself, her first one, when she was still very young, and another, equally impressive, made in her later years.

The crowded shelves in the carefully guarded museum library are treasure chests of information. Curator Dia apparently knows each book and its contents, and locates immediately the answers to questions concerning Hatshepsut and her people, as if they were known to her in life.

But it is in Room Fifty-two that the presence of Hatshepsut is felt most strongly. She dominates over and above the massed personalities of the long-dead kings and queens.

Once they, too, were Egypt. These are the all-powerful Pharaohs whose names and dynasties we memorized in history classes. Now we are seeing them immobilized, powerless in death, in a city called Cairo that was unknown in their time, many miles "downriver" from their, and Hatshepsut's, native city of Thebes.

"Macabre!" whispers an Egyptian friend as we study the calm, dry faces of the dead.

But not to me! Because there was a woman named Hatshepsut, and these are her people!

In this room her presence grows stronger, merging with her

illustrious dead, in a funeral-parlor silence so strong that even the groups of school children brought here by their teachers lower their shrill voices. Older visitors move quietly between the cases, silenced by the pressure of ancient death.

The leaf-dry faces under glass are darkened by preservatives and by the millennia spent underground. In many ways they resemble one another. All wear expressions of serenity, save for one who died the most violent of deaths.

Several unsealed lids reveal the glitter of glass eyes. Many of the withered hands are flexed as if they still gripped the royal crook and flail that once gave them powers of life and death over their subjects.

Several, both men and women, wear wigs. Some lips are rouged. Those of the Thothmesid, whose mouths are partly open, show the protruding upper teeth that were a family characteristic, a disfigurement Hatshepsut escaped. The closed mouth of "Amonhotep the Magnificent," the father of Akhenaton, conceals long-past agony in gums ravaged by disease.

Some of the bodies have been mutilated by the robbers that ransacked the treasure-filled graves. Royal fingers, hands, arms, legs, and even heads were ripped off in the ruthless hunt for jewels. One arm, torn off and tossed aside, still bears the imprint of its vanished bracelets. Perforated ears are slit where earrings were ripped away. A royal mummy was found torn into three parts. All that remains to the great ones are the resin-soaked remnants of the linen wrappings in which once were hidden, layer after layer, their personal fortunes in jewels, amulets, and tiny precious images of their gods.

Dr. Bakry has written, ". . . one may feel pity for them, seeing them stripped of their regalia and even of simple attire and only partially shrouded in the embalmer's wrappings and rags."

Each of these motionless forms was once a magnificent chapter in the history of Egypt. Man or woman, each sat arrogantly on the gold throne as the earthly counterpart of Re the sun god, not only regent, but in their own persons goddess or god.

As Hatshepsut took pride in being—a direct descendant of the sun!

The royal mummies in this room are the opening chapters in her history. What miracle brought them together here, from their secret tombs in the Theban hills?

If we were permitted to lift the glass covers of their cases, there would drift from the dry bodies the fragrance of spices thousands of years old. The preservative scents came from the coasts of Africa and Asia and from the fabulous land of Punt that Hatshepsut helped to make famous, and that added to her own fame. Such fragrances once tantalized the sensitive nostrils of Hatshepsut. Was there ever an Egyptian who did not love perfume? Hatshepsut's most notable achievement was motivated in part by her passion for myrrh.

The remarkable preservation of the mummies is due to these spices and other elements used in the art of mummification that reached its apex during the Eighteenth Dynasty, when such innovations were developed as removing the brains by means of a hook through the nostrils, and refilling the emptied abdomen with resin-soaked linen rags.

The discovery of these bodies is as much of a miracle as their preservation. They were found stacked together in two secret caches in Western Thebes. Curator Dia refers to these as the First and Second Discoveries.

The first was due to pure chance.

Rain is a rarity in middle Egypt, and on the western side of the Nile the hills and cliffs are arid ridges of stone and gravel, slashed through with the dry, sandy gullies that are those ancient royal burial sites known today as the Valleys of the Kings and Queens. But in the year 1875, rain drenched the bone-dry hills. Temporary torrents formed, and waterfalls rushed over the steep side of the cliff chosen by Hatshepsut more than three millennia before as the site of her greatest building project, Deir el-Bahari. A crevice in the side of the cliff was washed open.

After the downpour, a citizen of Thebes, a member of the highly placed family of El-Rassul, chanced to wander through the drying gullies. Looking up, he noticed the new opening. He climbed, investigated, knew. The rain had washed open a shaft in the cliff that led down into an ancient crypt, where, centuries before, Theban mortuary authorities had hidden a cache of royal mummies whose tombs had been despoiled by even more ancient grave robbers. The mummies retained their jewels.

During the next few years he and his family kept the secret of the tombs and grew rich. Other families found other tombs and grew rich. Grave-robbing was ever a family project in Egypt. Generations of Theban families benefited by and kept the secret of the tombs.

The fortunes taken from Egyptian tombs can never be estimated. Tutankhamon was one of the last and least of the kings of Hatshepsut's dynasty. The discovery of his tomb offered a glimpse of the wealth that must have been buried with the despoiled bodies in Room Fifty-two, of the jewels stolen, the gold coffins and grave furniture stripped of their gems and gold, and the gold melted down and sold. Antique shops all over the world welcomed loot from Egyptian tombs.

Worst of all from the archaeological point of view were the priceless records scattered or destroyed—forever lost.

Grave-robbing continued to be big business in Egypt until the year 1881, when the dedicated Egyptologist Gaston Maspero noticed that many of the small artifacts being peddled as souvenirs bore the cartouche marks of long-dead kings and queens. His suspicions were aroused, and he was able to communicate them to the Department of Antiquities. An official investigation exposed a situation that scandalized Egypt. One of the robber clan was persuaded while under arrest to reveal the valley source of his family's apparently inexhaustible wealth.

Forty-eight hours of official digging brought to light a cache of coffined kingly dead. The rescue was made under threat from predatory Thebans whose revenue was being cut off at the source, as well as by honest Thebans who were infuriated by an action they considered an invasion of the privacy of the dead. Fists and guns were shaken as the rag-wrapped bodies with the meager articles and sarcophagi that remained to them were carried to the western bank of the Nile. On July 14 the royal ones sailed downriver, away from Thebes, in the direction of Cairo. Kings and queens who had traveled the Nile in their resplendent royal barges were now inert cargo in boxes and rags.

The grisly cortège made its slow progress down the Nile, followed on the shore by men firing their guns at intervals, as is customary at Egyptian funerals, while the women keened their protests, casting dust on their tangled hair in the traditional ritual of mourning. The archaeologists had won at the risk of their lives.

So a delegation of the most famous Pharaohs of ancient Egypt came at last to Cairo, a city of which in their most grandiose planning they had never dreamed.

In this First Discovery were the bodies of kings outstanding in the dynastic lists. Among them were distinguished members of Hatshepsut's family.

These were King Sekenenre III, who had given his life in the first rebellion against the Hyksos; King Amose I, who resolved the war and founded the Eighteenth Dynasty; the great warrior and builder, Amonhotep I, and his three descendant kings named Thothmes, whose destinies were so strongly and strangely interwoven with Hatshepsut's.

Victor Loret made the Second Discovery in 1898 when he uncovered another royal hideaway in the Valley of the Kings. More of Hatshepsut's relatives were among the famous dead: Kings Amonhotep II and III, and Thothmes IV. These went prosaically to Cairo on the train.

In 1916 the arrest of another Theban grave robber led to the recovery of three Syrian princesses who had been secondary wives of Thothmes III. Hatshepsut would have known these women during her turbulent years with him.

In this way, slowly and carefully, the great ones of the past were brought together in Room Fifty-two in the Cairo Museum, which became their mausoleum, and, incidentally, Hatshepsut's family portrait gallery. It was opened to the public in the winter of 1959.

An amazed world could look with awe into the faces of men who had been masters of their world two, three, four thousand years before.

Of the twenty-nine bodies in this room, fifteen were related to Hatshepsut. They represent twelve generations of her line. Some were ancestors who lived far back in the Seventeenth Dynasty. Among the inert shapes are the warrior kings and their strong-minded queens who were the leaders of the most powerful dynasty ever to rule Egypt, in which she, Hatshepsut, played the strongest role.

Others followed her in the royal descent.

Ancestors, contemporaries, and descendants—what other family can we view entire, as it were, in the flesh? Hatshepsut would have been well tutored in the histories of her people. The ancestral faces would have been made familiar to her by the portraits and statues and records they left. History in Egypt was genealogical and composed of the accounts each ruler kept of his own life.

But she was never privileged to see many of these, as we can, and look upon face after face sealed in the dignity of death, and wonder, what did each contribute to her?

She thought them safe in the afterlife in their secret hiding places deep in the Theban hills. She thought them preserved in their multiple sarcophagi, surrounded by the treasures they had amassed in life. She pictured their hidden graves watched over by Anubis, the jackal-headed god-protector of the dead. She looked forward to similar security eternities long and began its preparation when she was very young.

Like all Egyptians, rich or poor, she cherished a prayer: "Grant me long life, oh Amon, an easy death, a resting place undisturbed."

Neither death nor vandalism have robbed Hatshepsut's people of their dignity. Their frail shapes have been pillaged and despoiled, but through them we glimpse the being and character of Hatshepsut.

To see her clearly we must move back with them through history, into a time centuries before she was born.

> No country in the ancient East has handed down its history so faithfully as Egypt . . . No other people have recorded so meticulously their important events, the activities of their rulers, their campaigns, the erection of temples and palaces, as well as their literature and poetry.
>
> —Werner Keller,
> *The Bible as History*

We study the faces of Hatshepsut's most ancient dead as she did their stone replicas. The fifteen representatives of her family share many good features. Dominant characteristics were emphasized in the royal line as the leaders practiced not only polygamy but marriage within families. Dr. Murray and others have pointed out the ways in which the system of consanguineous marriages has confused Egyptian history. It also confused Hatshepsut's personal history, and she herself, in her strong-mindedness, would confuse it even more.

Interfamilial marriage intensified family power, and we can follow the power line in Room Fifty-two that developed Hatshepsut's family into the strongest ever to rule Egypt. History holds no more complicated family tree. And still we can trace it, face after face, leading away from Hatshepsut back into the Seventeenth Dynasty.

Beyond these royal forefathers, as she and all Egyptians knew, loomed her heavenly ancestors, the eternal gods!

She would owe her dynamic personality to these people, and, above all, to three ancestresses who were outstanding in a line of powerful queens.

These women who so strongly influenced her life were never seen in life by Hatshepsut. But she was reared amid recorded praise of their influence over the kings whose lives and thrones they shared, and for their political acumen and the influence and powers they held without damage to their feminine image. The records describe the trio as lovely in appearance and dearly loved.

The first of Hatshepsut's three great ancestresses was Queen Tetisheri, who was the wife of King Sekenenre II, back in the Seventeenth Dynasty. They were the great-great-great-grandparents of Hatshepsut.

The only authentic portrait of Tetisheri is a small figure in the British Museum. It shows her as a young woman, delicate of body, beautiful of face. Also, a small mummy in the Cairo Museum may be hers. It is that of a very old woman, and it is known that she lived to be very old.

The kings of Hatshepsut's line married exceptional women, and Tetisheri's character was outstanding. She founded a long line of victorious warrior-kings and strong-minded queens. She was not of royal blood, but her life was regal. She needed her inborn courage. She lived in troubled and exciting times and played a dynamic role in tremendous change.

This was in the time of "the great humiliation." Egypt was held in bitter bondage by the Hyksos, those mysterious invaders of unknown origin, who, sometime in the eighteenth century B.C., had swarmed out of western Asia and down into Egypt by way of the Delta. They were like invading monsters. No one knew who they were or where they came from. They brought terrifying weapons made of bronze, which was unknown in Egypt, and war chariots drawn by horses, animals that no Egyptian had seen before. The Egyptians were gentle pastoral people who had never been asked to defend their rich, narrow, Nile-nourished land. They yielded in terror to the alien hordes.

The Hyksos stayed in Egypt. "Like mice in the wheat," the Egyptian historians described them. They razed and looted towns, raided farms, robbed, murdered, and enslaved. They built Hyksos garrisons and inflicted upon the Egyptians a series of puppet Egyptian kings manipulated by Hyksos kings.

A century passed, and another. The Egyptians stayed crushed, afraid to move under the Hyksos heel.

When revolt finally began, it started far from the Delta. Tetisheri in Thebes would have seen the beginning. It is only reasonable to believe she was among the early plotsters fomenting the rebellion that was spearheaded by her son, King Sekenenre III, whose body occupies one of the glass cases in Room Fifty-two.

Sekenenre III had been chosen by the Hyksos overlords to serve as their puppet king because he was the son of the respected royal pair, King Sekenenre II and Tetisheri. It was an unfortunate choice on the part of the Hyksos. Hatshepsut's great-great-grandfather was no puppet, but a young man of fury and fire.

Visitors linger in horror over his mummy. It is that of a man who died by violence while still in his thirties. Death has not sealed the marks of the final agony of the rebel king. The long, fragile-appearing skull is slashed by five deep wounds, probably made by battle-axe. Any one of these would have caused his death.

It is believed that Sekenenre received these wounds in battle action in 1575 B.C. in the revolt against the Hyksos that failed. Maspero, who unrolled the body in 1886 after the First Discovery, believed it to have been hastily embalmed, probably on the battlefield.

Hatshepsut, born long after, would have revered this rebel ancestor with special rites on the Day of the Dead, when, with all Egypt, she went into mourning for those who had died, or, as it was described, "gone into the West." And she doubtless learned with indignation the true details of an incident described on a fragment of papyrus that has baffled and amused students of Egyptiana.

The hieroglyphs describe a curious exchange of messages between King Sekenenre in his palace in Thebes, "the City in the South," and his Hyksos overlord, King Apophis, whose palace was in the Hyksos capital, Avaris, in the Delta.

The Hyksos messenger brought the first demand to Thebes:

"King Apophis . . . bids me say to you . . . get rid of the hippopotamus pool in the east end of your city. I cannot sleep for them. . . ."

The command was insulting and ridiculous. The sleep of the Hyksos king in his palace in the Delta could not possibly have been disturbed by the roaring of the royal hippopotami in the Theban palace zoo. The two cities were hundreds of miles apart. Temporarily, at least, the manuscript continues, the indignant Sekenenre curbed his temper. He did not punish the messenger, as another king might, or command his death. He ordered that the man be "treated with courtesy . . . given good things, with meat and cakes," and sent back to his Hyksos ruler with the pacifying words: "All that you have told me to do, I shall do."

Did he carry out his promise, or was it this insult from a foreign overlord that brought on King Sekenenre's rebellion against the Hyksos? We shall never know, for the papyrus reads, "then one and all remained silent for quite a while. . . ." And there, in the middle of a sentence, the paper is torn, and the report breaks off, and only the five deep battle wounds suggest a possible ending.

The rebellion did not end with the death of Sekenenre. His mother, Tetisheri, survived her martyred son. After his death, the full force of her personality was revealed when she devoted her love and influence to assist the extraordinary career of a son of her son who had died of the five wounds. This grandson took the Hyksos-ruled Egyptian throne circa 1570 B.C. under the name of King Amose I.

And with Amose the Eighteenth Dynasty began, and with it that triumphant division in history known as the New Kingdom.

Hatshepsut would revere the memory of her great-grandfather Amose. He was her most famous ancestor and the founder of her line. To history, he was "the glorious liberator," "the unifier of Egypt," "the great Conquerer," and "the final Conqueror." She would quiver with delicious terror as her teachers recited and court singers chanted the deeds of King Amose. She flamed with pride for his ruthlessness, his courage, and the terror he inspired in entire armies, so that when he approached across a battlefield, mace in hand and wearing on his forehead the flaming uraeus, the cobra crown, entire phalanxes of the armed enemy fell prone in the dust, immoblized with fear.

So she was told. So the historians wrote of Amose I.

There is nothing in his appearance now to inspire terror.

A small, meek-appearing man, Amose lies under glass near the mutilated mummy of his father, King Sekenenre III.

The body structure is delicate, like that of his grandmother, Tetisheri. He is less than five and a half feet tall. The nose is thin and arched, the skull narrow and covered with long brown curly hair, the hands and feet are narrow. Is there in that sleeping face a trace of Nubia? The wide, expressive mouth is slightly open, showing the first of the protruding upper teeth that would become a family characteristic. But the shoulders are broad, and the small form presents an innate appearance of power that is another dominant characteristic of Hatshepsut's line.

Maspero, who unwrapped the body of Amose, found it badly damaged by grave robbers. Limbs and wrappings had been torn off in the savage hunt for treasure. Wisps of linen are left to this great king whose appearance once caused his world to tremble and whose fortune was the greatest in that world.

Amose took the Theban throne after the death of his older brother, King Kamose, who had been made king by the Hyksos after Sekenenre III died in battle. Kamose followed his rebel father's attempt to protest the Hyksos rule, fought them, and lost. Then Kamose was dead, and Amose was made king. He must have been a mere teen-ager at the time, for he held the Egyptian throne until 1550, and his mummy is that of a man less than forty years old.

His was a meager inheritance. He took over a puppet throne in a captive Egypt, under alien kings who had been made furious by his father and brother's attempts at revolt. Theirs were deaths the boy-king determined to avenge.

In this, as in all he did, he was encouraged and advised by that Egyptian Medea, his widowed grandmother, the delicate and graceful Tetisheri.

The continuation of the revolt was planned as a campaign to the death. It had to be all-out victory, or the end of their family on the throne.

Somehow, without the Hyksos king in the Delta knowing, Amose organized a tremendous, well-trained army made up of Egyptian regulars, mercenaries, Asiatics, Negroes, and Nubians. Before the Hyksos overlords knew what was happening, a lethal struggle for independence was launched against them by Amose. He led his troops into the Delta, driving the Hyksos out of garrisons and towns, and reported his first major victory in proud words sent back to Thebes: "Avaris (the Hyksos capital) was taken!"

It was the first taste of victory. The thirst of Amose became unquenchable. All Egypt was aroused by the reports of his victories as he herded the Hyksos back over the border of the Egypt they had invaded three centuries before, until their armies "fled before his advancing steps, even to Asia, and southward, into the Sudan." As they fled, he followed, driven by the need for vengeance. His armies drove the Hyksos into western Asia and on, all the way to the Euphrates. He marched on, leading his men through Canaan. Palestine fell and became a province of Egypt.

The king of Kush was captured. The last of the Hyksos kings disappeared. The once-great Hyksos empire crumbled under the heel of Amose I. Wherever he marched, he conquered, and set up Egyptian garrisons to keep subject and enforce revenue from the newly captured lands.

Behind his fierce advance, the kingdom of Egypt swelled in size and power. Now it was becoming a great empire. The death by the five wounds had been avenged.

Egypt was free.

Amose was content. The struggle for independence ended. The two lands, north and south, so long divided, were joined by him into one country. His enriched and replete soldiers could hold firm the boundaries of an expanded and unified Egypt. Amose wore the double crown of the two Egypts, as sole regent, answerable to none, and, as one of the great conqueror-kings, he founded the Eighteenth Dynasty and fathered a line of royal heroes, who, upheld by invincible military power, would continue to rule an Egypt dedicated to prosperity and achievement.

The hated Hyksos became memories, but they had left behind them certain innovations the Egyptians would develop and cherish, such as bronze weapons and tools, and, above all, the horse and chariot, which would contribute greatly to the military effectiveness and private pleasures of all Egyptian kings starting with Amose I.

Amose maintained his great army. There were flurries of unrest from time to time. The Hyksos continued to threaten at intervals, and there were minor uprisings inside Egypt and in Nubia. He quelled these with an iron hand, and guaranteed the peace by ruling as wisely as he did in war.

He started a sprightly correspondence with rulers of other lands that widened the artistic and economic horizons of Egypt. The country grew steadily richer, in cattle, products, and world trade. Under his leadership, Egypt continued its rise to world power.

This Egyptian king, so ruthless in war, had his gentler artistic side. He was the first of his line to show the reverence for art and architecture that would be so strong a feature of the Thothmesid, including a girl named Hatshepsut, still unborn.

Amose restored temples that had been vandalized by the Hyksos. He refurnished them with idols and sacred possessions, and installed schools of priests to serve the gods.

He built, in part, the great temple of Amon at Karnak.

He directed the building of his own tomb in the Theban hills on the west side of the Nile, near the tombs of his Seventeenth Dynasty ancestors. He built largely, as he lived, but his cenotaph is the memorial temple he ordered for himself at Abydos. He could write with greater honesty than many of the others: "I have done more than any king before me."

We regard his quiet form in Room Fifty-two with the respect Hatshepsut felt for Amose, as did all Egyptians who lived in his time or who followed him. During the quarter century of his reign he changed his country's history and established himself as one of Egypt's great conqueror-kings.

His brilliant life has been overshadowed in history by the

effulgence shed by certain of his descendants, among them the girl Hatshepsut.

All that King Amose won, built, developed, or restored became part of the magnificent Egypt inherited by a great-granddaughter he never knew.

There was still another part of the inheritance Hatshepsut would receive from Amose I. This was the standard of respect he set for women and their abilities. It would aid Hatshepsut in developing her self-esteem, and it is still felt in the mores of Egypt. It began with the woman whose delicate form is preserved for us in the British Museum figurine.

Amose recorded his deep love for the women of his family, and, more astonishing, he gave them authoritative powers that equaled his own. He recorded their virtues and physical appeal. But the highest praise was reserved for his grandmother, Queen Tetisheri.

He preserved her memory on stone. He recorded the ways in which he had sought her advice, and how, during her long life, she never failed him. Her name is inscribed beside his on many monuments. He built a pyramid, a tomb, and a mortuary temple for her, and, at Abydos, a chapel staffed with priests. He made offerings to the gods and led prayers in her name, and planned other temples in her memory.

Amose must have ordered many portraits carved of her. Hatshepsut would have been familiar with the appearance of this great-great-great-grandmother. And still, only the small figure in London can be considered authentic.

Tetisheri was the first Egyptian Queen to bear the awesome title, "God's Wife of Amon," an honor Hatshepsut was to inherit—and discard.

And still, Hatshepsut would revere the memory of this great ancestress. She could stand in the vastness of the great temple at Karnak, and, looking up, read the hieroglyphic memento mori her great-grandfather Amose had ordered carved on his own stele:

"It is I, who have remembered the mother of my mother, the mother of my father, great king's wife and king's mother, Tetisheri, triumphant. . . ." This statement from the Seventeenth Dynasy testifies to the ancient tradition of inter-family marriage.

Hashepsut, princess of Thebes, reading the words generations later at Karnak, might tense her slender body with the need to be worthy of such an ancestress, to be as dearly loved and honored and praised in her own lifetime. And, when weary of life, she might be granted an easy death, and be placed safely in the arms of Osiris, surrounded by tremendous riches, where she would be remembered "for all the million million years."

She could look forward to a treasure-filled tomb, for she would be told of the riches Amose had hidden in the graves of the women he loved. Even more lasting were the tributes paid in words.

For his mother, Queen Ahotep I, he recorded his debt for her support and understanding, for himself and for Egypt, in peace and in war.

On his stele at Karnak he praised her: ". . . one who cares for Egypt . . . who has looked after her [Egypt's] soldiers; she has guarded her; she has brought back her fugitives and called together her deserters; she has pacified Upper Egypt, and expelled her rebels."

According to Charles Nims, Amose buried his mother with "the finest collection of jewelry, other than the Tutankhamon treasure, ever found at Thebes." The Cairo and other museums treasure the objects once owned by Ahotep, silver and gold jewelry set with turquoise and lapis lazuli and other stones, and curious oddments such as gold needles and the long gold tubes in which braids were inserted. There are many bracelets, worn by the women he loved and by Amose himself. The kings of Egypt were warriors; they took delight in jewelry created for them by the master goldsmiths. These gold and silver articles are often in such exquisite detail that one marvels how the jewelers could have fashioned them without magnifying lenses.

There was still a third queen beloved by Amose, who would be revered in memory by Hatshepsut.

Against the southern wall in Room Fifty-two lie the tragic bodies of Egyptian queens. Two of these were wives of Amose. They were found with his in the First Discovery.

One fragile form is that of a secondary wife, Queen Sitkamose. It is that of a woman less than thirty years old. Head and chest have been crushed by the robber despoilers. She was not of royal blood, and it is indicative of the kindness of Amose that he gave her the title of queen. But she was never the Great Wife, and she died without contributing either to Egypt's history or to Hatshepsut's, to whom she evidently bore a remote in-law relationship.

But the deepest marital love of Amose was expressed for another, whose mummy lies near that of Sitkamose in a togetherness neither wife would have tolerated in life. Queen Amose-Nefertari, Hatshepsut's great-grandmother, was probably his full sister; she is recorded as wholly royal. To her he awarded the most impressive titles borne until this time by any queen, including "God's Wife," and that first given Tetisheri, "Great Royal Wife."

The mummy of Nefertari is that of a woman who lived to be very old. She was five and a half feet tall. Her husband, the Great Conqueror, was smaller. Her bald head is concealed by a wig of twenty braids. The upper teeth protrude in the way now familiar.

Great honor was paid this queen while Amose lived. He recorded his gratitude to her for encouraging all his ambitions, and for helping to plan his many projects, including his own chapel at Abydos and the pyramid honoring his grandmother Tetisheri. He praised her for her devotion in paying honor to his ancestors, which were also hers. He raised her name on stone from Senai to Nubia. His stele at Karnak shows the royal pair with their son offering gifts to Amon. Until this time, even royal wives were usually pictured as much smaller than their husbands. They were shown as small, stiff, doll-like figures, with one hand grasping the arm or knee of their lord to show their dependency upon him. Nefertari, on this stele, is as large as Amose! As we have seen, she was taller.

Tetisheri! Ahotep! Nefertari! These were the royal three whose success as women and regents would set the pattern of life for Egyptian women that has lasted into the present day. Their strength of character would reappear in concentrated form in their slender young descendant, Hatshepsut.

Nefertari was still living when Amose died in 1550 B.C. Their son took the throne as Amonhotep I. The presence of Hatshepsut comes closer as we look at the dead face of this monarch, for Amonhotep was one she may have known in life.

He was her grandfather.

Amonhotep I was a true son of the great Amose. His mummy, with its stocky body, broad shoulders, and inevitable protruding teeth, might be a composite study made of all the Eighteenth Dynasty kings. The height is approximately theirs—five and one-half feet. Even in death there is that aura of tremendous physical assurance that was to appear dominant in Thothmes III.

With a vast kingdom, Amonhotep inherited his father's ideals in war and in peace. They were not easy to uphold. He was encouraged and advised by his widowed mother, Queen Nefertari. She supported him as she had his father, the Great Conqueror.

For although Egypt had become a storehouse of wealth under King Amose, the mice were still "nibbling in the wheat." The Hyksos had been driven out of Egypt, but they were still lurking on the rim of western Asia, nursing the hope of returning to the rich Egypt they had once conquered. It may be that their hopes were reactivated by word of the death of the once terrifying Amose, for warnings reached Thebes that the hated ones were massing armies outside the border. At the same time, flurries of protest started like fires in various places inside Egypt. Nubia, always restless, showed signs of rebellion.

It was the thankless task of the new king to restore order.

Amonhotep had been king only a few months when he was forced to leave his luxurious palace and quiet an uprising in Nubia. Nubia was the country's principal source of gold.

"With the energy for which his family was famous," he sailed with his armies up the Nile, annihilated the Nubian forces, made Nubia into a province, and subdued the "wretched land of Kush," thereby extending his kingdom up to the Third Cataract. He built a chain of garrisons along the Nile to guard the quarries and gold routes of the Sudan. He returned swiftly by ship to Thebes, bringing with him fortunes in battle bounty and cattle and slaves, and set out again to attend to growing unrest in the Delta.

Hatshepsut's grandfather was forced to re-fight and re-win crusades that had made his father famous. With armies built by Amose, along routes set by his father, Amonhotep led his armies out of the quieted Delta, and, evidently in the wake of the Amose campaigns, set out in pursuit of the still threatening Hyksos. He drove them farther and farther back into western Asia, all the way to the Euphrates.

Even with victory he did not cut down in size the great armies built by Amose. During his quarter century on the throne, Amonhotep maintained Egypt's military power, insured its peace, and helped develop its prosperity. He preserved

Thebes as the capital as established by Amose. Memphis was no longer the richest city. The patron god of Thebes, Amon-Re, who before this dynasty had been a local god of Thebes, had become the chief god of Egypt. Revenue flowed in to Amon and the king from every section of Egypt and its provinces. The priests gained in wealth and political power.

Amon was the recipient and the source. All good came from him. This Hatshepsut would believe, as did her grandfather, Amonhotep I.

The victories of Amonhotep I are long forgotten, but many of his works remain. Like all the kings of his line, he was a builder. He built with blocks of granite and bricks of sun-baked clay. He brought alabaster from the eastern mountains and slate from the Sudan. The child Hatshepsut would see in their newness, perhaps in their actual construction, many of the works left us by this tireless king.

He raised shrines and temples in upper Egypt. He built in the city of Thebes and in Western Thebes. A shrine of his remains in the great Temple of Karnak. On clearest alabaster against a double façade of white limestone are carved the words: "Amonhotep I, King Zeser-ka Re, son of the sun, living forever."

But even a king could not live forever. Royal or non-royal, rich or poor, all Egyptians while living had to plan for an abundant future after death. Hatshepsut's grandfather was no exception to the rule. With unlimited manpower, material, and funds, the kings had always built on a gigantic scale in Egypt, and always to insure their own immortality after death.

Amonhotep gave special attention to the necropolis on the left bank of the Nile. There he had seen his father safely to his grave. There were still other graves for Amonhotep to prepare for his mother, his many wives, and himself.

In keeping with family tradition, Amonhotep had married

two of his sisters or half sisters. Also in tradition he had other wives, including the non-royal Senseneb, of whom we shall hear later. The two most highly placed were the royal sisters Queen Ahotep II (Hatshepsut's grandmother), and Queen Meritamon. Of these three, only the mummy of Meritamon remains.

Hatshepsut as a child must have known Meritamon, for the body is that of a small woman who lived to be very old. It has been badly treated by robbers. The tiny wrinkled face wears a thoughtful expression. The hair, still dark, is neatly braided, and there is still to be observed the element of pride. Evidently this was a woman of orderly domestic habits. She was found with household articles, including dishes and a beer jar, at her feet, and around her body were bunches of tied persea leaves. Persea is a species of laurel.

Queen Meritamon outlived Amonhotep by many years. As a conscientious husband he would have planned for her burial while he lived.

The costliest final rites were planned well in advance for his mother, Queen Nefertari. She had been closely associated with him in all his projects. He gave full credit to her devotion, as had his father before him.

The construction of the royal graves required endless manpower. Amonhotep brought armies of mortuary workers—gravediggers, artisans, guards—to Western Thebes. Their families moved with them across the river. He installed the first workman's village at Abydos.

Nefertari died. In keeping with a growing tradition among Egyptian queens, she had outlived her husband by many years. She was given funeral honors befitting a great heroine by her son Amonhotep. Her mummified body was placed next to that of King Amose in the western necropolis. She would be worshiped there for centuries as guardian-goddess of the dead.

Amonhotep did not limit his west bank energies to the digging of graves. He raised a temple at Deir el-Bahari to the cow-goddess Hathor, the beloved deity who decided at birth the fate of every newborn child.

Was it the construction of this shrine that first drew Hatshepsut's attention to the magnificent site under the Theban tor?

Then King Amonhotep died, in 1528 B.C., and joined his royal ancestors in the west, close by the graves of the parents he had so lavishly and reverently buried. He would be worshiped with his mother in the necropolis as a co-guardian god.

His death was recorded in the customary terms: "His Majesty, having spent life in happiness and the years in peace, went forth to heaven; he joined the sun."

His is one of the few mummies to retain traces of the magnificent trappings a king took with him to his grave. Amonhotep's mummy was found during the First Discovery. His age is unknown, for the body was found in such perfect condition that Maspero and Elliot Smith left it in its funeral wrappings. He is believed to have lived between fifty and sixty years.

The wrappings hint at the splendor of his interment. Hatshepsut's parents would have seen to his goodly burial. The strips are of orange linen. The head and chest of Amonhotep are masked; his face is gilded.

He had served his country for more than twenty years and earned the right to the title, "the Conqueror." It had been won before him by his famous father. But his record, and that of Amose, was promptly overshadowed by the sturdy young prince who took his place on the throne and who augmented his own fame by being the father of that lovely young enigma named Hatshepsut.

For at last we have come to her place and time, in Room Fifty-two, and in history.

Following King Amonhotep in the mummy room and in descent are the four Thothmesid kings. One lived after Hatshepsut. The first three were closely related to her. She shared their common ancestry, their lives, their thrones, and, perhaps with each, their beds. Kings Thothmes I, and II, and III, rank among the greatest of the Eighteenth Dynasty kings. Once they were all important to Hatshepsut and to Egypt.

We study their impassive faces, so similar and still so unlike. These men are of similar physical structure and features. She knew them, heard their voices, anointed their bodies with her own hands, as women did those of the men they loved. These three out of all her world knew her best. Their emotional violences, ambitions, arrogance, and goodness were her own.

One was her father. One fathered her children. And one, the strongest, was her nemesis.

We study the face of Thothmes III and wonder, Why did such hatred exist? Their lives were irrevocably linked. What act of hers generated such enmity in one allied to her in status and blood—enmity so vicious that he tried to wipe away all proof that she had ever lived?

We shall meet later the three Thothmesid kings and learn what they meant to her.

For a more immediate question assails us. Where is Hatshepsut?

Her place is here in Room Fifty-two. Twelve generations of her people are here. Why is her mummy not in line with the other Eighteenth Dynasty queens, or, as she would have preferred, with the kings?

Those who contributed to her being are present, all the way back into the Seventeenth Dynasty. Each is a step leading up to Hatshepsut.

Here, too, are others who followed her narrow footprints over the Theban sands. They followed the diminishing path of the strongest of all the dynasties. Each silent form is, in itself, a dramatic chapter in history. But they were the followers. Our concern is not with them, but with the missing Hatshepsut, who lived out her own absorbing drama before they were born. Still, they were the heirs to her personality and her heritage. Some would take to themselves the results of her achievements.

So we linger, passing her three kings, wishing dead lips could reveal the unreachable secrets of their own distinguished and often tragic lives.

Review the principal post-Hatshepsut monarchs briefly, in the rhythm of the Biblical begats.

Here lies Amonhotep II with his son Thothmes IV and grandson Amonhotep III.

Their physical appearance demonstrates the ebbing powers of a powerful clan. Amonhotep II was a son of the colossus Thothmes III, but his mummy does not exude the impression of invincible strength as does that of his father. Do his features resemble those of the "Napoleon of Egypt"? We do not know. The arched Thothmesid nose has collapsed during thousands of years underground; the face has darkened, the skin is spotted from a disease unknown.

His son Thothmes IV gives the impression of being a dandy. His long brown curling hair, pierced ears, face clean-shaven, suggest a man who took pride in his appearance, and died in his mid-twenties. His reign was brief, his prowess negligible, but he fathered a son who in life rode the crest of the successful Eighteenth Dynasty, Amonhotep III, named "the Magnificent," who reigned from 1405 B.C. to 1367, and who achieved in that time one of the fullest of all the royal lives.

The mummy of this Amonhotep is that of a man only five feet tall, but he was a celebrated athlete and sportsman. Descriptions cite him as "the strongest man to draw bow," and it is recorded that he once slew one hundred and two lions in a single day.

Following tradition in a line of kings whose bloodthirsty proclivities were curiously welded to a love of beauty, Amonhotep built on a grand scale. Among his existing works are the

Temple of Luxor and the two gigantic statues of himself guarding the western necropolis at Thebes known as the Colossi of Memnon.

He married the fascinating non-royal Tye, and statues show them as a hearty, contentedly smiling pair. She appears plump and dimpled and cheerful; he portrays a man of physical and emotional content. They can only be described by the German adjective *lustige.* There is no explaining the odd result of this celebrated union, but their son King Amonhotep IV, of the feminine characteristics and mystical mind, founded the first monotheistic religion in history and built the fabulous city of Amarna to his disturbing dream. Renamed by himself King Akhenaton in honor of the one god, the sun disk, he brought the Eighteenth Dynasty to its highest peak of magnificence and madness, and here the mummy chain of descent is broken for the first time since Hatshepsut's defection, for the body of Akhenaton has not been discovered. It is not in this room. Missing also is his beautiful and mysterious Queen Nefertiti, whose bust is the most famous in the world.

Akhenaton may have fathered two young princes who reigned briefly at the end of the Dynasty. The mummy of Smenkhare, "beloved of Akhenaton," is here. One lingers over the damaged face and wonders, What was his history? He ruled as co-regent with Akhenaton, married his and Nefertiti's daughter, and in death yielded the throne to the boy king Tutankhamon, evidently his younger brother, whose gold-encrusted mummy has been returned to its tomb in Thebes.

These two boyish kings were the last of Hatshepsut's family line to rule Egypt.

So many links are missing in the royal chain. Where is Aye, the last of the Eighteenth Dynasty Kings, who maneuvered for more than a half-century to keep the sons of the Thothmesid on the throne, who defended Nefertiti to the death, who may, in fact, have been her father?

But, above all—where is Hatshepsut?

She should be with the three Thothmesid kings.

Her two richly decorated sarcophagi are in this museum in Cairo. The museums of the world are enriched by Hatshepsut statues. Her memorial temple, obelisks, and tomb in the Valley of the Kings—all are known to us.

But where is the body that was "more beautiful than anything," whose perpetual care she planned over so long a period of time and at such a tremendous cost?

In these generations of strong men and strong-minded women, we have glimpsed the tremendous struggle for royal power that she inherited. We cannot see the intangible elements handed down to her. On record elsewhere are her foibles, femininity, vanity, and her determination to match her strength against the greatness of Egypt.

To grasp the full image of Hatshepsut, we must leave this museum and a Cairo that did not exist in her time, and make our way southward upriver.

Flying with disappointing brevity over the Nile that winds far below like a vein in the scaly hide of the desert, we pass over the site of ravaged Amarna where Akhenaton and Nefertiti lived out the glowing chapters of their love story, and fly on to the city of Luxor, which was known as Thebes in Homer's time, and, long before that, when Hatshepsut was born there, as a city honoring the chief of Egypt's many gods, a city known as No-Amon.

I made the boundary of Egypt as far as the circuit of the sun.
—Thothmes I to the Priests of Abydos

The ruins of Karnak lift their shattered columns over the Nile two miles north of modern Luxor. Mutilated pillars, columns, walls, obelisks, and the colonnades of temples, chapels, festival halls, courts, shrines, altars, and tombs, reach up into the cloudless Egyptian sky. This forest of broken stone is the skeletal remains of a carefully planned and magnificent city, apparently built by giants for their gods.

Man walks dwarfed beneath the ruins, reduced in image and imagination by the works of men who, with primitive tools, built so splendidly, and with such precision of detail, so many thousands of years ago.

Luxor, as the modern city is called, means "the palaces." The name describes the complex of ancient temples that were palaces built for the gods. It was in Hatshepsut's time the southern suburbs of Thebes.

The Egyptians were the first people to build with stone. They had attained supremacy in architecture centuries before Hatshepsut was born, developed engineering on a massive scale, and erected mammoth temples and tombs intended to last "for a million million years."

Thebes was the supreme flowering of their artistry.

This was Hatshepsut's city. Here her life began, under the powerful influence of the man who was her first love—her father, Thothmes I.

We do not know the name by which Hatshepsut first knew her father. Thothmes was a "throne name" assumed at the time of his coronation. He was the first to adopt that name, which would be taken, in turn, by the three succeeding Thothmes kings. The histories spell it in various ways, but its meaning remains, "he who is born of the moon god."

He was not entirely royal. True, he was a son of the great Amonhotep, but not by either of that king's royal sister-wives, Queens Meritamon and Ahotep, who had been the daughters of the foundling father Amose I and his Great Queen Nefertari. Amose had taken many wives, and among them was a subsidiary non-royal wife, Senseneb. She gave birth to the child who became Thothmes I.

Little is known of her. Her name is included on a form which Thothmes devised to be used in the taking of oaths.

"Let them swear by the name of His Majesty . . . born of the royal mother, Senseneb."

Again, in his funerary chapel, Thothmes recorded her as "royal mother, princess of the two lands, Senseneb." But her name is not on the dynastic lists, and there is no proof that Amonhotep ever gave the rank of royalty to the little-known mother of Thothmes I.

Thothmes followed tradition when he married Hatshepsut's mother, the sweet-faced Crown Princess Amose, who was his half sister, and, being fully royal, the heiress to the throne. The three Kings Thothmes who followed him also married their royal half sisters. The mysterious alchemy of marriage made these men automatically regal, and gave them a legitimate right to claim the throne.

Thothmes would earn the right to that claim.

The adult Hatshepsut was to order many carved and colored portraits made of her father and mother. Queen Amose was always shown smiling. "More beautiful than any woman." So Hatshepsut described her mother. Thothmes too is often shown with a half-smile. The records indicate that they were a cheerful and compatible pair. Thothmes had taken the name of a moon god. Queen Amose was descended from a royal line so ancient that her earliest known ancestor was the sun.

So the child Hatshepsut knew herself to be born with vested rights in day and night, the two worlds of heaven and earth, and the two Egypts.

Hers was an auspicious beginning. She was born in the effulgence of her first ancestor, the sun god, Amon-Re. She was the second of four children of Thothmes and his wife Amose. Many other children of her father's get lived in the Theban palace, but the four were fully royal, and only children born to a Great Royal Wife were eligible to claim the throne.

We do not know the year of that birth or that of any other early Egyptian monarch. The rulers recorded only the years they reigned. There are many places in Egypt's history where the record blurs. This is particularly true of Hatshepsut's story —her painstaking inscriptions were viciously chiseled away.

Still, Egypt had developed the world's first calendar and astronomy was an advanced science. New Year's Day, when life began anew, was known by the appearance of the star Sirius. Knowing this, it has been possible to pinpoint events that took place three and one-half thousand years ago. Sometime before 1500 B.C., in the long-fallen palace, Hatshepsut was born and given the name of Hatshepsut.

Hatshepsut. Pronounce the name quickly, with the accent on the second syllable. Still, who can say how it was spoken in her time, so many centuries ago?

But we know its meaning, which is, "Chieftainess of noble women," and we know why it was given her. From babyhood on she held authority. In time, she would have other names and titles, as did all regents, but Hatshepsut remained her personal, cartouche, and dynastic name.

She was blessed with excellent health, a quick mind, and the inexhaustible Thothmesid energy. These priceless attributes were evidently lacking in part or completely in her brothers and sister. There are strong indications that Hatshepsut was always her father's favorite.

But she was not the heiress born. There was the older sister, Crown Princess Neferukheb, who had first rights as a future claimant to the throne. There were also the two brothers, Madjmose and Amonmose. They were younger than Hatshepsut, but they were boys, and would take precedence if there was eventually a contest for the right to rule.

This fact could not have troubled their minds while they were children. Hatshepsut was only one of many small youngsters running the rooms and corridors of the great palace, frankly naked as were many of her elders in the hot dry days and nights. She did not resent the presence of the dozens, even hundreds, of half-royal brothers and sisters. One of the king's august titles was "Mighty Bull of Maat." Hatshepsut could take pride in a father who had sired so many children.

She was a bright child, and it could not have been long before she understood that she was one of the most royal. She was given special attention and care. She was surrounded night and day by tender guardians. While pampered in many ways, she was, in others, held to stricter rules than children of less exalted birth. Even if she was never to advance in closer line to the throne, she would have great influence. She learned to give commands that were obeyed on pain of death. Courtiers fawned on the child. Nurses and servants tended and anticipated every wish. Slaves did not raise their eyes to the little princess, but groveled with faces in the dust.

Flattery and sincere praise sounded in her ears from infancy.

But there were nursery rules, even for her. She was trained to show deference to her parents, obey them in all things, and never to fail in courtesy to other highly placed elders. She stood up when an older person entered the room. She was taught to speak softly, to eat neatly, to submit to hours of body care in the luxurious palace bathrooms. She was taught the primary prayers to the gods which were part of the religious instruction of a royal child.

Her first memories were of the mud palace and its occupants. Its precious inner circle was her own family. The lives of the hundreds of others, many of them related to her, revolved around the king and queen and their children.

Dependent upon the monarch for their very lives were his "secondary" wives, ladies-in-waiting, ladies of the harem, and other women, often of royal blood, brought back as hostages from conquered foreign lands. Dependent upon him were the many half-royal children born to these women. Dependent too were the nobles, court officials, priestly advisors, scribes, clerks, superintendents, courtiers, and official adorers, all in attendance on the king, and the queen's personal retinue, and smaller groups tending each royal child. Others attached to the court were dancers, musicians, acrobats, storytellers—entertainers of every kind—and servants for each department and person, and slaves in endless supply.

All these, even the nobility, were lesser beings than the child running naked and free in the great palace. This Hatshepsut was told. This she believed.

There were hundreds of rooms in the palace. There were salons and halls, and rooms for eating and sleeping and bathing, and private chapels with altars to the many gods. The walls and floors were brightly painted with river scenes, and brightly dyed drapes of finely woven linen were drawn over the latticed windows when the strong winds blew in from the desert in the days of the *khamseen*. Even the eyes of royalty were not exempt from the wind-driven blades of sand. At such times, sand penetrated every crevice and corner of the palace and defied the continual sweeping of the slaves with their palm-frond brooms.

On the hot days, large leather-bladed fans on the roof drove freshening air through funnels and down into the thick-walled rooms. While the building itself was of bricks made of sun-baked Nile mud, the palace and its furnishings were designed for comfort, beauty, and luxurious living.

The finest art of the cabinetmakers contributed to the beauty of the interior. Furniture was carved and painted and gilded. Upholstery, cushions, and draperies were of brilliantly dyed handwoven wool, cotton, or linen. Some of the seats were upholstered with beautifully painted leather. Beds, chairs, stools, footstools, the small stands that served as tables, and the handsome storage chests where bedding and draperies and clothing and sandals and wigs were stored, were not only serviceable, but colorful works of art, inlaid with ebony and ivory and precious metals.

Everywhere in the palace were bowls and vases of flowers, and trays of fresh fruit, and fine glass and faience and pottery—priceless treasures, these, for future world museums. The rooms were scented with the fresh flowers and the heavy Oriental perfumes worn by both men and women, with the odor of myrrh dominating, which would become Hatshepsut's favorite.

Radiating from this building, in spokes covering the known world, were all the sources of power; and within, wherever her small feet carried her, was beauty. In the inner heart of this splendor she was a small princess ordained for greatness, the jewel in the lotus.

Her life was not confined to the palace. The roof of the palace was flat, as were all the roofs of the clay residences, and on them children rich or poor played between the great earthen jugs that stored wheat, emmet, and corn. The carefully guarded child Hatshepsut could look down from the roof into the palace gardens where hundreds of gardeners worked naked in the sun. Set between other buildings were other gardens, all a-burst with brilliant flowers. In the gardens were pools stocked with fish that gave life to the water while helping to deplete the larvae of the mosquitoes that in certain seasons were, and are, the plague of Egypt.

She stared down into the royal zoo where hippopotami still roared in defiance to the defeated Hyksos, and other alien animals stalked, brought back after conquest from far-away lands.

The wide-set, thoughtful eyes surveyed the city beyond the gardens. Thebes sprawled beneath her, a noisy Oriental metropolis. She saw it with the certainty of possession. It was her city, made great by her forefathers.

The first Theban settlers had constructed their mud village along the banks of the Nile in a wide, rich valley replenished every fall by the river's swollen waters racing downstream to the Mediterranean, five hundred miles to the north. It became an agricultural town, a waterways trading post, a world center of trade, and, eventually, due to Hatshepsut's ancestors in this Eighteenth Dynasty, the capital of Egypt. It was still a mud city of thick walls constructed of bricks made of sun-baked river mud.

Traffic was clotted in the narrow streets between the one- and two-story mud buildings. Women leaned from the deep-set windows, shouting gossip, tossing the family slops onto unwary passersby. Children played their ancient games on the flat roofs. Hatshepsut watched with interest; these children she would never know. She heard shouts and curses rise from the streets as burdened camels and donkeys and human beasts of burden fought for the right-of-way. There would be eddies of silence as a space widened before the approaching chariot wheels of some dignitary or man of wealth whom lesser men had reason to respect or even fear.

Plying their trades amid the activity were the tradespeople and craftsmen. Some dealt in the open air markets, others in small, crude shops. There were no stores; for that matter there was no money. Still, values were exact, and everyone knew the exchange value of a deer shot on the desert, or a pound of goat meat, or an egg.

Such values would remain as meaningless to Hatshepsut as the lives of the poor whose tenements formed a mud wall between the city and the desert.

The child looked down on the darkling green of palms on march along the river. Between their pointed fronds she saw the roiled waters of the Nile. Craft of every kind plied the waterway, naval ships of her father's fleet, trade ships from the Mediterranean, the pleasure barges of the rich, and the reed boats of the poor. Her father's royal barge might flaunt its banners at the long wharf, and on holy days the priests would roll down to the water the sacred barque of Amon. The river was the source of all Egypt's good, and supplied food and pleasure to all its people. Hatshepsut loved the Nile. It was more than a river. It was Hapi, a god.

On the other side of the river the sun lingered on the rose-gilt hills of Western Thebes. Below those folded cliffs were the secret graves of her family. There in the second largest necropolis in Egypt lay the royal, the great, the powerful, and the merely rich of Thebes. On the sandy fringes of the cemeteries, the poorer dead slept precariously in shallow graves, at the mercy of the packs of jackals that prowled the graveyards. All slept with what possessions they had managed to amass in life. All had gone to their graves with the hope of being undisturbed forever. Those who oversaw their burials did their best to keep them safe, but jackals ravaged the poorer graves, and there had been graverobbers since burials began. Hatshepsut would learn to fear for her own future safety, and for that of those dear to her.

On either side of the Nile, memorial temples, obelisks and statuary commemorated the lives of the illustrious dead. The child eyed these with precocious interest. Many were family memorials. From these monuments, ant-sized as viewed from the palace roof, and their graven messages, the little princess was to learn her country's history, and her own.

The slender body turned toward the north, where rose the pillared stone complex of Karnak. The Luxor temple did not exist in her time, and the city of Thebes was spread over the level river land in the direction of the temples. The view between them was unbroken.

From a distance, Karnak appears today much as Hatshepsut would have viewed it from the flat roof of the palace. It is a monument to an Egypt past.

The buildings where the gods lived with their armies of attendant priests were built of enduring stone. Like the gods, they were intended to last forever. A house for humans, even a palace, was to be used only during its owner's lifetime. It was built for that brief period of the mud bricks. The tomb was man's only eternal home, and every Egyptian wealthy enough built his of stone while he lived.

But historic Thebes was an adobe city, resembling certain agricultural towns along the Nile where the buildings are still constructed of sun-baked clay. Theban houses were comfortable and cool within, and often lavishly decorated and furnished, but mud they were, and have long since been washed back into the rich river ooze from which they came.

Gradually during the centuries, Thebes was to vanish. Luxor rose on the site of Hatshepsut's city.

Somewhere in the ancient dust of Thebes is the rubble of the palace where her life began.

Hatshepsut's first experience with a family death may have been that of King Amonhotep I. She must have had early memories of this grandfather, who was fifty years old when he died. She would certainly have known her grandmother, his widowed Queen Ahotep II, who lived to be "very old"—old enough to see her daughter Amose on the throne as the sister-spouse-Queen of Thothmes, who was Amonhotep's son by another wife.

Hatshepsut may have participated with her family in the complicated religious rites that followed the death of an Egyptian king. She would have been awed, even terrified, by the ceremonies carried out by the hundreds of leopard-skin-clad priests in the great Temple of Amon. All Egypt was plunged into mourning for the seventy prescribed days of mummification. Then the body of the old king was carried "to the west" in the night by processions of priests and mourners, and laid to rest in his fine orange-colored linen swathings, wearing the gilded mask and covered with the flowers that were to outlast the centuries.

Her small feet may have imprinted the coarse sand with others of the torchlighted throng that left the mummified body of her dead grandfather in his sealed "beautiful tomb" under the western hills. She would be a frequent visitor to this lonely region of death.

She may have fallen asleep as any child would on the royal barge returning across the Nile, lulled by the sad voices of her parents, the subdued keening of the official mourners, and the rhythmic splashing of a hundred oars in the night waters. She could sleep, thinking him safely at rest now forever—the mighty King Amonhotep I, who as a warrior prince equally great in peace had preserved the heritage handed down by his father Amose, founding father of the line. Amonhotep had ended the "long humiliation" of Hyksos domination, and brought Egypt into a period of prosperity and security that was advancing it toward world power.

Hatshepsut would revere his memory.

The funeral rites ended, and on the day Egypt ceased its mourning her father's coronation ceremonies began in the Karnak temple.

Thothmes was well prepared to rule. His apprenticeship had been long and severe, and he had waited a long time for the throne. The records describe him as being "middle-aged" at this time. He was in his mid-thirties. He had been born in the second year of his father's reign.

His might have been an easy, luxurious palace life. His marriage to the Crown Princess Amose insured his sometime inheritance of the crown. Instead, he had chosen to follow the grueling life of a soldier in his father Amonhotep's army. Like his father and grandfather, Thothmes became famous for his skill in handling weapons. He was also a born leader. There were always wars to be fought for Egypt. Thothmes was still a young man when he was made the commander of his aging father's legions. Long before that father died, the military victories of Prince Thothmes had won the respect of Egypt.

Many times Hatshepsut was to watch the metamorphosis of a tender parent into a fierce man of war. With her mother, she saw the small man turned avenger, terrifying in his glittering war chariot, with foot soldiers running alongside carrying the royal bow and mace, driving out of Thebes at the head of his armies to lead them on punishing raids, north toward Asia or upriver to Nubia. After him, in dust storms stirred by their marching feet, thundered his legions—well-trained, well-nourished, well-provided with all available weapons of war. After him marched the spearsmen, the archers, the axe-men, and the fleets of war chariots drawn by the horses that were still too small to be ridden even by the light-boned Egyptians but were capable of racing the silver and gilt chariots over battlefields in pursuit of the enemy. Both horses and chariots had been left by the conquered Hyksos.

Hatshepsut listened avidly as reports from Thothmes came back by chariot or human runner to the family waiting in the Theban palace. Every word sang of victory. She thought of her father, as did Egypt and all its enemies, as a superman who was in every place at once, sweeping his tremendous forces to victory after victory, and leaving terror and devastation in his wake.

Again and again before he became king, Thothmes led his father's legions out of Thebes to hold the peace of Egypt.

Hatshepsut may have seen him before these forays, prostrating himself before the altar in the Temple of Amon, humbly begging the Hidden One to insure his success in the coming conflict. She might see him there after his triumphant returnings, humbly reporting his victories and offering up to Amon the god's share of the spoils of victory.

Amon had been a local Theban deity until Hatshepsut's ancestors made him "Ruler of Thebes." Thebes had risen to power, and Amon became the leading god of Egypt. His tremendous temple stood, and still dominates, in the heart of the stone complex of Karnak. It was known as lpet-esut, and was not only the largest building at Karnak but the largest in the world. It was the cathedral of Egypt. The massive buildings sheltered armies of priests of Amon. Clad in leopard-skin robes, they carried out never-ending rites in honor of Amon and the king. All the kings added to its greatness.

Clustered around it were other stone temples, sanctuaries, and chapels dedicated to lesser gods of Egypt who were known as the Lords of Thebes. The temples of the minor gods were rich, and the priests who served them were men of substance and power. But none were as rich and powerful as the priests of Amon. The thousands of priests in the service of Amon shared authority and revenue with the king. A large part of the fortunes taken in battle or in taxes went to them. Amon owned cattle and lands; Amon garnered tremendous wealth as rich and poor Egyptians poured endless tribute into the gigantic stone coffer in tribute to the patron Ruler of Thebes.

In the inner sanctuary of the Amon temple, the gold image of the plumed and powerful god stood higher over the altar than the statue of the king. The king's will yielded only to Amon.

Still, when a long view is taken of Egyptian history, it is noticeable that the king had the last word.

Important events were celebrated with religious rites in the inner hall of the Amon temple. Every public episode in Hatshepsut's life would be celebrated there. In that vast, dim interior, clouded with sweet-smelling incense sparked by the multi-millioned glitter of silver and gold and electrum, and precious and semi-precious stones, Hatshepsut may have been one of the multitude that, in the year 1528 B.C., crowded below the Amon altar to see her father enthroned.

We have seen that father, in the mummy room at Cairo, as Hatshepsut saw him as he took the Kingdom of Egypt.

He was a smaller man than his father Amonhotep; he was only five feet tall. In size and personality, he was a throwback to his grandfather, the great Amose. His shoulders and torso were those of a powerful man. Even dead, his appearance is authoritative. The narrow face, arched nose, and protruding teeth were Thothmesid characteristics. Like many of the males of his line, Thothmes was bald.

Still, she saw him, splendid, terrifying, in his magnificent coronation apparel, standing with his warrior's stance among the leopard-skin-clad priests before the altar in the inner hall of the temple, under the gold statue of Amon. She heard him taking the oath of Amon to serve his country with nobility and justice, according to the laws of Maat. She heard the solemn pronouncements chanted by the hundreds of priests and the responses by the thousands of worshipers. Sistrums were shaken, priestesses danced the sacred dances. Clouds of fragrant myrrh blurred the walls glittering with jewels and the blazing gold of the crown and the throne.

Amose sat beside her husband, no longer Princess, but the one true Queen.

The pair were resplendent, a-flash with jewels, beings not of the earth that designated them king and queen, but also, from this moment, of the stuff of gods. A small girl who was still mortal might adore such parents from her place among the palace worshipers, and know their value and her own. Did glances warm with love flash her way from the golden throne?

Did she wonder if some day that glittering chair would be hers?

She knew in that moment, as she had always known, that out of all the world she owed allegiance only to this man and woman on the throne. None other dared give an order to Hatshepsut. Her head need bow only to them and to Amon. To her and to Egypt they were the trinity of power.

The father she had known from infancy changed as she watched. All eyes were fixed on the small, terrifying figure holding the tall double crown of the two Egypts.

And Hatshepsut, awed, would have heard the stone walls echoing to the sounds of her father's new throne name and his many new titles, called out in solemn intonation by the high priest of Amon.

King Thothmes I, entitled Okhepernere, Mighty Bull of Maat, Favorite of the Two Goddesses Golden Hours . . . making hearts live . . . Son of Re, living forever and ever. . . .

From the outer walls of the temple, trumpets blasted the news to the four corners of the earth, and the city shouted acclaim to Thothmes I, third Pharaoh of the New Kingdom, first bearer of the Thothmes name.

There was free bread and beer and celebration in the streets. The shouting was heartfelt, wishing long reign to the new leader of Egypt, and all lips voiced the ancient plea to the Hidden One: "Lord Amon, grant long life to Egypt's king."

The coronation decree was duly registered:

". . . His Majesty has dawned as King of Upper and Lower Egypt."

And with Thothmes I, in that moment of crowning, the girl Hatshepsut rose over the horizon of history.

Ruined Karnak is no longer a treasure chest built for giants, but it remains as in Hatshepsut's time a priceless depository of historic records that were carved on stone, "never to be broken . . . to endure forever."

On the walls, statues, pillars, obelisks, and stelae, the rulers of Egypt registered in turn the histories and achievements of the gods interwoven with accounts of their own personal lives.

These records are in hieroglyphic symbols and illustrated with brightly colored paintings and carvings. They are actually hymns of self-praise, and while many enlarged upon the accomplishments of the royal authors, still they have served to make Egypt the best documented of all ancient lands.

We know the child Hatshepsut stood dwarfed under walls towering above her apparently into infinity. All the great ones were listed there, back to the founding of her dynasty. Their portraits and statues of the warrior-kings and their "Ladies of the Two Lands" looked down upon her with a demanding love. They would ask much of her. The awareness of their majesty and hers must never leave her while she lived.

Now she was a king's daughter, and to be worthy of him, and of them, the child Hatshepsut had much to learn.

Thothmes I was given little time in which to enjoy the pleasures of royal living. As in his father's time, he had been king only a few months when a major outbreak started in Nubia.

The royal barge became a battleship. Thothmes sailed with

his soldiers upstream to Nubia, as far south as the Third Cataract.

The Eighteenth Dynasty had its Homer. Amose, the son of Abana, was a soldier-author who fought with a series of warrior-kings into his ninetieth year. He campaigned with the armies of Amose I. He would be with Thothmes III. He recorded all their victories.

He chronicled the conquest of Nubia in stark terms, describing the way King Thothmes "subdued and slew" the Negroes with his mighty sword, slashing through their legions and leaving them on the field where "their severed bits of flesh were carried off by the birds." The king in battle, Amose wrote, was "as a young panther among the fleeing cattle."

He recorded the death of the Nubian chief on that field.

"His Majesty [Thothmes] raged like a panther of the south; His Majesty cast his javelin, and it remained in the body of that enemy chieftain, whose army was powerless before his flaming uraeus, made so in an instant of time."

Thothmes raised garrisons along his line of conquest to guard the rich trade routes into Nubia and the Sudan. Returning downriver, he paused in places to subdue minor outbursts. His military historian described the triumphant return to Thebes.

"His Majesty sailed downstream with all countries in his grasp, and that miserable troglodyte, the Nubian foe, hanged head first from the bow of the royal barge."

There was no rest for Thothmes. Reports of threatened Hyksos invasion came from the Delta. He rushed his soldiers downstream, quelled internal disturbances in the vicinity of Memphis, and crossed the borders in the north to hunt down the ancient enemy. Victory followed victory as his armies raided Palestine and Syria and chased the Hyksos farther and farther back into Asia, all the way to the Euphrates, "that inverted water which goes downstream going upstream." His armies and his country were enriched with plunder from Palestine and Syria, and the kingdom of Mitanni.

The monuments Thothmes raised on the scenes of his victories marked the widening extent of Egyptian power. They have been found on the Euphrates and along the Nile.

He commemorated the defeat of the Nubians in the second year of his reign with inscriptions cut into the granite cliffs of the Third Cataract:

"He marched to the ends of the earth with his conquering might, seeking one who would fight, but he found no one who would turn his face against him. He pressed on into valleys which the ancestors had not known and which the wearers of the vulture and the serpent diadems had never seen. . . ."

"Subject to him are the islands of the sea, and the whole earth is under his two feet."

This was Thothmes I, father of Hatshepsut.

He was one of the greatest of Egypt's greatest line of warrior-kings.

How was it that his daughter Hatshepsut was to become her country's outstanding protagonist of peace?

Her father was a king who wore many faces.

There was the savage mien of the soldier that had glared from the royal barge drawing up to the Theban wharf, with the enemy he had slain, the Nubian chief, hanging head down from the prow. There was the stern-faced warrior-king who never lost and who recorded his victories on stone. There was the benevolent visage of the king, who, having won every victory, turned his tremendous energies into the improvement and beautifying of Egypt, which was also in the tradition of the Eighteenth Dynasty kings.

The country was never wholly free of war threats. Thothmes held his person and his soldiers in readiness. The result was an era of peace and prosperity, and during this happy interim

Hatshepsut knew a father as effective in peace as he had been in war.

A wave of progress swept over Egypt. Agriculture, trade, and mining zoomed. A more lasting advance was the forward thrust in architecture, literature, and art. A passion for building was dominant in the Thothmesid strain.

At the very beginning of his reign, Thothmes had started on a vast scale the building of the processional temples that were to add so much to the future glory of Egypt.

He chose with care an architect-engineer who could put his plans into being. This was Ineni, a famed master builder in stone, and a man understanding of the ways of monarchs. He had built for Thothmes' father.

The architect always held a vital place in royal planning. Every Egyptian monarch from Zoser on had his chief architect, whose buildings have awed students of architecture down to the present day.

King Thothmes made his building plans on the grand scale. He turned his attention first to the temple of Amon. It had been standing for hundreds of years. No one knew how old it was. Even before that, a temple had stood on the Karnak site, dedicated to gods no one remembered. The father of Thothmes had enlarged the temple. Ineni had made certain additions for Amonhotep. To Ineni, versed in the ways of kings, it could have been no surprise when his first order from Thothmes was to destroy the additions he had made for the king's father and replace them with others, thereby adding to the size of the temple and the glory of Thothmes I.

Ineni started construction with the enthusiasm that made him a favorite with the kings he served. He understood the fine art of yielding. In time, rich and honored, he would be made Mayor of Thebes.

He began by replacing the Amonhotep construction with the still existing Fourth Pylon of Thothmes I. (It was before this pylon that a later warrior-king, Amonhotep II, son of Thothmes III, was to set his often-copied stele showing himself in his chariot, drawing the bow he called by its own personal name, "Great in Strength." The arrow, so the legend attests, "pierced a copper slab three fingers in thickness.")

Ineni also raised before the Temple two great gates of gleaming copper brought from Asia, and sandstone walls with columned porticoes in which were set statues of Thothmes I in the sheath robe of the Sed-Festival. Other statues of the king in jubilee dress were set under the pylons. The architect constructed the tremendous gallery to the temple court, with its broad towers crowned with cornices, brightly painted, their tips sheathed in gold. The colors of Thothmes I flew before the gates from tall fir flagpoles brought upstream from Lebanon.

Colonnades, courtyards, chapels, sanctuaries—all Ineni built was adding to the glory of Amon and the king.

The temple grew. It became the Great Temple and a lasting memorial to the Thothmesid line.

Later, in a sensational feat of engineering, Ineni brought downriver from the quarries of Aswan two obelisks of red granite sixty-four feet high. They were convoyed down the Nile on a specially constructed barge that was two hundred feet long and sixty feet wide. Before they were set in place and while still on the ground, their sides were carved with the names and titles of Thothmes I. The tips were coated with silver and gold to return the flashings of Re, the sun.

On the two massive temple gates erected by Ineni were recorded the many victories of Thothmes I. They duplicated other data set on stone from the Euphrates to Aswan. But the temple records stressed not only success in battle, but the joys of peace.

"He brought the ends of the earth into his domain . . . subject to him are the islands of the Great Circle, the entire earth is under his two feet . . . his beauty, stability, health . . . all pray for him."

The king's own appraisal of his life was inscribed on his memorial at Abydos:

"I did more than any other king who was before me. The gods rejoiced in my time and their temples were in festival. I made the boundaries of Ta-mery [Egypt] as far as the circuit of the sun, and I caused Egypt to be the head of every land."

The growing Hatshepsut could stand slim and straight beside her father, watching the carving of the inscriptions, and recognize the value of praise being awarded while one still lived. She heard the kingly praise given Ineni, and saw the rich rewards he was given. She saw her father express on stone the hope that she and all his descendants would follow the standards in building he was setting.

Certainly the impetus Thothmes gave to architecture in Egypt would inspire future building, as he had hoped, and helped to inflame the imagination among others of that later king of his dynasty, the strange Akhenaton, who, with his wife Nefertiti, would create the fabulous city called Amarna.

And Hatshepsut, watching the strangely shaped letters memorized in childhood, made into words by the sculptor's chisel, could share her father's pride in the raising of pylons and walls and colonnades, and sense the first fire of an ambition to commemorate a life she intended to make glorious. In time, she, too, would be able to command the genius of a man like the great Ineni, who could immortalize the dreams of a monarch in sandstone and quartzite and granite and alabaster.

She must have been very young when the fierce determination came to Hatshepsut: "In time, I too shall build!"

Her majesty grew beyond everything; to look upon her was more beautiful than anything; . . . her form was like a god, she did everything like a god, her splendor was like a god; her majesty was a maiden, beautiful, blooming . . .

—Description of Hatshepsut,
Ancient Records

At puberty the lock of childhood was clipped away and Hatshepsut's head was shaved. She was growing up.

It is permissible to imagine her mother Amose directing the laying away in the decorative storage chests and baskets of the small-sized chairs, boxes, beaded sandals, hair ornaments, necklaces, rings, and bracelets that had been Hatshepsut's as a child. With them would be stored the painted and jointed wooden dolls and toy animals and games. Hatshepsut would enjoy these in another world. Egyptians took all their possessions, saved lifelong, into their graves. One cannot but be touched by the slingshot and other boyish articles found in Tutankhamon's tomb.

Was her clipped lock added to these stored articles? It is likely. Nothing that belonged to a royal person was thrown away.

Also, there may have been superstitions concerning hair.

While the ancient Egyptians were fickle in their love of fashion and often changed the styles of dress and hair, the headdress of the Pharaoh was never changed. The portraits of the monarchs show them wearing the concealing gold beard attached to the double crown. It has been suggested that the royal head was shaved for religious reasons and that a taboo kept it from public view.

Other Egyptians, men and women alike, clipped their heads for coolness and to provide a closer fit to the heavy sheep wool wigs that had been worn in Egypt ever since man could remember.

None of Hatshepsut's childhood relics have been found.

The loss of the childish tress marked a turning point in any girl's life. In Hatshepsut's it began the specialized training suitable to one who some day might be queen.

The education of Egyptian royalty stressed morality and good manners. Hatshepsut could look forward to pleasures unknown to ordinary people, but also to responsibilities almost too heavy for a man to bear. Dr. Murray has observed that the queens appear "to have been often well educated." There were nurses and governesses for Hatshepsut when she was small. These were replaced by tutors chosen from the wisest men in the kingdom. They were priests of Amon.

The ability with which Hatshepsut was to meet future responsibility is proof that she was well taught.

Thebes was the capital of a country that had become not only a world center of trade, but of culture, moral precepts, and civilized living. The Amon priests were masters of medicine, science, ethics, and the interpretation of dreams.

They showed no leniency toward a student who was their king's favorite child. It was apparent to her advisors from her earliest years that the youngest daughter of King Thothmes was likeliest to reach the throne. More was demanded of Hatshepsut than of the other royal children.

There was a well-equipped schoolroom in the palace. Each royal child had his slate and papyrus textbooks, reed pens, ink, and writing paper made of the pressed pith of the papyrus that grew so plentifully then along the banks of the Nile. (Our word "paper" stems from "papyrus.")

On the wall over the children's heads hung the ibis-headed image of Thoth, the god of writing, learning, science, mathematics, astronomy, and magic. He was patron of the scribes on earth, and in heaven served as the scribe of all the gods. He also kept the records for the gods during the solemn rite of the weighing of the heart of the dead.

Reading, writing, and mathematics were essential, but history and religion were major subjects. Hatshepsut learned to write, first on slate, then with ink on papyrus. She had to memorize all the six hundred phonetic signs.

The Egyptians had developed the first writing symbols. Due to this, Egypt was leading the world in literature, poetry, songs, and fables—even cartoons.

The signs would enable Hatshepsut, if ever she came to rule, to express to her friendly or unfriendly correspondents exactly what she wished to say. The time would come when she would have her own palace scribe to take her dictation while he crouched cross-legged at her feet; still it was important in royal circles, where treachery was in the air, to be able to make certain that one's words were recorded as they were spoken.

She doubtless hated arithmetic, as most girls do, but was certainly impressed, as were all Egyptians, by the magic qualities in numbers, and the way they could be adapted into potent formulas by the priests by using the most mystic numerals, seven, fourteen, and twenty-one. Egypt was highly advanced and deeply respectful of the science of mathematics, but the fundamentals of algebra and geometry and the method of finding the area of a circle that were being taught then could have held little interest for Hatshepsut.

She would know in time the values they held for her. Due to their knowledge of geometry the royal surveyors were able to measure every mile of Egypt. Hatshepsut learned the width and length of her father's kingdom. It consisted of two lands, upper and lower Egypt. Someday, it might be hers.

She learned of other lands and other people. There were Hebrews and Babylonians and the ancient enemy, the Hyksos, who had been driven out by her forefathers. She would know vaguely of Crete, Sumeria, and of a country the location of which we are not certain, known then as Mitanni. She would know something of India, although not by that name. Many of India's arts, and certainly its spices, had crossed the Mediterranean into Egypt. But the land that gripped her imagination was the fabulous land of Punt, source of that rarest of incense, the myrrh.

She was taught that Egypt was the center and apex, and, in fact, virtually the entire world. She could not have known that her country was but one of three great civilizations traveling slowly along the same level but far apart. She could not have known that India had already firmly established a caste system that was to lock its people into divisions which they have not broken to this present day. Egypt had no caste system. A peasant might become a king, given brains, determination, and luck.

She could have known nothing of China, developing on its own terms into a gigantic peaceful empire under a series of energetic dynasties whose emperors were to command a great civilization for the next three thousand years.

But her own records show the interest she took in Egypt's history. It was her family's story, and her own.

The hieroglyphs she learned to read opened doors to the past. The importance of the records they kept was impressed on her developing mind, and she knew that in time the phonetic symbols would document her own life.

She learned the names and intimate histories of the ancestors she had never seen, but whose time-darkened bodies we have seen in the Cairo Museum. She knew them better than we shall ever know them, for the details of their lives were verbally handed down, as such matters are in families, and their sculptured forms and the records they had left were everywhere in Thebes.

She was one of the sacred few to be told where their bodies were hidden.

Everything she learned emphasized the importance of the lives leading up to her own.

The burden of heritage was heavy. While all surrounding her praised her, still more was being asked of her. Her family and her teachers never let her lose sight of the fact that she must live up to the standards set by a long line of men and women possessed of strong bodies and strong minds. Even as a child this had been impressed upon her. She lifted her face to the towering statues of Thebes and let her reverence for the colossi melt into the sense of her own majesty until she knew that even the long-ago dead still lived, and were still watching and demanding much of her.

It was a heavy responsibility that had been placed on a child.

She studied the stone faces of the ancestral queens who had been chosen by their royal mates for their strength of character and mind. She would never lose touch with an early prayer, "May my life be worthy of them!"

Did she know, this slender girl, with the precocious glances no longer shadowed by the youth lock, that she was to be the strongest of them all?

Her upbringing was different from that given any other Egyptian queen.

According to the pictorial records left by both Hatshepsut and her father, whose devotion to his immediate female ancestors never flagged, and to Egypt's strong matriarchal trend, Hatshepsut was never to regret having been born a girl. Even as a small girl, Hatshepsut is shown wearing the jaunty brief pleated boyish kilt, belted and stopping at the knees.

The teen-age years demanded much of her. She had a great deal to learn, and the certainty was growing that she had been chosen by the gods for an exceptional destiny. It was no light matter to be the favorite child of her world's most powerful king. Hatshepsut was the pampered darling of a large and loyal family circle, but all evidence shows she was growing up under her father's personal supervision and that her training was as rigid as that which Thothmes would have demanded for a son.

There are bas reliefs showing her in her boy's clothing hunting in the marshes. Balanced on rafts made of bundles of papyrus reeds lashed together, the girl-child imitated her father's famed skill with the javelin, stabbing with the forked wooden spear and lifting from the water the fat Nile shad about which so many songs were sung. She hurled nets to trap the coveys of quail startled in feathered clouds from the papyrus covers. She learned to throw a boomerang at protesting ducks or to taunt the crocodile that nosed its leathery shapes between the reeds. The Nile was alive with wild fowl, fish, and water animals.

There were popular games to be played in and out of doors. There were brief pleasure journeys on the royal barge.

Some of these amusements were shared with her father. He evidently approved and encouraged interests and habits that were usually those of a growing boy. And still, we observe from the records, Hatshepsut was also the daughter of her mother, the gentle Queen Amose, and was developing along other lines that were feminine and even frivolous.

There could be no boyishness when it came to good manners. Hatshepsut was beautifully trained in court etiquette. Protocol and courtesy and ritual were necessary to an orderly palace life. Polite conversation was a fine art in itself. Hatshepsut learned who merited the distant greeting and who the warm. She learned to walk as queens walk, unseeing of the earth under her feet and its minions.

The teaching that went deepest with her was religious.

Reverence was in the air of Egypt. There were so many gods. Some were the outgrowth of even more ancient deities, but all were jealous and to slight one of their holy days and observances was to risk terrible retribution. Nearly every day of the year was the feast day of some god and each must have its own day-long celebration ending, inevitably, in a feast.

Hatshepsut had endless prayers to recite and rituals to perform. She learned to present offerings, to dance and prostrate herself before altars.

The gods' peculiar habits of changing their names, shapes, and places of residence were problems that concerned only the priests. Certainly Hatshepsut was not one to question why the leading trinity of Thebes—Amon and his wife Mut and son Khons—were worshiped in northern Egypt as Osiris, Isis, and Horus.

Again, confusing no true believers, for one month out of every year Osiris-Amon-Re achieved another godly transfiguration and became the lettuce-eating god of sensuality, Min, whose celebration in the southern temple of Thebes, one mile from the Great Temple, was known as the "beautiful festival of the Harem." All Thebes was left exhausted annually by this celebration. Hatshepsut was learning to take part in all these festivals as royalty did in all festivals, but any role she may have played in Min's honor we do not know.

She was told a great deal about death and its importance in life.

She learned that there was no death. After the brief pang of extremis and the confrontation in the hall of the gods, life went pleasantly on in the tomb. There, the ceremony of the opening of the mouth having been carried out by someone near and dear to the dead, all the departed faculties were restored as in life. To complete future enjoyment, every object the dead person had used in life, or might need, went with him into the tomb.

It was a comforting belief, and one that entailed maintaining a respectful intimacy with the gods during every Egyptian's lifetime. Royal persons received extensive early training in the complicated rituals due the gods since they were themselves divine.

Religion overlapped with politics in a satisfying way. The political leaders were priests of Amon. They were not only wealthy and wise, but they also had access to the royal ear. Priests were put in charge of Hatshepsut's education as a matter of policy. She learned early she would have to depend upon the Amon hierarchy if ever she came to rule. In turn, the brotherhood respected her for her potential and because her forefathers had set their Theban god above every other god of Egypt.

Hatshepsut worshiped all the gods, but her greatest fealty was to Amon.

Religion was also morality. The moral code was firmly incorporated into the legal, and both rested on a religious premise. The Egyptians may have observed their laws no more carefully than we do ours, nevertheless the laws were clear. Each Egyptian was taught, and Hatshepsut herself was taught, that king or serf must stand before Osiris on the day of judgment in the great hall of the underworld and watch their hearts being weighed on the scales of justice by the goddess Maat, whose feather headdress symbolized the moralities.

"When my heart is weighed before the great Re. . . ." Hatshepsut offered up this prayer as humbly as did the lowliest slave.

For all one's deeds were under observance, and placed on record in the book of doom, to be explained after death to the Great Questioner. Even a queen must have her answers ready for that terrible confrontation in the underworld. Good deeds were richly rewarded after death. Bad acts meant the punishment of being endlessly devoured by the hideous goddess of evil.

So ethics were simplified for Hatshepsut, since religion, morality, and the law were one, conceived by the gods and upheld by the temples and the courts. Those who broke the law were punished while living, but no earthly punishment could contend with that promised in the after-life.

Murder, grave-robbing, and treason were crimes punishable by death.

The moral ideal was toward order, in matters both regal and divine.

"Control your hand, restrain your heart, and seal your lips," was part of the ethical ruling.

There were odd lesions in the moral code. Adultery was frowned upon but not punished by law, while a sex act performed in a sacred place or the entering of such a place after the act, was a serious crime.

Good deeds were listed in the graves. "I fed the hungry, sheltered the widowed, aided the orphaned. . . ."

Honor to the dead was demanded by religion. Hatshepsut had many prayers to learn to insure the eternal content of her people. Food, flowers, gifts, even letters, were carried across the river and placed in the tombs. The dead left certain requests: that their records be kept, their monuments be preserved, and their names be kept alive on earth as in heaven.

"That I may in turn be remembered. . . ."

So the young Hatshepsut prayed, with reverence for her ancestors, and memorized many commemorative prayers to be recited in the memorial temples of those who slept on the western side of the Nile.

We can only believe that Hatshepsut, according to the records, would do her best to live by the words laid down by Egypt's ancient seers and prophets and priests.

By her time, a thousand years before Buddha and Confucius were born, a religion had developed in Egypt satisfying to its people even if they did not always adhere to its principles. There was a happy sense of cosmic unity in believing that all living things shared godhood. Man or plant or animal were all of the stuff of gods. The humble scarab, known to us as the dung beetle, was a god symbolizing the sun. It was worthy of mummification and subsequent burial, or it could be made into a jewel. The hounds wearing beautifully colored leather collars with which Hatshepsut raced under the royal acacia trees were the living symbols of Anubis, the jackal-headed guardian god of the dead. The kittens she tumbled on the palace floors were the playful representatives of the great cat goddess Bastet, a deity so powerful that cat mummies had their own cemeteries or were buried in the tombs of the humans who had shared their brief lives. Cats were highly esteemed. Men used them as retrievers in hunting, women made of them favored pets and dressed them in jeweled belts and collars, even clothing, and perhaps gold hoops in their ears.

This belief in the sacredness and relativity of all that lived made for a serene present and a perfect hereafter. Hatshepsut became exceptionally religious.

While her mystical sense was developing to an extraordinary degree, her parents and teachers were not neglecting the practical side of her nature. More was demanded of her than of any other royal child in the palace. Her deportment must be the best, her knowledge the widest, and her capacity for winning and retaining loyalty second to none. Any natural capacity she may have had for inspiring friendship was developed into a genius for commanding fealty. She saw her father reward his devotees with gold and titles and advancement. She learned early the returns to be gained by lavish giving. Hatshepsut had early training in consolidating court circles into a chain that might eventually aid her in a rise to power.

The death of her older sister, the princess royal Neferukheb, brought the adolescent Hatshepsut a step nearer to the throne. Nothing is known of this sister. Her brief life contributed little to Egyptian history, and her death went unexplained. At this time the most carefully nurtured children everywhere were likely to die young, and even the death of a princess royal was not commented upon in the records.

Again, very close to this child's death, two other brief records were made when Hatshepsut's two little brothers died for reasons equally unknown.

With these deaths, her childhood ended. Hatshepsut was now the sole remaining heir to the throne of Egypt.

We use the word "heir" with authority. It was her father's term.

The growing Hatshepsut continued to wear the shorter and narrower kilt of a boy, perhaps to please her father and make him less regretful that he had failed to bring to adulthood a fully royal son.

Other adolescent girls in the palace were beginning to wear the fashionable long pleated linen skirts that gave such fluid lines to blossoming young bodies. Hatshepsut continued to flaunt convention. The brief pleated boyish kilt did not detract from her graceful form.

She was the last fully royal child left to Thothmes I, and the relationship with her father deepened.

There was no dearth of semi-royal sons! The secondary wives, concubines, and harem women of Thothmes had kept the palace well supplied with boy children.

Hatshepsut had known since childhood that in time certain biological facts must be faced. The jaunty boyish kilts could not conceal the fact that she was a growing girl. Nothing could prevent the inevitable fact that she must eventually make her choice among the half brothers with whom she had run naked and carefree in their father's palace.

These princeling half brothers were well provided for by their father the king. They spent their earliest years with their mothers in the palace. After attaining puberty, they were placed as neophytes in the Great Temple of Amon where the priests trained them to reach any position they were qualified to fill. There was no goal these lads could not attain if they were ambitious and intelligent. Many a king's son rose to the highest ranks in the powerful Amon priesthood. Others turned to a more worldly life and founded families of great wealth and social position.

The death of the siblings made Hatshepsut more aware that she alone was left of both royal and divine descent, and that her delicate body must in time nourish the seed of the future Egypt.

For the purity of divine descent had to be maintained. Only one of royal blood was worthy of marriage to another who was royal. To save the succession, brother must marry sister, provided that sister was the eldest daughter of the Pharaoh by his one Great Wife.

Sooner or later, Hatshepsut must choose among the lads who were growing up with her in the palace and leaving, one by one, to be trained in the services of Amon.

She may have made her choice, even then.

We return to the stone inscriptions. King Thothmes had shown himself to be a man of iron determination. He had realized all his own ambitions since marrying the heiress to the throne. Now his fierce energies settled upon Hatshepsut. She was his last remaining hope for retaining the throne after his death for the Thothmesid family.

Three inscriptions record events following the deaths of the three royal siblings.

In the first drawing, the child Hatshepsut is shown being consecrated by the gods. Wearing her boyish garb, she is standing between the gods Amon and Khons, undergoing the ritual of purification. The presence of her father is implied in that of Amon.

The two gods are pouring water on her head. They speak in unison.

"Thou art pure, together with thy ka [the spiritual duplicate] . . . [for?] the great dignity of the King of Upper and Lower Egypt."

In the second scene, Amon and his son hold the child between them and are evidently promising her their protection and a brilliant future.

The last interview shows the gathering of many gods. Anubis is present rolling a heavenly disk. Amon, the great god (also her father), is seated on the throne holding the child on his knees. A god kneels at her feet. Above them are three figures representing "all the Gods of the South," and below, three others presenting "all the gods of the North."

Amon is presenting the child to all his fellow gods and explaining that she is now the heiress to the throne.

Then Thothmes I placed the final seal of his approval on her. Speaking not as a god, but as the king, and with the approval of all the gods, he named her officially the new heiress to the throne. He named her, not as the princess royal, but by the male title he would have awarded a fully royal son!

When Hatshepsut left the presence of her father, she bore the new title. She was now Hatshepsut, Crown Prince of Egypt.

The pictorial records at Deir el-Bahari and Luxor show she was still little more than a child.

It is not right to inject a fictional suspicion into an account of a life based on records made during or shortly after a woman's lifetime. But a theory is prevalent in Egypt that many deaths in the ancient royal circles were not due to natural causes, and it is permissible to wonder why the oldest daughter and two young sons of Thothmes I and Amose, his Great Queen, should have died so conveniently and so close together, leaving the bright child Hatshepsut the sole remaining claimant to the throne.

She had certainly been very young when her precocity and good looks attracted the admiration, not only of her father the king, but of certain strongly placed political leaders in the Great Temple. Some of these may have decided that the favorite child of Thothmes I would be more capable of eventually ruling Egypt than his other royal children.

While this is guesswork, it is still along the strong lines of suspicion laid down in ancient times. The politicians were priests, the priests were the medical authorities and skilled in the uses of poison. Royal deaths were often suspect. Down into Cleopatra's time the royal scion with the strongest political backing was able by fair means or foul to sweep the way clear to the throne. The practice certainly existed long before Hatshepsut.

She had been taught as a child one of royalty's ugliest lessons.

It was suspicion.

Treachery was part of her heritage. Envy, hatred, and conspiracy moved in shadowy forces around the throne. Young royalty were taught never to wholly trust a friend, never to be fully at ease in their gilded beds. Did the evening cup hold poison, a woven curtain move, a blade stab forth in a once trusted hand?

Hatshepsut could take heed of the warning a long-dead king had left to his successor son.

"Fill not thy heart with a brother, nor know a friend . . . guard thy heart against thyself. . . ."

But she was strong in affection and the time would come when Hatshepsut could no longer guard her own heart.

CHAPTER 5

> The Southerners came downriver, the Northerners came upriver, and all lands together bring their tribute to the Good God (the king-deity) . . .
>
> —Inscription in praise of Thothmes I

Tribute poured in from every part of the kingdom and its tributaries to the throne of King Thothmes. He, richest of kings, was preparing to turn his revenue and his kingdom over to his last remaining fully royal child, addressed now by her new title of Crown Prince Hatshepsut.

It was her privilege and her duty to observe the daily life of this energetic father. As the royal heir nearing womanhood she had to learn everything a king would need to know. Hers would be the difficult dual role of both woman and regent. Under the guidance of her parents and the priests, she learned the meaning and manipulation of unlimited wealth and unlimited power.

She saw the richly laden processions thread the narrow streets to the gates of the great mud palace in Southern Thebes. She saw treasure and produce of every kind heaped at the feet of the aging king who sat furrow-browed and watchful, glittering like a god on his golden throne. Now she knew for a certainty her place would in time be there.

She watched while produce and yield and taxes were catalogued and divided—so much to the throne, so much to the gods. Outside the royal gates herds of cattle and other domestic beasts, taken as taxes, were divided and driven away, some to the palace pens and corrals, and always a goodly share to the Great Temple.

Everything was listed and distributed under the cold eye of the king.

Hatshepsut, watching, saw the collectors of taxes and the emissaries from foreign lands conquered by her father offer him tribute while lowering their heads before him seven times seven. (Collectors sent to foreign lands knew the language and customs of the distant places and no scrap of revenue could be hidden from them.)

Hatshepsut listened, hearing their reports and the brief acceptance speeches of her balding father, watched the king's share being carried off to swell the royal coffers, and knew that in time this too would be hers.

Now she saw the importance of the hundreds of clerks who flitted like bats through the palace with their papyrus pads and pens. They kept the records of the taxes collected from the farmers in cattle, sheep, geese, ducks, and honey, wine, linen, and grain. Crouched in rows under the throne, with the state treasurer standing proudly before them announcing the tribute received, and watched keenly by the Grand Vizier as well as the king, they listed the mounds of tribute rising like a tide over the royal knees.

She knew the great circle of flatterers and sycophants surrounding the throne, and saw beyond them to the greater areas of those who gave to it their loyalty and their lives. She learned respect for the minor and major officials who kept order in the city and the land.

She had been taught the fundamentals of Egyptian laws and their alliance with the moral and religious precepts. Established law had existed in Egypt long before the first records were set down. She heard her father pronounce the final judgment on matters political and moral, and took part in the daily religious observances that claimed so much of a monarch's energy and time.

Thothmes was a deeply religious man. He shared much of his life and his riches with his gods. The major share went to Amon in the Great Temple. Hatshepsut watched reverently as the greatest of kings humbly abased himself at the golden feet of the plumed idol. Thothmes the Conqueror lowered his head before Amon like any conquered subject before the King, seven times seven in the dust.

Placed lower than her father, prostrating herself before the altar, Hatshepsut chanted with Thothmes the great prayer to Amon:

> Thou art the One, maker of all things that are;
> The Only One, Maker of what has been. . . .

Clouds of burning myrrh rose to the rhythm of the sacred sistrums held in the hands of the priestesses of Amon, chosen from daughters of the Theban nobility. The gold image, bathed and dressed anew daily by the priests, heard the prayer rise to crescendo:

Father of the Father of all Gods!
Amon!
Who did stretch out the heavens and spread all the earth. . . .

Amon accepted all that was given and poured largesse over Egypt. The young Hatshepsut saw the wisdom in her father's giving to the gods. In that as in all else she would follow him.

Now that she had been named Crown Prince by her father, Hatshepsut's way of life changed.

It was an Egyptian royal custom to give every king's child its own separate establishment as it approached adulthood.

Sometime between puberty and marriage, he or she left the royal household, and, while remaining in close contact with their parents, they set up their own households. Hatshepsut probably made this change shortly after assuming the title of Crown Prince, but it is not known if she moved into a palace constructed especially for her, or into a larger, completely staffed apartment that was virtually a palace in itself, within the big palace. She would reveal at Deir el-Bahari her love of gardens, so it is not stretching the imagination too far to picture her in her own mud palace with its own great garden, with the inevitable pool and "sunshade houses" and relays of gardeners.

The change brought no household cares. Every great household had its own staff, and that of a palace was tremendous. She would have her own superintendent and housekeepers, and, most important, her own scribe. He not only had charge of her correspondence, writing her letters and notes, but he attended to all household economics, kept the lists of the vast army of employees, assigned them their duties, and settled their disputes. No problems reached Hatshepsut. The multitudes who tended her household, the clerks, accountants, valets, nurses, maids, cooks, chefs, butlers, waiters, and scullions, and the attendants for the bedrooms, bath, and massage rooms, were, to her, invisible beings. They answered only to the scribe.

The visible ones were her courtiers and ladies-in-waiting—the powerful and great of her land, including the Amon priests. An advantage in a separate life was the opportunity it gave a "Crown Prince" to develop her own strong influential circle. A capacity for friendship was evidently one of Hatshepsut's most invaluable attributes. During these post-adolescent years she was developing a social-political following that could be depended upon to help defend her against potential enemies. For she would have enemies, as her parents knew. Every Egyptian ruler, in fact every leader who has ever lived, faced hatred for one reason or another, or for no reason.

To her growing circle of devotees, to her family, and to her public, Hatshepsut had bifurcated responsibilities. She had to be both beautiful and wise.

The royal life held every incentive for deterioration. The jaded faces of some of the Pharaohs show the ravages left by sybaritic living. In a world where almost every evening ended in a feast, where drunkenness was tolerated, and Oriental temptations, luxury, and flattery pressed the ruler from every side, only one of extraordinary physical and moral strength could retain his stability. Many weakened and died young.

It testifies to the innate normalcy of Hatshepsut that her head was not turned at an early age. Her sense of moral responsibility deepened with her religious devotion, and if, along with these, her love of frivolity grew, it was never permitted to interfere with her career.

The responsibility of beauty required her to appear before her people always as a goddess. She had her good looks and her youth, but ritual made its demands. Any royal person's morning in Egypt began with a prolonged session in the bath.

This was no ordinary immersion. It required the presence of courtiers and attendants worthy of the honor of crowding into the ornate bathroom with their naked young "prince." The bath was one of the most attractive rooms in any fine home. There were alabaster tubs and bottles and jars and boxes of rare unguents and perfumes, a separate toilet, an adjoining massage room. One of the most important of the ladies-in-waiting was in charge of cosmetics, who accentuated the provocative lips of the young Hatshepsut with rouge and outlined the wide, questioning eyes with kohl.

The brief boyish kilts were becoming, and no girl, not even one spoken to as "Prince," could have resisted the jeweled sandals, many of them so beautiful they are copied today; or, if she was leaving the palace, a pair of the exquisitely stitched linen gloves both men and women wore. Men delighted in jewelry and perfumes, as did the women: Hatshepsut in her role of male heir could indulge her taste in these.

Bejeweled, perfumed, anointed, she was ready to conquer her immediate world. Royalty did not visit. Royalty presided. Hatshepsut's subsequent political successes are evidence that she was a notable hostess. The beautifully trained servants moved in relays about their designated tasks. The salon and dining room furnishings that have come down to us from the Eighteenth Dynasty show how lavish were the settings over which a royal or wealthy hostess would preside. Small stands served as tables, which were set with dishes made of the gold that was so plentiful then, or of silver, copper, bronze, and even alabaster. The most beautiful dishes were of painted pottery or molded glass. The wine or water goblets were masterpieces of art. Glass-making was new in this dynasty, and took the shape of small, beautiful flasks that held condiments, and larger flasks and jugs for beer, water, and wine. Bowls served as plates, and smaller bowls held dates and the honey used as a sweetener. Between the tables were set vases of flowers, roses and the favorite blue lotus, cool and sweet.

The Egyptians had made an art of fine food. The kitchens in the great houses boasted a small army of chefs and their aides. There were specialized cooks for pastries and vegetables and meats. There was always one chef whose sole responsibility was the meat roasting on spits turned by a slave or a dog. One pastry cook made nothing but the cakes craved by the sweet-loving Egyptians. One papyrus cookbook of that era contains recipes for forty cakes. The favorite in Hatshepsut's time was the shat cake, made of date flour and honey, and fried.

In the great dining halls the diners lolled on comfortable cushioned stools, like benches, as they made their way through the apparently endless courses. Waiters came and went, covering the small tables with trays and dishes of roasted beef and veal and mutton, and wild fowl and game, with many varieties of vegetables—onions were the favorite with rich and poor—with dishes made of eggs, cheeses, melons and grapes in season, and, always, the sun-dried dates.

There were round loaves of excellent bread made of wheat and barley and date flour, and an assortment of cakes.

Bread and onions were the staple foods of rich and poor. There is a saying in Egypt that the great monuments were built on a diet of onions.

Hosts and guests lingered at the tables, savoring the many courses, drinking their beer and wine, and gossiping or observing the varied forms of entertainment that were indispensable to any feast.

Some played games on small taborets placed by their chairs, a current favorite being a game like checkers that used pieces shaped like jackals or hounds. Others rolled dice while they ate and drank. The Egyptians, rich or poor, were a playful people, and in the city outside the less fortunate were watching paid entertainers or gaily playing their games, in and out of doors, on the flat roofs in the warm nights, or under the palm clusters, or in the market places that served the poor as parks. For these were people loving parties, military parades, religious processions, pageants, performances of every kind. In the market places were always to be found the acrobats, dancers, magicians, jugglers, musicians, and storytellers that enlivened the hard-working lot of the poor.

The nobility, and the wealthy, limited their pleasures to the banquet halls and the privacy of their gardens. They, too, had their dancers, musicians, singers, jugglers, acrobats, and professional storytellers, who maintained a perpetual vaudeville performance through the long courses of the feast. A palace, or any great house, had its own performers; Hatshepsut would have maintained her own orchestra and dancing troop. The musicians played their oboes, lutes, lyres, perhaps drums. There were famous visiting harpists who went from one feast to another and were highly honored.

Music played an important role in religious ceremonies and in all entertainment. Palace musicians were respected members of the court. Hatshepsut herself learned to play at least one musical instrument; this was required of all Egyptian queens.

Poets were in high favor. They recited poems of their own or by famous dead poets. Most of the poems dealt with love. The verses did not rhyme, but the rhythm was exact and recited to a resounding beat that stirred Egyptian hearts.

The storytellers were among the most loved entertainers. Listeners laughed, wept, shouted with indignation, as the narrative gained in tension or sorrow. Sometimes it was spoken to the haunting music of Egypt.

The diners listened in the warm night, eating the rich foods, drinking the cool drinks. Men or women, they might be lightly dressed or wear nothing at all, but on their heads were strapped cone-shaped cakes of what was apparently marrow fat, mixed with oil and perfumes and herbs. The cones melted in the heat of the rooms. The fragrant oil bedewed heads and shoulders, "to smell sweetly and provoke erotic desires."

The wine and beer never ceased to flow.

Behind the diners stood lines of little naked slave girls holding bowls of perfumed water and towels. Ever watchful, they were quick to spring to the side of a noble guest who had eaten or drunk too well. Drunkenness was not discouraged. Inebriation was referred to as "the sweetness of death."

The rescued one, cleansed and perfumed, returned to his table to eat and drink again.

The harp singer did not interrupt his song. One favorite of this dynasty expresses the current philosophy of a pleasure.

> . . . follow thy desire as long as thou shalt live . . . Fulfill thy needs on earth, after the command of thy heart . . . Wailing saves not the heart of a man from the underworld.

And Hatshepsut, listening, could ponder the continuation of the warning:

Behold, it is not given a man to take his property with him.
Behold, there is not one who departs who comes back again!

(Omar Khayyám would not be born for another two thousand years.)

Her life widened. It was not confined to palaces and the temple. She would have her own gilded chariot by this time, and, since she imitated her father in every way, we may be certain she drove it herself, gripping the reins with small hands sheathed in finely stitched driving gauntlets.

Thebes was her city. It was explosive with activity. She saw it intimately now, in the streets the millers delivering their jars and sacks of grain, the professional hunters peddling their netted game from the marshes, the fishermen their silvery take from the Nile. She looked into shops and small factories where men wove ropes and basketry, turned potter's wheels, pressed oil and wine, brewed beer, and spun and wove cotton and flax.

Over these people in status, and in more elegant shops, were the makers of sandals, jewelry, furniture, and armor, and the craftsmen who fashioned the magnificent furniture.

The same respect for fine workmanship was demonstrated by the shipbuilders who toiled with their copper-edged tools in the shipyards, fashioning the wooden sections of the ships designed for pleasure or for carrying cargo to and from Thebes to all the ports of the known world.

The Egyptian standards of workmanship were high. The artist and the artisan were respected citizens.

Lowliest of all were the slaves. They were mainly from Nubia or Syria, and had been captured in battle or purchased by traveling merchants. They were bought and sold like cattle and some were branded with the cartouche of their owner, as cattle were. Even a low-income family could own a slave.

They were everywhere, beyond all counting, underfoot and active, but as helpless as the mud bricks from which the city was made. They toiled, prayed, and died in obscurity. No one suspected then, and least of all a girl who was a Crown Prince, that they were the foundation of Egypt's economy.

The slaves tended the herds, grew the crops, fished the rivers, explored the mines, made Egypt rich. They built the monuments conceived by the kings. They cut and set in place the stones for the memorial buildings that were being built for Thothmes I by the great engineer-architect Ineni, that were adding to the greatness of Egypt. The naked thousands, fed on bread and onions and a little beer, formed the wave that was carrying Egypt to world supremacy.

And still, they were not wholly submerged. They were listed in groups, like herds of cattle, but each individual name was written down in the official records, along with his parents' names, his place of origin, and the name of the Egyptian official registering him. So it has come about that, while the names of the slave owners are lost, those of their slaves remain.

The slave was protected by law. He had to be fed and clothed by his owner, and a marriage could be arranged for him with another slave and even, in caste-free Egypt, with a member of the family who owned him! Class barriers were not insurmountable. A humane owner could set a slave free and help him to develop any ambitions he might have. A state official, a craftsman, was not an impossible goal for a freed lad with ambition. The means were there; the winning was up to him.

Hatshepsut went on longer trips with her father, up and down the river by boat, and by litter or chariot inland. She saw the peasants working their farms and plantations of palms in the rich level valley.

Did it matter to this glowing girl that the peasant was little better than a slave, and that in some ways his lot was even more severe? He had to scrape his living from the dry sandy soil he watered with water brought from the Nile, and much that he grew was taken from him in taxes for the king. He was permitted to own property, but he had no way to acquire it. He was at the mercy of the great landowners. He worked on a farm and out of so many days of labor he was permitted one day of gleaning for himself. If he did manage to become a tenant farmer, he was heavily taxed, and if suspected of withholding so much as an egg, he was beaten without mercy. Unlike the slaves, the peasants were listed in groups as so many farm workers, or construction workers, and only the official in charge of them was listed by name.

To the peasant was given the struggle to make fertile the arid land of Egypt, to build and maintain the irrigation ditches, to tend the fields and groves and cattle and sheep, ducks and geese, to gather the figs, olives, dates, pomegranates, and wild honey, to fish and hunt for the markets, and somehow survive. The terror of the tax collector was always with him, and he also lived in constant dread of conscription, of being torn from his family and placed in the military or the work armies, where he was made to carry stones and labor on the monuments to the glory of the king.

And Hatshepsut, with her father and her smiling mother, saw these things and saw in them only the growing prosperity of Egypt. What did she know of the back-bending labor that grew the flax? The finished product was hers in the woven linen, in the boyish kilts that rustled with the softness of silk around her slender loins.

She saw only the purpose and the end to the labors of Egypt. The lives that went into these had no meaning to her. These living creatures were the toilers. They toiled for her.

Her father's kingdom was an orderly Egypt. The laws of Maat and the king's officials kept order. The system had developed through one thousand progressive years. In Hatshepsut's eyes, the system was perfect and invincible and destined to last forever. The multi-tentacles of power stretched from her father's palace and Amon's temple over an ideal and timeless land. Egypt waited—for her.

And she, Hatshepsut, was being prepared for Egypt.

Thothmes I had given Egypt a new incentive to build and grow. His daughter was part of that forward movement.

Now the great warrior-king was showing his years. It may be he was beginning to weary of his many governmental responsibilities when he made his daughter Crown Prince. He had fought many years for Egypt, widened its boundaries, and brought it and its possessions to a durable peace. Now his still tremendous Thothmesid energies turned to other interests. They centered on Thebes and the dream of making it the most beautiful of all Egypt's cities.

Grant me an easy death, Oh Lord, a goodly burial. That my beauty be remembered.
—Prayer expressed in varying forms in Egyptian tombs.

Kings, queens, and commoners voiced the above wistful plea from their graves. Was it their appearance they wished to commemorate, or the beauty of their achievements while living? Royalty were convinced of their physical perfection by the thousands who paid them lip service. The tombs echoed praises heard in life, and the paintings and carvings were hymns of adulation for those who slept within.

To insure this perpetual recognition, all Egyptians of substance prepared their tombs and obituaries well in advance while they were alive.

Thothmes I was preparing for his own endless glory in the prime of his life and at the peak of his reign.

It was the good fortune of Hatshepsut to be associated with her father during the years of his revolutionary building that was to immortalize the Thothmesid name and add greatly to the beauty of Egypt.

Thothmes had no interest left in conquest. The great warrior-king had conquered all he had set out to win, and the Egypt he had enlarged and pacified was running smoothly under his devoted officials and the laws of Maat. Now he threw all his tremendous Thothmesid energies, his love of the beautiful, his unlimited labor sources, and almost unlimited wealth into the dream of architectural development that would be the eternal pride of Egypt.

His daughter Hatshepsut would share in, and carry on, the dream.

With the genius of the great engineer-architect Ineni to carry out his wishes, Thothmes had built lavishly of temples and monuments at Karnak and Abydos and other places. His stone memorabilia were scattered for hundreds of miles along the banks of the Nile.

Now he who had built so much in so many places determined to make the cemetery section of Thebes on the western side of the river into the foremost necropolis in Egypt.

So it was during Hatshepsut's youthful years and in the reign of Thothmes I that the series of great funerary temples began to rise on the western bank. Here Ineni began the construction of the last resting places for King Thothmes, his wife, and their daughter.

Hatshepsut, in the bloom of her youth, went often with her parents to the region of death to watch the preparation of the graves and temples that were to keep her parents and herself immortal on earth and in heaven "for the million million years." Any Egyptian of means, no matter how young and strong, planned early for his final home, and royalty above all others had need to plan, for the construction and furnishing of their "beautiful tombs" entailed the work of many years.

To Hatshepsut the necropolis had become a friendly and familiar place. It was the home of the dead, and there was nothing unhappy about death. Death was called "the resting of the ka," and it prepared the owner of the "ka" (doppleganger, physical replica, or soul?) for a triumphant entry into the next world.

She was profoundly impressed by her father's building on the western bank, where, with a final thrust of his energy, Thothmes started construction on a colossal scale.

Hatshepsut paid many visits to the necropolis, crossing the river from the city on the royal barge, and proceeding by litter, even walking in places over the thickly graveled sand, to the area of death. King and queen and daughter accepted with grace the knowledge of a time to come when the royal barque would wait for one of them in vain. Which would be the first to go? No matter, their graves, and their hearts, would be ready. There was no sadness in the knowledge, only a sense of togetherness as they discussed future meetings, plans, celebrations in the hereafter when they would again be with all they had loved. Queen Amose could look forward to seeing her three children again as they had been in life, before their burials at Western Thebes. And Hatshepsut, did she contemplate with joy the certainty of meeting again with her sister and little brothers, and would she have welcomed their return to earth between herself and the nearing throne? This is speculation of the wildest kind; we pass over it hastily, and return to the burial place on the Nile.

Western Thebes, the necropolis of the Thebans since their city began, is a strange terrain dedicated to the eternal silence. It is a lost and lonely region between the river and the Libyan hills, with bone-dry stretches of granite and sand, cliffs and wadis. Until the reign of Thothmes I, the Theban kings had always been buried on the sandy plain above the river, where the city of the dead started, at the hill site known to us as Deir el-Bahari.

It was not called by that name in Hatshepsut's lifetime. It took the name later when the temple became a Coptic convent and paintings of Christ were superimposed over those of Hatshepsut. Deir el-Bahari is Arabic, meaning "Residence of the West."

This site under the mountain of Gurn (the Horn) was the

burial ground of the ancient Theban kings. Seven regents of the Eleventh Dynasty were buried in this awe-inspiring setting. The towering cliff was honeycombed with tombs. It would be the site most associated with Hatshepsut; its splendor was worthy of her.

Stretching southward from the cliff was the otherwise empty desert under the hills, its monotony broken only by ancient tombs and mortuary temples. Here, close to their kings, were buried nobles, courtiers, high officials, and wealthy Thebans who had died back in the Eleventh Dynasty, during the Middle Kingdom, one thousand years before Hatshepsut was born.

For centuries this area had been the burial ground of the royal, the rich, and the distinguished of Thebes.

This was the necropolis, the eternal city that was the halfway station between two worlds. Across the river could be seen the towering stone temples of Karnak. They were built in memory of the gods. But the temples of Western Thebes commemorated the glory of the Theban kings whose bodies lay deep in the cliffs, near the temples they had raised to their own eternal glory.

The death area was consecrated to the goddess Hathor, protectress of the dead, "she who loveth silence."

The royal trio chose their burial sites cheerfully. Queen Amose would be buried on the plain near the graves of her ancestors. But her king-brother-husband and their daughter were innovators.

Thothmes broke with many traditions. He had violated custom when he made his daughter Crown Prince and permitted her to wear boys' clothing. His newest reversal of tradition was his choice of a place of burial in a lonely spot where no grave had been dug before.

This was a rocky cleft between hills, north of the manytombed cliff behind Deir el-Bahari. The valley ran hundreds of feet between the steep rocky walls of the hills. A stony ridge

1. Front and profile pictures of the only known statue of Queen Tetisheri, the great-great-great-grandmother of Hatshepsut. She was the wife of King Sekenenre II during the troubled Seventeenth Dynasty, preceding Hatshepsut's, and, noted for her beauty and courage, became the foundress of a long line of warrior kings and strong-minded queens.

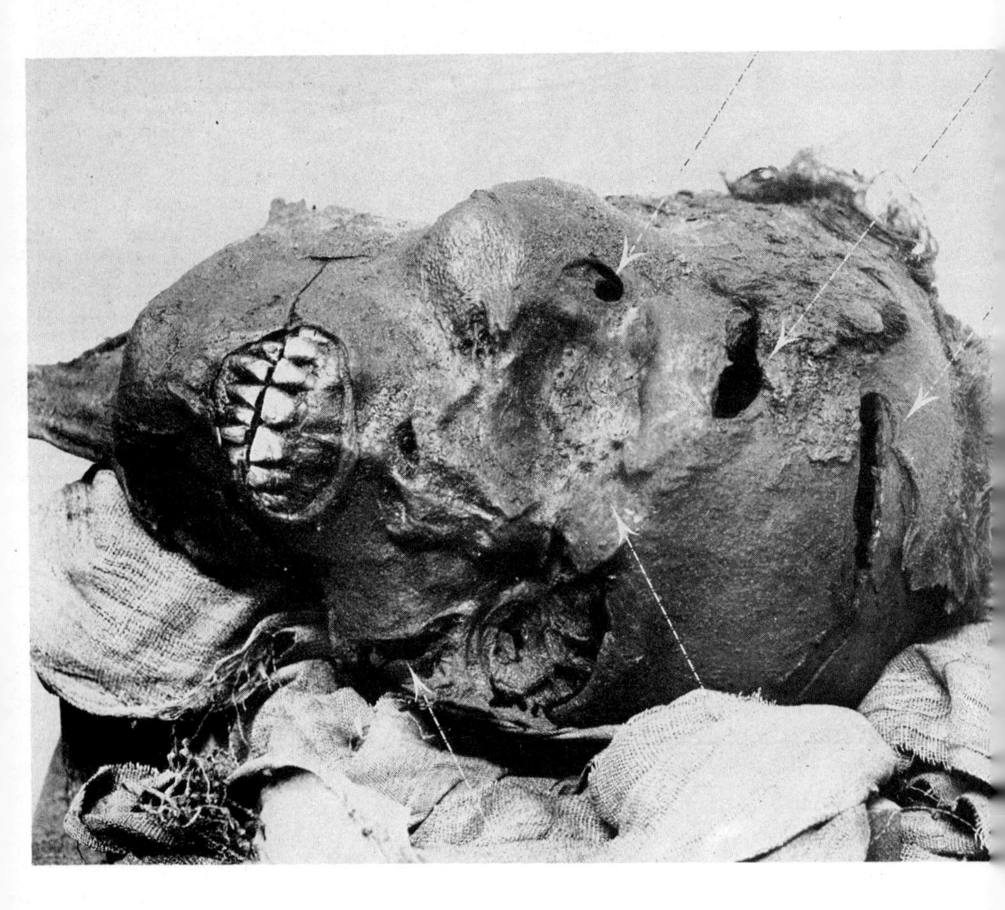

2. A horrifying object of interest in the Cairo Museum is this head of the mummy of King Sekenenre III, the son of Tetisheri who led the rebellion against the Hyksos overlords, and died, presumably in battle, of the five terrible wounds. He was Hatshepsut's great-great-grandfather. His death would be avenged and Egypt redeemed by his son, Amose I.

3. King Amose I, the great grandfather of Hatshepsut, avenged his father's death, freed Egypt from the Hyksos, and founded the Eighteenth Dynasty, the richest and most powerful in the history of Egypt. The head of this king, and the hand of a god, are shown on the fragment of a relief from the temple at Karnak.

4. Amose-Nefertari, sister, wife and queen to the great Amose, and the great grandmother of Hatshepsut, was paid the highest honors by her royal husband. He raised her name on stone from Senai to Nubia. Her mummy in the Cairo Museum is that of a woman who lived to be very old.

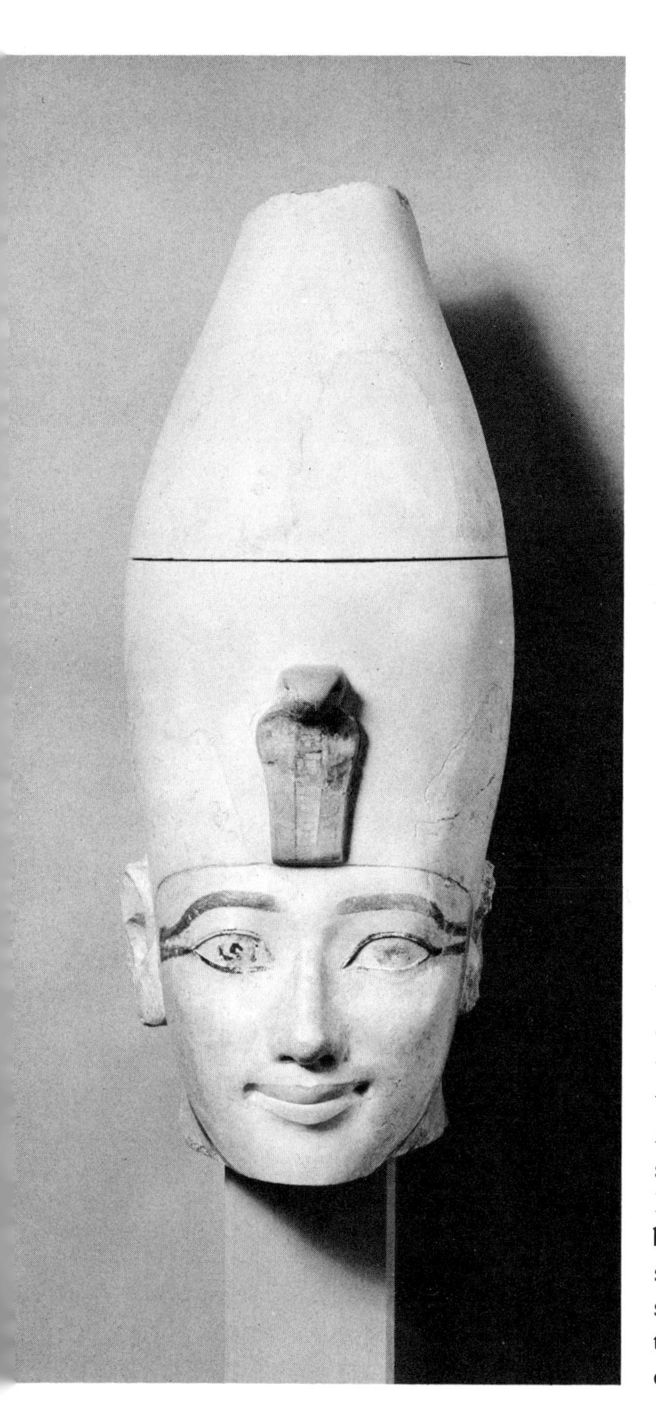

5. Hatshepsut was still very young when, according to her biography, her father placed upon her head the White Crown of Egypt and other crowns that signified the authority she shared with him. Responsibility rested heavily on her young shoulders but in nearly all her portraits, as in this Theban statue, the mobile mouth seems about to break into a smile. On her forehead is the "flaming uraeus," the cobra head worn by kings.

6. This sandstone relief of Thothmes II is as shadowy as the life of this half-brother and husband, with whom Hatshepsut shared the throne until his early death. His mummy, with its artificially curled hair and careful pedicure is responsible for the belief that this king lacked authority. He did not play an important role in the history of Egypt, nor apparently, in Hatshepsut's life.

7. Left young and widowed and in control of Egypt, Hatshepsut proceeded to cover the country with monuments and temples and statues of herself. Her favorite pose was that of the Sphinx, the royal male image she as a woman had no right to assume. She also wore the false gold beard on her chin that was another symbol of masculine royal power.

8. Hatshepsut considered the raising of the giant obelisks at Karnak one of the great feats of her career. On them, for the first time, she proclaimed herself to be, not Queen, but King of Egypt. This portrait of herself as king, wearing the false beard and crown, is on a fragment from her fallen obelisk.

barred it from Deir el-Bahari. It was a secret, silent, lonely place. Its isolation gave a promise of security that appealed to Thothmes.

He determined to be the first to be buried there and ordered Ineni to start the digging of his grave.

With this order he chose a new burial site for Egyptian royalty. The strange valley, widening under the hills, is known to us as the Valley of the Kings.

He was the first to have his burial shaft sunk there, but he would not be alone in the valley. His daughter Hatshepsut was another who defied tradition. She was still young, a teen-ager, still uncrowned, she was aburst with health and life, when she asked that her burial shaft be dug in the Valley of the Kings near that of her father.

If Hatshepsut had been an ordinary girl she would have chosen her final resting place nearer her mother's selected burial site with the other royal women whose tombs were guarded by the serpent goddess of silence. But Hatshepsut would not look forward to rest in the Valley of the Queens. True to her role as her father's son, she chose to remain close to her father in death as in life.

May we be permitted to listen in on a conversation that could have lingered thousands of years ago in the pure air of that secret valley? Father and daughter might rejoice together for their planned good future. Perhaps the royal mother of whom we know so little stood with them, listening and wondering at these strange beings who made up her living family, and approving, as Amose did all things, with her gentle smile.

"Here you will bring me." The King of Egypt braced jeweled sandals on the sunbaked gravel slide and looked with arrogant satisfaction down the treeless stretch of the valley. "Here I will be the first one. And you will visit me."

"I will visit you." So Hatshepsut promised. "I will bring gifts for you and for the gods who will guard you so none other will know where you sleep. You will be well hidden. No robbers will reach the great treasure you will take with you into the eternal happiness. And here, I will follow you in death."

Then all three were content, certain that all would come about as Hatshepsut promised and that Thothmes I would be the first to be buried in this place while Amose slept dreamlessly on the plain below, and that in time their beautiful daughter would follow her father into the Valley of the Kings.

But between this imagined conversation and the first entry into the new royal burial ground, a great deal happened to Hatshepsut of Egypt.

Now Ineni was hard at work developing in stone the dreams of his royal patrons. He began the construction work at the necropolis on a massive scale. There were the three graves to be dug and furnished for the royal family and their memorial temples to be designed and built. Other important Thebans would want their temples built close to those of their king.

Ineni had many construction problems. The temples must be beautiful and the graves safe.

The funerary temples were like chapels, or temples, and were, in effect, sumptuously furnished mansions, where the "ka" might visit when it chose, and the families of the deceased hold annual banquets in memoriam. Centuries of grave-robbing had taught Egyptians the wisdom of placing the temple at some distance from the grave.

The priests of Amon were skilled in the secret burials of the kings, but, still, robbery was rampant. King Amonhotep I, the father of Thothmes, lay deep under his own chapel where a shaft led down into the tomb, and, still, his grave had been violated shortly after his death.

Ineni began the mortuary temple of Thothmes near that of his father, and not far from the newly dug grave in the Valley of the Kings. The temple was nearer the river. Meanwhile, the new royal burial complex was developing behind the cliff of Deir el-Bahari. Other graves would be sunk around those of Thothmes and Hatshepsut. This was the beginning of the Valley of the Kings.

Hatshepsut saw the lonely region of death change to an explosive construction site as Ineni imported armies of workmen to the necropolis. He brought their families along to insure contentment.

Thothmes ordered a workman's village built in a wadi between the hills. It was named Deir el-Medineh.

Once a workman's family settled there, they stayed there the rest of their lives. The workmen were known as "Servitors in the Place of Maat." Generations of people were born, married, raised families, and died, without leaving Deir el-Medineh.

The village was gateless and open to the desert. The small and comfortable houses were built of the same sun-baked mud bricks as was the city of Thebes. The name of the householder was printed by the door. Life centered around work, and, as in most Eastern villages, around the community well. An efficient police force kept order. Thothmes built shrines to the gods for the people to worship. The principal shrine was that of his father, Amonhotep I, whom Thothmes had deified as a god and made the patron deity of the necropolis.

It was a curious community, devoted solely to the business of death. The howl of Anubis, the jackal-god of the dead, sounding through the wadi and over the plain, was the voice of death. The workmen were all expert in their various fields, but their labors had only one goal, which was the preservation of the dead.

They worked in gangs that were changed every ten days. The gangs were in charge of overseers who were answerable to the Royal Scribe who kept their names and accounts. He, in turn, answered only to the Grand Vizier.

There were levels of status, even here.

Lowliest of all were the quarry men who dug the graves with wooden copper-edged tools that penetrated the stony sides of the great cliffs with endless corridors and shafts, culminating in the deep-set secret rooms that were the graves. Armies of these men toiled deep in the earth, working by the light of shallow saucer lamps where cotton wicks burned in oil.

When the graves were completed and the walls smoothed and lined wth bricks, the artists and sculptors carved and painted under similar lamps the scenes that were to preserve for unborn generations the complete picture of life as it was then.

It is always stressed that it was the Egyptian faith in the afterlife that has saved for us a brilliant panorama of early Egypt.

The graves, chapels, and temples were art galleries and halls of record. The finest artists and sculptors gave their best to Western Thebes and art reached its supreme peak during this Eighteenth Dynasty. The artists worked underground in poor light, but the colors remain, clear and strong. They painted or carved, on papyri scrolls, limestone, granite, quartz, and alabaster. The bas relief, murals, portraits, and scenes recorded the lives of the dead and the Egypt of their time.

The artists used the new art style that was developing in Egypt during this dynasty and would achieve its apex under Akhenaton. In previous centuries the human figure had been shown angular, rigid, one-dimensional. Children were portrayed as miniature adults. Adults were shown one-sided, as children draw.

But now the artists painted and the sculptors carved their subjects with body curves and flowing draperies that foreshadowed the future Grecian art. The face and form of the growing Hatshepsut was their delight, and they portrayed in detail her developing womanly curves.

Tehuty was well known to her. He was the rich and famous, foremost sculptor of the land. He carved figures of the gods and of Thothmes I, whose sculptor he was, and he must have carved many portraits of the king's young daughter.

Sculptors were privileged. They could sign their works and ornament their own tombs, which were built to their own design.

The finest tomb paintings in Egypt are in Western Thebes. They date from Hatshepsut's time.

The recognized masterpiece is the tomb of Rekhmire, who later, as the Grand Vizier under Thothmes III, was to be in charge of all the construction in the necropolis. His tomb is a treasure chest of Egyptian art. The colors on the walls remain as fresh as if painted yesterday.

It is this famous tomb that shows the mysterious ceremony of The Opening of the Mouth. In this an ankh-like instrument was placed in or over the mummified mouth, which restored to the dead the ability to eat, drink, and be merry as in life. The paintings also show a family banqueting, and Rekhmire's own official duties as Grand Vizier. He directed the tasks of the work armies in his charge, including those of artists and craftsmen of every kind, and the raising and collecting of taxes foreign and domestic. Hatshepsut would have known Rekhmire, perhaps to her sorrow. As the most powerful aide of her arch enemy, he may have conspired against her.

Other celebrated Theban tombs, notably those of Nakht and Ramose, show scenes of funeral banquets with girl orchestras and dancing girls. The guests, or mourners, are tended by little naked girl slaves. These funeral banquets were annual events, celebrated in the temples on the annual feast day of the dead.

Because the tombs were the permanent homes of the dead, they contained everything conducive to happiness in the future life, when all human faculties were restored and all human wishes would be granted. Actually, there was no death. There was a brief pang of severance and a time for sleeping, a short journey by boat on the waters of the underworld, and a confrontation with the gods. Then the "ka" and the body, reunited, turned afresh to the pleasures of life, to eat, drink, and make love again. So everything that could contribute to the pleasure or comfort of the departed went with him in eternity.

To the tombs we owe our knowledge of the details of the funeral rites, the mourners and rituals of mourning, and the scenes of daily life of rich and poor, the hunting and fishing, the tending of the land, the sowing and the reaping, and all other details of daily living, large and small.

The lives of the families of the great were carefully pictured. Their battle scenes and hunting prowess, their victories and feats of strength and valor, their acts of kindness and dispensing of largess, their sports, amusements, the clothes they wore, the foods they ate, even their moments of tipsy conviviality, were carefully portrayed.

Food has been found in the tombs, left for renewed appetites, jars of grain and jars that once held wine or beer, and haunches of meat, preserved and wrapped like mummies.

Women took their cosmetic cases, their sewing equipment, and their jewels into the tomb. All took their most cherished possessions, even their childhood toys and small figurines that, restored to life, would be their servants in the other world. The rich men took small replicas of their favorite concubines, that they too might be available after death.

The poor had no fine graves to preserve their histories, but their lives were carefully portrayed at Western Thebes. A complete picture of Eighteenth Dynasty labor is preserved in the tombs. On the stone walls we can see today by electric torchlight the pictures of those who toiled for their masters in the fields and on the river and the monuments, who spun and wove and planted and reaped, and tended the cattle domesticated far back in times unknown. They are shown as living skeletons during the years when Hapi, god of the Nile, became angry and refused to flood the valley. Then dreadful months of famine swelled the ranks of Egypt's dead. But the poor had no graves. Their unpreserved bodies were rolled in papyrus mats and interred on the desert outside the necropolis under thin layers of sand which the jackals, attendants of death, had no difficulty removing.

Death was the leading occupation of all Thebes, and many other craftsmen, in and out of the workmen's village of Deir el-Medineh, labored in shops and studios all their lives in the service of Anubis.

There were the cabinet makers who fashioned the beautiful grave furnishings. The finest examples of these would be found in the tomb of Tutankhamon. There were the shipfitters who made the wooden boats buried with the dead, to carry them through the waters of the underworld.

There were the papyrus makers who stripped the reeds of their pith to make the paper scrolls on which the mortuary scribes recorded in beautiful inscriptions the virtues of the dead. There were the makers of charms and amulets designed to keep the dead bodies safe from robbing hands. There were potters who shaped memorial vases and plates and trays, and the small images of gods and animals, and the blue clay cow images of the goddess Hathor that have been found by the hundreds at Deir el-Bahari. They fashioned the small "soul houses" that were placed on the graves. These were small mansions like doll houses, in which the soul, or "ka," might rest. They were prettily colored and furnished with small-scale pottery furniture and minute servants shown in the variety of tasks that insured a comfortable life in the tiny home. The pottery figurines of the women are charming. They have pierced ears.

Many of the "soul houses" are very old, dating back to the Twelfth Dynasty. It is interesting to note that similar pottery offerings to the dead, dating from the same period, have been found on the banks of the Dnieper. Egyptian trade was wide-flung and far away, long ago.

Among the aristocrats of the death workers were the craftsmen who made the magnificent sarcophagi. Coffin within coffin was demanded by many preparing for their deaths. Some were shaped in human form, but all were beautifully carved and painted.

Thothmes I and his wife, Amose, had their handsome coffins prepared and in readiness. Hatshepsut also ordered her first sarcophagus long before she was crowned. It was a receptacle worthy of a Crown Prince, but it would not be considered adequate when in time she became a queen. She ordered others prepared during her lifetime, each more splendid than the one before.

Coffins were made of wood until her time. Hatshepsut, protestor of convention, was the first to order one carved of stone. Regents who followed her would also have stone sarcophagi, but hers was the first. She was a leader, an innovator, as was her father, Thothmes I.

The stone temples rose on the western bank. The cemeteries spread below Deir el-Bahari to Deir el-Medineh where the workmen lived. It was not an unhappy place. The citizens not only built the tombs of the great, but they were privileged to build their own. They also built temples to their favorite gods. They had their own complete little world.

Deir el-Medineh grew in time from a workman's village to a workman's city. It remained devoted in its entirety to the development and beautification and maintenance of the temples and tombs. The necropolis came in time to rival in importance the great stone complex of Karnak on the eastern side of the river. Deir el-Medineh reached an important milestone in the story of labor relations when the workmen, left without work for some months and therefore without food, staged the first sit-down strike in history. This, however, was long after Hatshepsut's time.

She was aware by this time of every aspect in the intricate craftsmanship of death. She knew of the men who preserved the bodies of the dead that they might return to life complete in body. These experts in mummification were of utmost importance, and it was to them Egypt owed its detailed knowledge of surgery and medicine. Other civilizations, centuries later, would be stopped in medical advancement by a reluctance to examine the bodies of the dead.

Mummification reached perfection during the Eighteenth Dynasty, and, while the art itself was highly respected, those who carried it out were apparently rated among the lowest in the working scale.

It was an unpleasant but necessary process, usually lasting a prescribed seventy days. During this time the soul rested; the mourners grieved, awaiting the final interment in the well-prepared and waiting grave.

Many death notices remain in the tombs. The customary wording explains that while the "ka" rested, the body was placed "in the hands of Anubis." In the mortuary workshop it was stretched over four wooden blocks on a wooden table in an embalming room that resembled a modern autopsy room. At each corner of the table stood a wooden emblem of the ankh, the symbol of life (recently adopted by certain elements in the United States as an emblem of peace).

Around the body were pots of salt and other preservatives, spices, knives, scrapers, and bundles of linen rags.

An incision was made on the left side. Abdomen and chest were emptied of all soft organs save the kidneys and heart. Wire hooks inserted through the nostrils extracted the soft material that was the brain. Organs and cavities were washed in palm wine thickened with spices. Then the cranial, abdominal, and chest cavities were stuffed with linen rags, straw, or other vegetable fibres, impregnated with salt and resin. Lastly, the emptied body was washed with the spiced palm wine and anointed with oil. It was placed on a slanted table and covered with dry salt. Vases placed under the table caught the body liquids. These too must be saved.

The long days of mummification began.

At the end of seventy or more days, the mummified body was taken from its salt coating. The linen padding was removed from the cavities. Head, chest, and abdomen were stuffed anew with linen rags soaked in melted resin. The incision, mouth, ears, nose, and eyes were sealed with the hot resin. Then the body was anointed with oils and fats scented with myrrh and cedar and other fragrances, and melted resin was poured over the entire body to close the pores.

Now there began, layer on layer, the wrapping of the mummy in strips of resin-soaked linen. Between the strips were placed amulets, and small sacred images of the gods in human or animal forms, and the fortune in jewels that had belonged to the dead and would prove so irresistible to the ever-waiting grave robbers.

Everything that had been taken from the body, including the treated rags from the cavities, was washed in the spiced wine and treated with perfumes, salt, resin, fats, and oil. Even butter was sometimes used. All these, and the liquid collected in the vases, were sealed into four handsome canopic jars. These would be carried with the body to the tomb and buried nearby in the sand, to be ready when the dead person reassembled his body and began enjoying his future life.

The mummy-makers also specialized in the preservation of scarabs, the worshiped beetle, and favorite pets, to companion the deceased in death as they had in life. Many mummies of cats, dogs, falcons, monkeys, and even a donkey, have been found in the Theban tombs.

The morticians left inscribed reports of their work in the mortuaries. It was written of one woman:

> There was done for her all that can be done for any blessed dead person. She was placed in the mortuary workshop in the hands of Anubis. She completed seventy days in the House of Embalmment, being content, safe, and prosperous in the venerated state.

Of another, a man, it was written:

> He completed seventy-two days in the House of Embalmment. Becoming content with the venerated state, he was drawn to his house of eternity, resting therein forever.

A more complete description of the actual burial is quoted by Dr. Bakry from an Eighteenth Dynasty tomb:

> . . . when thy seventy days are completed in the mortuary workshop . . . thou art placed upon a bier and art drawn by young cattle. The roads are sprinkled with milk until thou hast reached the door of thy tomb. The children of thy children, united all together, weep with loving heart.

The family of Thothmes I could face whatever might happen with loving hearts. Their graves were dug, their coffins prepared, the memorial temples of Thothmes and his wife Amose towered in splendid stone over the other western monuments. Hatshepsut, Crown Prince of Egypt, had readied her grave and sarcophagus, but as yet no temple had been reared to immortalize her name.

Her interests divided between the city and the cemetery side of the Nile. She went often to watch the monuments Ineni was completing for her father.

Toward evening, the western cliffs burned with a rose-copper tinge in the ebbing light. The cliff over Deir el-Bahari towered like a mountain of warm metal against a blazing sky.

The graves of many kings were there, each buried with the promise made by the gods that they would live forever.

We may imagine the royal litter halted and the slender girl in boy's clothing standing under the cliff, looking upward with the greatest dream of her life beginning to show in the wide-set, observant eyes.

Against the cliff stood the ruins of the mortuary temple King Mentuhotep I had raised in his own honor during the Eleventh Dynasty. His life and works were well known to Hatshepsut. He it was who had sent an expedition to Punt, hundreds of years before, and the impression his partially ruined but distinctive temple made on her was soon to be made apparent.

We can imagine her slim body tensing in the dry desert air as she felt awareness of the knowledge that here in this world of the dead she was still on the mobile side of existence and that life on earth stretched before her unlimited in its promises. She breathed the never-forgotten prayer, "That my name be remembered! That my life be worthy of these who sleep underground!"

The warm face of her ancestor the sun looked down on the small royal figure standing with the pride of ownership under the strange, lonely cliff of Deir el-Bahari. When did she first decide, ignoring the rights of the kingly occupants long dead, This place is mine?

Then the day came when Queen Amose II smiled on her king-brother-husband and her princely daughter Hatshepsut for the last time, and left the Theban palace for her "beautiful tomb" in the West.

Now there was the donning of white robes of mourning and of funereal leis of live flowers, the favorite being the cornflower of the hue that was the royal color of Egypt. Now there was ululant wailing and the casting of dust on the heads of men and women, who, naked to the waist, beat their breasts and bewailed the presence of death.

There was also the funeral feasting, and the gathering of family and friends. After the seventy days of rest there was no delay in placing the mummified body of the little queen in her well-prepared tomb. Now the advantage was seen of having a grave prepared in advance which had been enjoyed by the occupant in life. Hatshepsut could take comfort in knowing her mother was safe and amply provided for and that in the grave as in life she would be upheld by all the majesty of worldly power. For the royal dead did not lose their authority. Deep underground, they felt concern and could still give powerful aid to those they loved who were still living.

Hatshepsut would continue to bring gifts to her mother, leaving presents, flowers, and food in the tomb. She would continue to consult her in affairs domestic, political, or emotional, with the priests acting as intermediaries. She might even write letters to her.

Hatshepsut and her father returned to Thebes on the royal barge after the burial, knowing the lovely smiling Amose was safe and comfortable forever in the shadowy West, as they too would be, in time.

Thothmes I raised other memorials to his dead wife. He was nearing the end of his long, auspicious reign, and it may be that the fierce Thothmesid energy was waning. Shortly after the death of Queen Amose he made one more of his unprecedented moves.

Defying all that had gone before in Egyptian history, he placed his daughter Hatshepsut beside him on the golden throne.

. . . exceedingly good to look upon, with the form and spirit of a god . . . a beautiful maiden, fresh, serene of nature . . . altogether divine.

—Description of Hatshepsut,
Ancient Records

Myth and mutilation obscure the accounts of Hatshepsut's coronation. Both she and her father recorded the stirring events, which monarchs who followed her would claim by erasing her name and substituting theirs. Still, the record of the long drawn-out and costly process remains decipherable in words and pictures at Deir el-Bahari and on a pylon at Karnak.

It was certainly a daring move for Thothmes I to foist a girl disguised as a boy onto the throne. Only a ruler with absolute power would have dared, and then only with the approval of the priests of Amon. He began with a summons, made in the royal audience hall of his own palace.

The king records the edict in his own words:

> My majesty caused that there be brought to him the dignitaries of the king, the nobles, the companions, the officers of the court, and the chief of the people [the Grand Vizier], that they may do homage, to set the majesty of this daughter of Horus before him in his palace . . .

(Horus was the god-ruler of the sky and stars.)

The illustration accompanying the text shows Thothmes seated on his throne in the hall in his dual role of both king and god. Hatshepsut stands before him, slim and boyish, in the ceremonial dress of a king. On their right, three groups of courtiers stand in rows. It is explained that the entire court is present, so it can be assumed that hundreds of people are postrating themselves on the floor of the great hall.

The king had summoned his daughter before him to be crowned. "She is embraced by Amon [the king]." Thothmes is shown holding her arm.

The god-king-father speaks to Hatshepsut:

> Come, glorious one! I have placed [thee] before me, that thou mayest see thy administration in the palace, and the excellent deeds of thy ka's that thou mayest assume thy royal dignity, glorious in thy magic, mighty in thy strength. Thou shalt be powerful in the Two Lands; thou shalt seize the rebellious; thou shalt appear in the palace, thy forehead shall be adorned with the double diadem . . . given to thee by him who presides over the thrones of the gods.

Then Thothmes, speaking over her head, addresses the court:

> This is my living daughter, Khnemet-Amon, Hatshepsut, who liveth. Behold! I have appointed her my successor upon my throne . . . She shall command the people in every place of the palace; she it is who shall lead you; you shall proclaim her word . . . be united at her command.

And then, the monarch thundered; was it her human father, or Amon, speaking?

> He who shall do her homage shall live, he who shall speak evil blasphemy of her majesty shall die . . . !

Then, to Hatshepsut:

> For thou art divine, O daughter of a god, for whom even the gods fight; behind whom they exert their protection every day according to the command of her father, the lord of the gods.

Hatshepsut describes her own reactions:

> There saw she [Hatshepsut] the majesty of her father . . . how divine is her great fashioner. Her heart is glad, great is her crown.

But she could not yet don the crown. There were more complicated rites to be observed. For the present, it was recorded that the court dignitaries who were present heard the royal command advancing the dignity of the king's daughter to that of "king of Upper and Lower Egypt, Makere (Kamere) [Hatshepsut] living forever."

The court dignitaries "kissed the earth at his (Hatshepsut's) feet and praised all the gods of Upper and Lower Egypt and Okhepernere [Thothmes] living forever."

Then, leaving the palace, they

> . . . went forth, their mouths rejoiced, they published his proclamation . . . All the people of all the dwelling of the court heard; they came, their mouths rejoicing, they proclaimed beyond everything, swelling and swelling was announcing in his name; soldiers on soldiers . . . they leaped and they danced for the double joy of their hearts. They proclaimed the name of her majesty as king; while her majesty was a youth . . . Makere [Hatshepsut] living forever . . . thus they were excellent in her great soul.

The king's threat was enlarged upon and broadcast throughout the city.

> As for any man who shall love her in his heart, and shall do her homage every day, she shall shine, and he shall flourish exceedingly; as any man who shall speak against the name of her majesty, the god shall determine his death . . .

So Thebes fell before Hatshepsut, promising her fealty and love, and the promise of death to any who might fail her.

Thebes was the capital, but further approval had to be won before Hatshepsut could wear the double crown of united

Egypt. Directly after the ceremony in the palace, King Thothmes announced that he and his daughter, accompanied in some mysterious manner by the god Amon, and all the members of the court, would set out on the royal barge for Heliopolis on the Delta, to show the budding Queen Hatshepsut "to all the gods of North and South."

She was less than twenty years in age, but by her own description Hatshepsut had "grown up." The pictorial records show her at this time as a slender, graceful lad, wearing the masculine kilt she would continue to affect while she lived. It may be that she was portrayed as male to strengthen her position of leadership.

The records are hopelessly confusing. Sometimes Hatshepsut is referred to as "he" and sometimes as "she." Thothmes writes of "the Majesty of Him my daughter."

It is not surprising that in earlier archaeological studies Hatshepsut's reign would be passed over entirely, or she would be listed as a king.

But in all the records her beauty was mentioned, and stressed.

According to the descriptions, she was developing into a young woman with a brilliant mind. She walked with the assurance of majesty. She graciously accepted adulation in the chapels, the theaters, at the great court festivals and religious ceremonies where hymns were sung lauding her beauty and her divine heritage. Heads lowered in the dust before her, courtiers waved ostrich fans over her head, musicians played to the rhythm of her steps, and singers chanted, "Sweet in love is the daughter of the king."

Now she would be a queen in her own right, sharing the throne with a father whose one true royal wife had died.

We cannot be certain in which year he named her co-regent. Egyptian dates B.C. resemble the Nile, that flows downward to the north, so that what would normally be considered the lower part of Egypt is known as Upper Egypt. Conflicting dates are given for all the reigns, but, since it is recorded that Thothmes had reigned since 1528 B.C., he had been more than thirty years on the throne when he conferred the insignia of royalty upon his daughter.

Was Thothmes beginning to feel the inevitable twinges of mortality when he made her his queen?

Hatshepsut was well prepared for the honor. She had served for many years—some believe as many as fifteen—as her father's Crown Prince. She had shared in his interests and activities and accompanied him on inspection trips along the Nile. Hatshepsut had inherited the iron constitution of the Thothmesid. Like her father, her interest and her energy never flagged.

An impressive cavalcade set out by water from Thebes, turning south on the river toward the Delta.

Hatshepsut had fished, hunted, and boated on the Nile. This would be her most impressive journey. Her father was taking her to Heliopolis on the Delta to be crowned there by the gods, and Heliopolis, the city of the sun, was Egypt's holiest city. The journey was in the nature of a pilgrimage, and it would mark the greatest change in her life.

And still Hatshepsut has left only a brief record of what must have been a dramatic experience.

With the innate Egyptian ability to combine religion, business, and pleasure, the royal party must have made the pilgrimage into a merry expedition as the royal entourage made its memorable journey down the Nile.

The king's barge and the accompanying boats made up a colorful pageant. The blue and white pennants of imperial Egypt streamed over the heads of Hatshepsut and her father. They spent much of their time on deck, seated in gilded chairs and shielded by parasols and plumes and a Conestoga wagon-type of tent, surrounded by favored members of the courts and priestly representatives of Amon from the Great Temple. The relays of naked oarsmen rowed in ceaseless rhythm, and there were court musicians and singers aboard to relieve the monotony of life aboard ship.

None of the luxuries of the palace were lacking on the royal barge. There were folding beds (such a cot would be found in the tomb of Tutankhamon) and comfortable folding chairs and head rests. These had been designed for travel. On deck the travelers might loll at ease, eat and drink, and be entertained and play their favorite games. There were tents and sunshades for picnics on the shaded banks along the way.

Every luxury craft had its own kitchen boat. Cooks and chefs and their helpers brought from Thebes prepared the royal meals skillfully as in the palace kitchens. One ancient painting of a kitchen boat shows haunches of meat hanging from the mast.

The royal hunters aboard did not have to go far to provide the royal table with game. At this time, the Nile was fringed all the way to the Mediterranean with feathery groves of papyrus from which clouds of waterfowl rose at the approach of the cavalcade. From their high seats on deck the royal party watched with interest the stately flight of ibis, the sacred bird, the scurry of gazelles and hyenas, the thundering roar and tread of hippopotami, and the submersion of another scaly Nile god, the crocodile.

Hatshepsut may have scoured the banks with the hunting parties. Her love of Nile sports has been commemorated.

The royal caravan passed majestically downstream, passing now coppery stretches of desert, then under cliffs flashing gold in the sun. Hatshepsut watched the stately march of palms proceed along either side of the river and admired the bursting floral fountains, yellow and pink and rose, that were tamarisk and acacia, and watched for the appearance of the river towns set far apart along the rim of the water.

How many towns long vanished lay then along the Nile?

Then as now, the Nile was the heart line of Egypt.

It was a well-traveled water highway, a moving panorama of boats and barges propelled by wind and sail, or men and oars, between Aswan, near the First Cataract in the south where a massed granite ledge formed the southern frontier, to the branching waters of the north in the Delta, and on into the Mediterranean. From Thebes, the mid-Egypt center of commerce, a steady flow of commerce moved up- and downstream. The records do not list the many places the cavalcade rested on the journey, but they linger rapturously over Hatshepsut's godlike appearance and the adoration she inspired in both gods and men along the way. Certainly, the royal party stopped at every village and hamlet, since every Egyptian community, no matter how minute, had its own sacred shrine to its favorite god, and each shrine must be visited by Hatshepsut! Not even the most insignificant country god could be passed by. It was dangerous to withhold homage from even the least.

Among the ancient towns was one unknown to us by place or name, but after Hatshepsut's time there would be born there one who was to change the thought of mankind. From that place an Egyptian-born Hebrew babe was set adrift on the Nile. Found in his rush crib or raft by Pharaoh's daughter, he was reared by her under the name of Moses, which is a variant of Thothmes or Amose, names so popular in Hatshepsut's family. This was Moses who would lead the enslaved children of Israel out of Egypt in the time of Rameses II, who, while a great king in his own right, was to lay claim to many of the triumphs and records of Hatshepsut.

But Hatshepsut, dreaming on the royal barge, knew nothing of these events that were to change the world, nor did she know, as the barge idled past an empty crescent of sand under cliffs in a bend of the Nile, that a nephew of hers still unborn, King Akhenaton, would build there in the following century the fabulous city of Amarna.

An important stopover was Abydos, between Thebes and the site of the future Amarna. This was one of the holiest shrines in Egypt. Devotees from all over the country made pilgrimages to Abydos. The head of Osiris was buried there, and each year the reunited body of the murdered and dismembered god was carried in a priestly procession to his tomb. Hatshepsut would perform elaborate rites at the shrine of Osiris, the "Great One of the West," who had been the leading god of Egypt before her ancestors set Amon over all the gods. He was still a spiritual force it was best to have on one's side. Hatshepsut made profound obeisance at his shrine.

Thothmes, her father, had constructed his own memorial at Abydos.

Here in the north, as they neared Heliopolis, by another of those mysterious changes peculiar to the alchemy of Egypt's ancient religion, their god Amon, who had accompanied them on this journey, became Atom-Re, and also Osiris!

There is no way of knowing how many shrines Hatshepsut visited on the way to the Delta. She prostrated her graceful body before every sacred image. She laid her smooth forehead against the base of altars, and proffered gifts and sacrifices and burned incense and poured out libations of milk, water, and wine to hundreds of gods.

Many villages and towns were scattered then at remote intervals along the Nile. Some have melted with their histories into the desert. Some have developed into modern cities. But each one, in Hatshepsut's time, had its claim as an abiding place of a god.

It is reported that Hatshepsut neglected none of them on this journey, and that all the gods she visited, according to the ancient records, "were well pleased with her."

She was seeing an Egypt few could know. Her father was her mentor and teacher. From the deck of the barge he pointed out the merits of the Egypt he had fought for, guided, made secure for her. She too must know and love the land.

They were threading a green ribbon of a country that was the rich and narrow valley of the Nile, in places only seven miles wide. The black land held the river as a man holds a woman. Both changed in shape and color with the changes of Egypt's year.

There were three seasons—Flood Time, Seed Time, and Harvest.

The journey to the Delta would logically have been made in Flood Time to take advantage of the currents racing from the snow-melting southern mountains down to the Mediterranean.

This was in late summer or September, nearing the time of the New Year, when the floods started from far beyond Aswan in the region no one knew. The hopes of the people rose with the muddy waters. Humans, homes, and herds might be washed away, but this remained a time for thanksgiving, for the god Hapi had relented once more and was replenishing the earth. Gruesome records told of the famine years when no flood waters swept down to replenish the land.

In every household small shapes of Osiris made of the river mud were sprinkled with seeds, and these, sprouted, symbolized the return of the dead god to life.

The waters reached their height in late November. On the night of the High Nile women drank nine times of the flood waters and prayed to Osiris. "Bless my children and my home." When the waters lowered, the rich land showed black rimming the river. It was Seed Time and the beginning of winter.

When the seeds were scattered over the wet earth, the drovers herded the cattle back and forth over the land to drive the seeds into the ground. The loin-clad men, up to their thighs in mud, drove the staggering animals to and fro as they sang one of the cheerful "labor" songs.

Your shepherd is a shepherd of the West
He will paddle in the water and salute the fish's daughter . . .

The irrigation ditches were left clogged with mud and had to be dug anew each year. The farmers were aided in watering their fields with the well-sweep, an innovation imported from Asia.

Spring was the time of the sandstorms and the great winds. Then men worked with eyes shielded against the fury of the sand-driving khamseen. But with summer, energy sank in both beast and man, and human veins burned as the sun filled them with longing.

Each season lasted thirty days.

Five leftover days remained, and must be added to fill out the year when it ended in the fall after Harvest Time, making the three hundred and sixty-five days of the Egyptian calendar (and ours), the first calendar in the world. Long before Hatshepsut was born, the astronomer-priests had made this calculation to allow time for the sowing and reaping and the many religious festivals.

From her gilded traveling chair, Hatshepsut observed the width and substance of her land and came to understand an Egypt at work. She saw the importance of the river and the allegiance all Egyptians owed to Hapi, who, as god of the Nile, gave Egypt the water that was its life's blood. She paid special devotions to him.

As they idled downriver, her father could tell her much about this fertile land. From the deck they reviewed a moving display of the wealth and industry of Egypt. Hatshepsut saw well-tended vineyards and plantations of pomegranate and olive trees, and everywhere stands of date palms that supplied a large share of the food of the people. She saw the dark-earthed vegetable fields which the fellahin tilled with copper-sheathed hoes or wooden plows drawn by cattle.

Every community had its mud-brick granaries filled with wheat and emmet and corn.

She saw the papyrus workers along the river's banks, cutting the tall, feathery shafts and binding them into sheaves that would be made into the thick, smooth sheets of paper.

The country was alive with commerce. There were signs of prosperity everywhere. The smallest hamlet had its market-place and its wharf where the boats and barges of tradesmen stopped to barter and exchange food, clothing, sandals, and pottery that made up most of the goods produced along the Nile.

Pressing close to the communities, like a tremendous dry maw waiting to swallow them, awaited the desert.

From her perch aboard the barge, Hatshepsut could see past the cultivated land to the wind-ruffled desert. In places there might be sighted, deep in a wadi or clustered around an oasis, small clusters of dark tents or mud huts that in time might become villages. Some of these have survived; others have sunk back into the eternal sands.

Along the river's rim, linking the hamlets together, ran pathways centuries old. Over these marched the donkey and camel trains bringing goods from one place to another along the Nile.

Other well-trodden roads led away from the river eastward over the Sahara. These were the ancient trade routes the caravans had traveled carrying Egyptian goods over the arid Wadi el-Hammamat to the Red Sea, where Egyptian trade ships waited to carry Egyptian goods to Somaliland and Sinai and Arabia and the Sudan. The caravans returned across the desert bearing imported goods from other lands, turquoise from Sinai and gold from the Red Sea hills for the jewelry beloved by Egyptians, the copper that had revolutionized the primitive wooden tools of industry and horticulture. Foreign trade had been active in Egypt since earliest times.

Where, now, is the road that once led across the desert to the gold mines in the hills rimming the Red Sea?

Hatshepsut saw the flow of commercial ships carrying Egyptian-made goods down the Nile to the Mediterranean, where

Egypt's largest trade ships waited to transport it to Byblos, Mycenae, Syria, and Palestine (these last two subject to Egypt), and to Crete and Greece. Egypt controlled the Aegean trade, and Greece absorbed from her in art and architecture. Egyptian pottery has been found in many lands, including Southern Russia.

All this Hatshepsut observed and understood as the barge traveled slowly toward the north. She was learning from her father the importance of a country's economy to that country, its people, and its king.

In the places they visited she met with the authorities who had charge, under her father's crown, of the land along the Nile. She met with the Grand Viziers of north and south and the leaders who worked with them under the laws of Maat that kept her world secure. She saw that every town and hamlet had its own squadron of police, and its civil and military authorities, who now pledged themselves to continue to enforce order in Egypt in her's and the king's name.

She realized that none of these human beings had the power or the terrifying authority of the river. The Nile was the source of her country's commerce and industry and of its daily food, and the media of communication between Egypt and the outer world. It provided her people and their herds with the grains, fruits, and vegetables that kept them alive. It provided Hatshepsut with her wealth and with the flowers she loved.

Now she knew her country and the Nile that fed so many—the beautiful land that was Hatshepsut's Egypt.

Her father was well versed in his country's history and legends. He could tell her much concerning the river.

> Far back during the Second Dynasty, so men say, the Nile once flowed with honey for eleven days.

She could not question the miracle. It was set down in the records; it must be true.

The two must have had many discussions on the long journey that was made longer than its over four hundred miles by the frequent pauses along the way. It may well be that on this trip Hatshepsut's thoughts moved closer to the mystery of Punt, the land that held for her an almost mystic fascination. She learned that not all commerce went over the desert by camel train to the Red Sea. There was a waterway leading from the eastern branch of the Nile, in the Delta, to the inland sea. It was a rudimentary forerunner of the Suez Canal.

Her eager thoughts formed questions.

> It is true then that goods can go to Sinai by water or land? That there is a way over water to the Red Sea? Could our ships go there, and down the Sea . . . perhaps to Punt?

And the father might have told her, yes, an Egyptian ship might go to Punt by way of the Red Sea.

Punt! The Red Land! The Land of God!

The magic of the name reached from far back in history to Hatshepsut. Punt was a glamour word, holding the touch of gold and ivory, the voices of strange animals, the odor of her favorite incense from the citrous-scented myrrh trees that grew in Punt.

She may have hidden her excitement, asking, "Has one done this thing?"

Then Thothmes could have told his daughter of the first King Mentuhotep, whose memorial temple she had seen at Deir el-Bahari.

Back in the Eleventh Dynasty, she was told, this king had sent a successful expedition to Punt. Three thousand of his soldiers marched across the Sahara to the Red Sea, each man carrying two jars of water and twenty loaves of bread, and poles for digging water holes along the way. They were five days without water. It had taken them almost a week to cross the mountains of the desert, and they had dug perhaps a dozen wells on the Wadi el-Hammamat.

"They reached the coast of the Red Sea," so the king could have continued the story as it had been told to him by his father, "and there they built a great ship, a Byblos ship. [This was a seagoing craft that could ride the deepest known waters.] They sacrificed to its success the sacred animals they had brought with them for this purpose, cattle of all kinds, and ibexes. . . . Then a crew sailed away on the ship to Punt, and returned with wondrous stories of the things they had seen in that land of fables, and with proof in incense brought back by the travelers, and gold and ivory and spices and strange animals and humans. And this was the first expedition to Punt. . . ."

(It was probably the first Egyptian venture into foreign trade which had become supreme by Hatshepsut's time.)

She would have wondered eagerly, "And where is this land?"

But this not even the king knew. The secret of the way had been lost for centuries. It was known only that the early expeditions had ranged the coasts of Arabia and Africa before arriving in Punt. Other expeditions had gone to Nubia and returned with stone brought from the trade route to the Red Sea that had been used in the building of the earliest pyramids that were appearing along the shore as the royal caravan progressed toward Memphis. But Punt had been long forgotten.

Hatshepsut would remember. Her agile mind raced ahead of the slow-moving barge. The waterway ran farther north, above Memphis, from the Nile to the Red Sea. There would be no need now to send armies marching across the terrible desert. And now she would be a queen, and could take advantage of every modern means of commerce.

Hatshepsut had been schooled in the victories of her conqueror-ancestors. She was not impressed by conquest. She admired the lasting memorials they had left. Her admiration was great for King Mentuhotep, who had sent his armies not to make war but to open up avenues of trade for Egypt. He had engineered the first expedition to Punt. He had built the mortuary temple she so admired in Western Thebes. She found in him a hero to follow.

Her thoughts were a girl's thoughts, but they held the determination of one who was about to be made a regent. Hatshepsut had been encouraged to form her own opinions. Now she shifted standards. Not to destroy, but to build. Not to conquer, but to explore.

Even carried along on the high tides of fall, the royal cavalcade would have taken many weeks in traveling from Thebes to the Delta. Everywhere, shrine appearances and receptions for Hatshepsut slowed down what the ancient records describe as a triumphant journey. They commemorate the impression she made on both gods and men.

"They came to hear," so one report runs,

> . . . in pleasant ways . . . they brought all life and satisfaction with them, they exerted their protection behind her; one preceded after another of them, they passed behind her every day . . . they did obeisance before her. . . .

Her father and forefathers had marched the length of this land as war heroes, acclaimed on every side. Hatshepsut also conquered. She held Egypt in her hand. The people along the river showed their love for their new queen. The priests of every shrine demonstrated their preference for her, and the priests spoke for the gods.

Time was spent observing the great monuments along the rim of the river. As they neared the Delta they sighted hundreds of these stone cairns that marked the burial sites of ancient kings. The pyramids increased in size and majesty as they traveled farther north toward the branching of the Delta waters, where the pyramid concept had started more than a thousand years before.

The immense monuments were to inspire Hatshepsut in plans that would add to the greatness of Egypt and her own.

So the journey increased in triumph, which reached its peak when they came at last to the Delta at the junction of the two Egypts. King Thothmes had chosen Heliopolis, the holiest of cities, as the setting for the coronation. Here his daughter Hatshepsut would receive the first of her Egyptian crowns.

> Her Majesty journeyed to the North country after her father, the King of Upper and Lower Egypt. . . . There came her mother, Hathor, patroness of Thebes; Buto, mistress of Dep; Amon, Lord of Thebes; Atom, Lord of Heliopolis; Montu, Lord of Thebes; all the gods of the South and North, and approached her.
>
> —The Crowning at Heliopolis, from *Ancient Records*

On this northern tour with her father, Hatshepsut was welcomed everywhere by priests of various cults and the political leaders of the land. Nearing the Delta she was shown the monuments of an earlier Egypt, older by thousands of years than those of Thebes. Many had been left damaged and even destroyed by the Hyksos, but hundreds remained on their original sites. Temples, pyramids, tombs, and pillars fringed the banks of the Nile like the stone fingers of gods pointing to the sun.

Here was the most ancient Egypt, preserved in limestone, granite, alabaster.

She saw its greatness when she was welcomed to Memphis, a thriving maritime city that lay seventeen miles south of the present Cairo, on the wide plain between two branches of the Nile that joined Upper and Lower Egypt. It had been the capital until Hatshepsut's family turned the current of power to Thebes.

It was an active river port, with commerce reaching its wharves from every branch of the Nile. The ships of the imperial navy were built in its navy yards.

Like all Egyptian cities, Memphis was constructed of the sun-dried bricks. Date plantations spread a green carpet for miles around, and the famous White Wall of Menes, built of white-washed bricks, which encircled the city, gleamed through the stems of the palms.

Memphis was one of the oldest cities, perhaps the oldest in Egypt. Thousands of years before a settlement had grown there around a temple dedicated to Ptah, who was still the city's patron god. He was worshiped as the creator of the world, from whose heart came thought and from whose tongue came the gift of speech. His wife, the lion-headed goddess Sekhmet, was a favored deity in Hatshepsut's time. There were many statues of her at Karnak. She was the patroness of lions and Lady of the Messenger of Death. Her son by Ptah was Nefertum, the fragrant lotus.

The mud palaces, religious images, monuments, and inscriptions of Memphis, were older than the time of Menes (Narmer), the first king of the First Dynasty (a date often given as 3000 B.C., but set by Petrie at 5500 B.C.). Long before that, no one could guess how many centuries before, Memphis had been a prehistoric city.

Menes lived in Memphis and is credited with having developed the ancient settlement into a city and surrounding it with the White Wall. Herodotus believed Memphis was built on marsh land which Menes drained in order to found the city, but the Greek historian often mingled history with legend.

The earliest kings of the First Dynasty continued to live in Memphis and began building their memorial temples across the river.

Nothing remains now of the great city of Memphis Hatshepsut knew but a scatter of broken stones on the plain that marks the site of the ancient temple of Ptah, a fallen statue, and the mud-brick ruins of what was once the famous White Wall of Menes. The city of clay has vanished.

But Saqqara, its burial ground, remains. It was built of stone.

Modern man, saturated with scientific miracles, is no less astounded than was Hatshepsut upon seeing the monuments of Saqqara loom like cubist mountains over the desert. Drawings of the reconstructed necropolis show its incredible architectural beauty. Not even in Thebes had she seen such magnificent building.

The cemetery was approached by a high ramp like a stone boulevard. It was walled and galleried. Visitors to the necropolis, like Hatshepsut, could climb that tremendous crest, and, looking down, survey the dreamlike panorama of palms and river and the city of Memphis. The ramp led to other ramps, leading into the necropolis that towered over the western bank in a stone complex of palely gleaming pyramids, temples, chapels, and tombs. The pyramids were the graveyards of the kings, and spreading around them were miles of mastabas, the groups of important tombs that surrounded those of the kings.

Dominating the stone city of death was the Step Pyramid of Zoser. It remains the most extraordinary monument dating from the Old Kingdom. The oldest stone construction in the world, and the first, it is the tomb of King Zoser (Djoser), the first king of the Third Dynasty. It was built for him by the famous architect-engineer Imhotep, who was the first man in the world to build with cut stone instead of the traditional wood and clay. So it was in Zoser's time that architecture took a mighty leap forward, and all the stone monuments we see in Egypt are tributes to the genius of Imhotep. He it was who chose the site for the Step Monument and constructed it, and, around it, the massive stone city that was the necropolis of Saqqara.

The step pyramid was two hundred feet high and formed of cut and polished stone blocks mounting to an apex. Upon these steps the soul of the king could ascend to his final meeting with the gods. Surrounding the Step were the pyramids of other kings whose architects built in the ways originated by Imhotep and around these rose miles upon miles of tombs built for lesser members of the royal families, and nobles and priests.

Temples and chapels and colonnades rose with the centuries, and more of the graceful fluted columns created by Imhotep that the Greeks would copy, thousands of years later, and which would be known as "Greek."

Imhotep's designs would reappear on columns, roofs and porticos in Greece and Rome. Churchs and cathedrals of Europe testify to the genius of Imhotep.

The monuments were connected by the long ramps and the entire complex was enclosed by an ornamental wall nearly a mile in circumference. There was no other cemetery like Saqqara.

And Hatshepsut, whose thoughts had been fixed so early on the practical side of burial, would be told how Imhotep had constructed this stone city in anticipation of the death of a single man, King Zoser, and how Imhotep, who had built the memorial and engineered the burial, had constructed an underground city for his king to live in after death, and a deeply hidden underground palace with chambers and chapels, and rooms that were tombs, complete with funereal furnishings and sarcophagi worthy of the majesty of Zoser.

How carefully the architect-engineer planned for the future security of his patron! The mummy of Zoser was hidden far under the desert, having been lowered slowly in its gigantic stone sarcophagus on a wooden platform while the sandy earth below was being excavated and brought to the surface through a side tunnel that slanted downward to the grave.

And still that august grave was ravaged; the treasure horde hidden with Zoser had been lost.

The treasures that have been found at Saqqara are scattered through world museums. But visitors to Egypt may view the pyramids and graves that remain, and gain an awesome vision of the Saqqara Hatshepsut knew. In the tombs, the wall paintings, fresh and clear in appearance, recreate an Egypt that existed even before her time. There remain mummies and statues and portraits that make real to us the personages we have read about in history. They would have been familiar names to her.

Her father Thothmes, one of whose sub-titles was the Great Bull of Maat, would have paid ceremonious attention to a richly decorated stable in Memphis that housed the current Apis, the sacred bull whose worship was as old as Egyptian civilization. The god-bull symbolized fertility. It wore the sun's disk between its horns. The death of one of these chosen bulls was mourned throughout Egypt, since it was connected in some mystic fashion with the death of Osiris, and was followed by funeral services similar to those given a king. The great carcass was embalmed and interred in the tombs at Saqqara sacred to the divine bulls. Mourning continued until a divine successor could be found. This entailed a careful search by the priests through the herds of Egypt, for the new god-bull could be no ordinary calf, but a white animal marked by the gods with certain black cabalistic spots. Once discovered, he and his cow mother (living symbol of Hathor) were brought to Memphis and reverenced in the sacred stall, where, as the young bull matured, he would be presented with a select bovine harem.

There are still to be seen at Saqqara the tombs containing the great mummified shapes of the sacred Apis bulls and the flat stone table where the bodies were embalmed. These Hatshepsut would have been shown on her way into the Delta to be crowned.

In view of her subsequent activities, we may believe that her most devout moments at Saqqara were spent in the chapel dedicated to Imhotep—architect, physician, engineer, scientist, astronomer, and author.

He had been dead for many centuries, but his memory was revered in Egypt. He had been deified and was worshiped as a god. Other chapels had been built for him at Deir el-Bahari, Deir el-Medineh, Karnak, and on the Island of Philae. But the chapel at Saqqara was his most sacred shrine where he was worshiped as the god of healing. Cripples made pilgrimages there to pray for his intercession, that they might be healed.

There the proud young Hatshepsut, prostrating herself before his image, may have known a moment of true humility in realizing that while the most powerful king might order the building of such places as Saqqara, the royal command was impotent without the architect's genius. A king's name, such as that of Zoser, was remembered by the monuments built in his name, but it was the architect who had built to the king's eternal glory, and to Egypt's.

On her journey down the Nile she had seen one hundred and fifty miles of pyramids and monuments, and all were tribute to the memory of Imhotep, who was the first to build in stone.

She had seen many statues of the famed Imhotep. World museums now possess small bronze statuettes of the man. The builder of Saqqara is shown seated on a carved stool with a papyrus scroll balanced on his knees. He is the image of thought. He has been called "the first intellectual in history."

She felt his presence at Saqqara. From this stone promontory he had surveyed his desert world, made his plans, drawn his designs, and chosen the sites where his monuments should stand. Here he had directed his armies of draftsmen, stone polishers, and the slaves who lifted into position the incredibly heavy cubes, and, with the care other craftsmen showed in making jewelry, fitted them together so tightly, sans mortar, that a knife blade cannot be slid between.

She pushed her small hand over stone polished to the smoothness of glass. How were entire edifices polished to such perfection, by hand? Ambition swelled in her thoughts like a bursting seed. To build, to match her own matchless beauty! That she be remembered. . . .

She may with reason have offered up a small but fervid prayer at Saqqara. Send me a man like yourself, O Imhotep! An architect like a god, who will build for me, that my praise for him will last forever . . .

Where could she find such a man?

Did she pause before a statue of King Zoser mounted on a pedestal inside the wall of the Step Pyramid? On it the name of Imhotep was engraved next to that of the king. She may have read and approved the praise and honors given to a master architect by the king he made immortal:

> . . . Chancellor of the King of Lower Egypt, the first after the King of Upper Egypt, administrator of the Great Palace, hereditary lord, the High Priest of Heliopolis, Imhotep, the builder, the sculptor.

Imhotep authored many books, and the tomb he was permitted to build for himself must have been magnificent beyond belief, but "the books he wrote have disappeared, like his tomb." This last observation is several years old. Recently the English Egyptologist Walter Emory, excavating at Saqqara, uncovered a complex of ancient tunnels, tombs, and structures. The tunnels leading to the underground rooms were packed with the mummies of the ibis, the bird sacred to Imhotep. A burst of excitement swept archaeological circles around the world.

Emory believed the tomb was Imhotep's.

The royal travelers were taking a leisurely route to Heliopolis. Evidently Thothmes was in no hurry to see his daughter crowned. There were many shrines she must visit, many marvels to see. After Saqqara there was Giza to be visited. It was the necropolis of Heliopolis, as Saqqara was that of Memphis. It lay on the western bank of the river to the north of Saqqara, and had been started during the Fourth Dynasty, later than Saqqara, but using the designs created by Imhotep. It, too, was a city of the dead in stone. Mastabas beyond counting fanned out in straight lines between its pyramids, an orderly stone forest crisscrossing the desert.

Giza is now a modern and charming city, across the river from Cairo. The pyramids that have made its name famous rise from a limestone plateau on the desert five miles beyond the city. They were the largest pyramids in Egypt, and Giza was the country's leading cemetery in Hatshepsut's time.

The largest and most impressive of the monuments was and is the Great Pyramid, commonly known as the Pyramid of Cheops. It was built as the tomb of King Khufu, second king of the Fourth Dynasty, who became known to the Greeks as Cheops.

Two million limestone blocks went into the making of this royal tomb. Some of the stone cubes weigh fifteen tons. One hundred thousand men worked on it for twenty years, living chiefly on onions and bread. The stones were cut and polished with stone tools, some ferried downriver on rafts, all dragged to the crest of the stone plateau on wooden sleds drawn by men, then pushed up wooden ramps and levered into place.

The Pyramid was four hundred and eighty feet high and covered thirteen acres. It was one of the Seven Wonders of the ancient world.

Other pyramids rose around Cheops' tomb. Under them, at incredible depths, were buried the monarchs of the Old Kingdom. Their fortunes went with them underground. Underground in pursuit went the professional grave robbers. Cheops learned that the grave of his mother had been entered and despoiled. He moved her body and its treasure to a deeper well in the sand, where, sealed in by stone blocks, they remained safely hidden until found by archaeologists after nearly five thousand years.

The antiquarians who have honeycombed Giza opened an inexhaustible account with the past.

Hatshepsut knew of the queens who had been vital forces in the Old Kingdom. She was shown their memorials. One queen had built a tomb for herself as large as a pyramid.

The Old Kingdom had been ravaged by revolution and war, but its noblest monuments remained, then and now. Hatshepsut, as would generations of tourists long after, must have sensed her own smallness in size and time as she stood between the stone paws of the Sphinx looking up at the calm mysterious gaze of that then-undamaged face. "The largest portrait in the world," it has been called. It is the face of King Chephren, who was the fourth king of the Fourth Dynasty and a brother, or perhaps a son, of Cheops. She would have seen it whole. Centuries later the face was mutilated by cannon fire.

The body was that of the "divine lion" of Egypt. The Sphinx was a favorite model for royal portraits, with the face that of the king whose monument it was. The Sphinx of Chephren was carved out of a single rock cliff rising out of the desert. The statue was two hundred and forty feet long.

The Sphinx was always male, until Hatshepsut. The hundreds of statues she would order made of herself in the guise of the Sphinx, with her pretty face mounted on the body of a lion, may have been born in her mind in that unforgettable moment when she first stood transfixed before the great Sphinx at Giza.

Visitors to Egypt may have been bored lifelong with pictured representations of the Sphinx, but they can still be moved by the sense of timeless majesty the sight of that crouching shape inspires.

That it played a strong role in Hatshepsut's history is proven by the many Sphinx statues she left of herself.

The great Sphinx remains, molded of its limestone ledge, below the great pyramids of Giza. Its calm eyes survey the site of the long-vanished city of Memphis and the crisscross of modern highways where speeding cars overtake and outdistance the burdened camel trains.

At Giza and Saqqara Hatshepsut had seen and would remember the building by kings and queens of dynasties far older than her own. The Eighteenth Dynasty was the richest and strongest. What could she do to perpetuate its majesty, and hers? The dreams were crowding her now that would shortly be frozen into stone memorials destined "to last forever."

She could lay seige to these dreams, now that she was to be a queen.

The delights and duties of the long journey ended at the mouth of the Delta. Sated by marvels, saturated with dreams, it was time to cross the river from Giza to Heliopolis, where their river journey ended and Hatshepsut would receive the first of her many crowns.

Heliopolis, the once sacred city of the sun, is now a city of modern villas that has been absorbed into the larger city of Cairo as it stretches toward the airport. It lies northeast of Cairo, which did not exist in Hatshepsut's time, nearer the desert and the mouths of the Nile opening into the Delta.

A solitary obelisk remains in Heliopolis. It is one of many that made spectacular the multi-pillared city Hatshepsut and her father visited. Back in the Twelfth Dynasty the first King Sesostris had covered this level valley with monuments and inscriptions to the gods.

Thothmes chose Heliopolis for his daughter's crowning because it was the theological headquarters of Egypt and the birthplace of the earliest Egyptian kings. The bull and phoenix and many other gods were worshiped here, but it was the original place of worship for Atom, the solar disk, original of Re the sun god. The stone from which the first sun rose was one of the sacred relics guarded by the Atom priests, who were the most learned of all the religious leaders.

They were famous for their wisdom and scientific knowledge. The Greeks would praise them later as "very learned in matters of astronomy." So the hierarchy of the Atom cult were present, together with the civic leaders of Heliopolis and the Amon delegation from Thebes, when King Thothmes led his daughter Hatshepsut into the Temple of the Sun to be crowned "before all the gods of Egypt."

Hatshepsut's accounts of her coronation were defaced by her enemies, but the recorded utterances of the gods were left intact because they were sacred. Through them we glimpse the colorful scenes of her crowning.

Two pictures remain. One shows her, a slender figure in male clothing, kneeling before the enthroned image of Amon-Re. Surrounding her in the sun temple are her father and members of the Theban court who journeyed with them to Heliopolis. Assisting Amon are other powerful gods: Thoth and Horus, Sekhmet the lion-headed goddess, and Set.

It is always a shock to novices in Egyptian mythology to find Set pictured as an important actor in historic scenes, for in appearance and morals he was a forerunner of Satan. His body had the long-limbed elegant shape of a greyhound, his face was a wolf's muzzle, his eyes were slanted and his ears pointed, and sometimes he wore ram's horns. He was a very ancient god and wholly evil. Set it was who had murdered Osiris and torn the eye out of young Horus (who castrated and flayed Set in retribution). For some reason his capacity for violence and his acts of "great anger" won the admiration of the Thothmes kings, who could be fierce in their own right, and they identified themselves with Set and stressed worship of him. So it was that he was present at many great events, as now at Hatshepsut's crowning in the North, where he shared with Horus the honor of presenting the new regent with the crown.

Set fell from grace a few dynasties after this. His statues were destroyed, his worship was forbidden, and, instead of being the admired god of retribution he became an outcast—an early dynastic fallen angel.

The inscription portrays a moving scene as Thothmes presented his daughter to the assembled gods. Holding her "before the world," he spoke to her. ". . . blessed one, whom I take in my arms . . . thou art my heir."

Then the assembled gods spoke together to the royal father, voicing their approval of the slender young prince that was the king's daughter, Hatshepsut.

> This thy daughter who liveth, we are satisfied with her in life and peace. She is now thy daughter of thy form, whom thou hast begotten. Thou hast given her thy soul . . . thy bounty . . . the magic powers of the diadem. While she was in the body of her that bore her, the lands were hers, the countries were hers, all that the heavens cover, all that the sea encircles.

(This last statement refers to a belief Hatshepsut would shortly inscribe in her records, that the gods approved her for the throne before she was born.)

The gods gave advice and promises of divine protection to Hatshepsut.

> Welcome, daughter of Amon-Re; thou hast seen thy administration in the land, thou shalt set it in order . . . restore that which has gone to its ruin, thou shalt make thy monuments . . . thou shalt pass through the land and embrace many countries. . . .
>
> Thy tribute is myriads of men, the captives of thy valor, thy reward is thousands of men for the temples of the Two Lands. . . . The gods have [endowed] thee with years, they present thee with life and satisfaction, they praise thee, for their heart hath given understanding. . . . They shall set thy boundary as far as the breadth of heaven, as far as the limits of the twelfth hour of the night. . . .

So the gods admonished Hatshepsut, because on her pilgrimage she had seen the country and the way it was administered, and she had seen the ruined temples left by the Hyksos and would rebuild them, and build monuments to the gods for their glory and her own, and in return they would keep their promises to her.

Thoth, the wisest of the deities, spoke finally for them all.

"Set the diadem upon his head . . . before the gods. . . ." The rest of the order has been chiseled away.

But the account resumes, telling how, in the presence of Amon, the gods Set and Horus set upon the head of Hatshepsut the jeweled diadem that was the cobra-shaped coronet known as the "Lady of Life," that had been worn by her mother and all Egyptian queens. With it Hatshepsut was given the titles that had been her mother's; she would be given more at her final crowning.

Then the king addressed the assemblage in the temple. "This daughter . . . Hatshepsut, the loving one, I put her in my place, henceforth she guides you." And again the protective king-father threatened, ". . . whoever obeys her will live, but he who speaks out against her–will die–!"

The royal party turned back to Thebes where the final coronation ceremony would be made before Amon, and Hatshepsut would celebrate her official ascension to the throne.

She had learned much on this journey into the North. She had been shown the greatest wonders of her world. Was she describing the gigantic memorials of Giza and Saqqara, or the events of her crowning in the Temple at Heliopolis, when she later inscribed in her Theban records,

> Her Majesty saw all this thing herself, which she told to the people, who heard, falling down for terror among them.

Her position was strong because of her birth and she had, it seems, the support of the rich temple of Amon.
—*Encyclopedia of Egyptian Civilization*

The official coronation in the Great Temple at Thebes was the last and most impressive of the crowning ceremonies. The important day, chosen by King Thothmes, was New Year's Day, which was the all-important day of Thoth. This is according to Thothmes' written testimony, although Hatshepsut, curiously, was to give a different date on an obelisk she raised at Karnak.

Thothmes made his explanation on stone.

> He [Thothmes I] recognized the auspiciousness of a coronation on New Year's Day as the beginning of the peaceful years and of the spending of . . . very many jubilees.

The power of Thebes was represented in the jewel-glittering hall of the Great Temple as the warrior-king Thothmes, resplendent in his royal robes, humbly approached the niche holding the images of Amon, chief of the gods, Mut his wife, and Khons their son. The king proffered his royal emblems, the crook and flail, to signify his subservience to a power greater than his own. In recorded words, he, who had always shared generously with Amon, now stated the case of his daughter's preferment and begged the god to reward the father's fealty by granting protection to her.

The king pleaded.

> I am before you, king of the gods. I prostrate myself. In return for what I have done for thee do thou bestow Egypt and the red land [the Sahara] on my daughter Ramaka [Kamare, child of the sun] living eternally, as thou hast done for me.

Then Hatshepsut approached the idol of Amon. She was "prostrate, smelling the earth, crawling on the ground, invoking the Perfect God and exalting his beauty."

There were terrifying moments of waiting. Would the god deny the rights of the crown to this young woman? All eyes were fixed anxiously on the glittering image. Then, it was believed, the idol bowed its golden head. Amon had consented! The priests and nobility crowded into the Temple shouted their jubilance, and the king, raising his voice, expressed his gratitude to Amon.

> My daughter . . . who loves thee, who is united unto thee, beloved, thou hast transmitted the world unto her, into her hands; thou hast chosen her as queen.

There then entered the scene, according to the illustration, Nekhbet and Buto, two goddesses of North and South, followed by the four gods of the cardinal points. Thoth, scribe of the gods, and the lion-faced Sekhmet, are shown recording the scene.

The inscription reads:

> Presented to thee is this red crown [of the North], which is upon the head of Re; thou shalt wear the double crown, and thou shalt take the Two Lands by this its name.
>
> Presented to thee is this white crown [of the South], mighty upon thy head; thou shalt take the lands by its diadem, by this its name.

With these words her father placed on Hatshepsut's proudly held head the double crown of the two Egypts. Then Amon the god spoke and displayed his chosen daughter "to all the other gods."

> Behold ye, my daughter Hatshepsut living; be ye loving toward her, and be ye satisfied with her.

With these words the Hidden One showed his acceptance of Hatshepsut as Egypt's queen and his daughter on earth.

This announcement, made by Amon through her father and proclaimed to the assemblage by the ritual priests, let all Egyptians know that their adored and beautiful Crown Prince was now Queen Hatshepsut I of Imperial Egypt.

There were further rites in the Great Temple which she must undergo before the coronation ended.

Water was poured over her in the purification by the gods with "the waters of stabilizing life."

She was brought to the golden throne beside that which held her father. Under it were placed lotus blossoms, the flower of the South, and sprays of papyrus, the plant emblem of the North. These were bound in separate bouquets, then drawn together under the throne to symbolize the unification of the two Egypts.

Then, wearing the tall crown, in the heavily gemmed robe of a king, and holding the flail and crook of Osiris, Hatshepsut began the mystic ceremony of walking around the wall of the tremendous sanctuary.

The coronation was finally complete. The announcement was made by the god Horus, who referred to her in the masculine gender.

> Thou hast established thy dignity as king, and appeared upon the Horus-throne.

An inscription explains:

> The first day of the first season, New Year's Day, the first of the peaceful years of the King of Upper and Lower Egypt, Favorite of the Two Goddesses, who makes the circuit north of the wall. . . .

It must be remembered that many of the inscriptions are Hatshepsut's and made after the events, during a time when she was deep in the building of Deir el-Bahari and other monuments. Much that she describes may be hindsight. It may be that she did not assume the masculine role this early. It is clear that she served as queen during her father's remaining years.

She had other names. Some had been hers as Crown Prince. Others were given her this triumphant day in the great temple. Thirty-five names and titles and a long list of descriptive terms were read off at her coronation. With them went two cartouches. From this day on her letters and inscriptions would bear the seal of the cartouches of Hatshepsut.

Among the greatest of her "great names" was that of Horus, living forever; Favorite of the Goddesses, "Fresh in Years"; Golden Horus, "Divine of diadems"; "Makere (Kamere), king of Upper and Lower Egypt, who liveth forever."

The fifth name was her own personal name which the gods had given her before she was born.

Hatshepsut! "Chieftainess of noble women!"

The Great Temple emptied and the mud palace in Southern Thebes filled with the sounds and glitter of the feast of her coronation. In the streets the piercing notes of flutes and the steady staccato of drums rose, and there was jubilant shouting from the people. "Let Egypt rejoice! Happy times have come!"

So the people of Egypt welcomed the New Year and their new queen, Hatshepsut I of Imperial Egypt.

Among her many new titles Hatshepsut inherited were those that had belonged to her mother. They were formally bestowed upon her by her father upon her ascension to the throne. One will seem strange to us.

> Lady of the Two Lands; the King's Sister; the King's Daughter; Great Wife of the King.

We cannot attempt to understand the mores of a people who lived many thousands of years ago. What to us is incest was to the Egyptians the highest morality. To retain the purity of the royal blood line, kings married their full or half sisters, even their daughters. In the century following Hatshepsut's, another regent of her family, Akhenaton, was to father a child by a daughter born to him by his wife Nefertiti.

The preservation of the royal seed was all-important.

Inter-familial marriage among the royal families doubled and redoubled the divine strain and eventually would weaken the imperial line, but that was in the future.

One of the few artifacts linking us to Hatshepsut is a small jar. It is inscribed:

> Divine consort, Great King's Wife, Hatshepsut; she made [this] for her mother, Great King's Wife, Ahmose, triumphant before Osiris.

This was apparently an "after death" gift from Hatshepsut, after her coronation, to her recently dead mother, Amose II.

Dr. Murray has written that the action of King Thothmes, in associating Hatshepsut with him on the throne, suggests that she was married to him. There are other leading authorities who believe Thothmes gave his daughter the title of Divine Wife because the coronation was synonymous with marriage.

Others assume no marriage took place, but that the widower-king gave his young unmarried daughter her "great titles" to build her authority in the eyes of her subjects and strengthen her position on the throne.

The official records are sadly damaged, but it is clear that during the rest of the life of Thothmes I his daughter Hatshepsut shared the throne as his co-regent and Great Queen.

The title of Great Wife gave Hatshepsut powers and responsibilities equal to those of the king. There grew about her the congealing armor of majesty that few would penetrate. Her own words testify that her deepest love was reserved for the gods and her parents, and it was now, as co-regent, that she began planning for the enhancement of their glorious names and her own.

She started to build in her own right. Her architect had been her father's and grandfather's. He was Ineni, and he served her through his lifetime. But he was not the builder of her dreams. She wanted another Imhotep, one who would make her immortal.

Ineni constructed small temples and chapels for her, and repaired other religious buildings that had been left in ruins by the Hyksos. These she had sworn to repair at her coronation. The inscriptions of this period were not entirely for her self-glorification. They commemorated her love for her dead mother and her deep respect for her father.

Thothmes supported her with his ebbing strength. An inscription on a pylon at Karnak illustrates the ways in which he tried to insure her continued allegiance from gods and men.

The illustration shows him pleading in her behalf before the Theban trinity, Amon, Mut, and Khons. He begged the powerful ones to continue their support of her.

A long and active life was nearing its end. Thothmes had completed his aims as conqueror and builder. He had developed the necropolis in Western Thebes until that sanctuary of death rivaled in importance the great stone complex of Karnak on the other side of the river. He had made many trips of inspection to the burial grounds. His memorial temple on the west bank was finished, and his personal history was recorded on stone at Western Thebes, and at Karnak, and in the Temple of Osiris at Abydos. Hatshepsut, visiting Abydos with him during their journey into the North, had read with him the king's own epitaph in the Osiris shrine.

> I did more than any king before me. . . . I made the borders of Egypt as far as the circuit of the sea. . . .

Then he was dead. Thothmes was about seventy years of age when he "retired from life, going forth to heaven and mingling with the gods."

He had reigned for thirty-five years. Hatshepsut had not known an Egypt without him.

Now, for the first time, hers was the sole responsibility of the dreadful rituals of a royal funeral. Once more the royal barge was a bark of death, and Hatshepsut wore the white robes and floral wreaths of mourning. Once more the procession of high priests and nobles and professional mourners went with the mummified body to its final resting place on the western side of the Nile.

The site was familiar to the dead man's daughter. Hatshepsut had watched the preparing and furnishing of her father's grave. He it was who had chosen the desolate hidden valley as his final resting place, and it was there she took him as promised, so that Thothmes I was the first to be buried in the Valley of the Kings. Later royalty would be buried there, and, of all their graves, only that of young Tutankhamon, who lived long after this, would be found unviolated.

She buried her father deep and with care, as they had planned. The mummy of Thothmes I in Room Fifty-two in the Cairo Museum was so well preserved when unwrapped by Maspero that it is often described as the finest example of Eighteenth-Century mummification.

It was a "goodly burial" he owed to Hatshepsut.

She left him to make his dark journey alone on the waters of the underworld, following the route taken every night by the sun, over the edge of the world in the west, and back, to the east. Her father would reunite with the body she had hidden away so carefully, which she would not see again.

She returned to Thebes, to the beautifully furnished mud palace, to the glory and pressures of regency. The father who had been her protector and earthly god since her babyhood was dead. He had fought for her against gods and men. Now she stood alone—the sole monarch of Egypt.

There had been strong-minded queens who preceded her, but none had been asked to serve as she must serve. They had acted as co-regents with their kings. She would be the first woman to rule Egypt alone.

Hatshepsut's mutilated records show the importance but not the sequence of the events that followed her father's death. She found Sennemut. She began the building of Deir el-Bahari. She married.

CHAPTER 10

It would have outraged all tradition and convention for a woman to crown herself with the double crown of Egypt and to assume the inheritance of the gods on earth . . . therefore, the sovereignty was passed on by the heiress to her husband, while she contented herself with the rank of "Great Royal Wife" . . .

—Steindorff and Seele

The above refers to Hatshepsut's mother, Amose II, who, by marrying her half brother, made him king. Thothmes I also won through that marriage the privilege of naming his own successor. Generation after generation of Thothmesid kings were sons born to subsidiary wives or concubines. This had been Hatshepsut's father's story. It was the way her future husband would arrive at the throne.

The smiling Amose had followed in family tradition and the half brother she married had been a successful king.

In many ways Hatshepsut did not resemble her apparently amiable mother. She was a daughter of tradition, true, but there was in her a rebel strain inherited from her father. Marriage was necessary, but she did not choose to marry at once. Now that both her parents were dead there was no one to tell her what to do. Her future rested with herself and with Amon, whose armies of Theban priests had pledged their loyalty to her.

She would need their fealty. The death of Thothmes I marked the beginning of that infamous power struggle around the throne that is known historically as "the feud of the Thothmesid." For the rest of her life a woman would compete against male relatives to retain her place in the sun.

We look back to the inscription showing her father, before his death, kneeling before Amon and begging the god's continued support for his daughter "Makere [Hatshepsut] living forever."

Her name has been chipped away. It can be deciphered, although over it has been placed in stronger letters the name of Thothmes II.

In other places his name has replaced hers, or the names of later kings are substituted. Everything Hatshepsut was to accomplish was claimed by men who followed her on the throne.

The official lists ignore her. Powerful enemies obscured her records and those of her father concerning her, and place the step of ascension from Thothmes I to Thothmes II. Only a careful study of the records was to uncover the fact that a queen once ruled Egypt, and was all that she herself had claimed to be.

Certainly it was not Thothmes II who replaced her name with his and claimed her regency as his own. His records and his personal appearance indicate that he was not an aggressive man. Those who substituted his name for hers had the justification that Thothmes II had the advantage of being a male scion of her father's, which Hatshepsut could only pretend to be.

Hatshepsut's self-assurance was beyond calculation, but her sex was against her.

Sculptors portrayed her wearing the boyish kilt, the gold beard and double crown, but they could not hide that graceful form. There was no escaping the biological fact that Hatshepsut was still a slip of a girl.

She might dress as a man and claim masculinity in confusing

records that refer to her both as "he" and "she," but the public that had watched her from babyhood knew the truth.

A queen, not a king, held the future. The body beloved by the sculptors was a chalice. She was the only remaining fully royal Thothmesid. If she did not produce an heir, her powerful dynasty would end.

The strong stone faces of her ancestors accused Hatshepsut. All placed an obligation upon her; she must marry, and within the family.

It is safe to assume that her father selected her future husband before his death, knowing that his choice would be respected by his loyal daughter, in her own good time!

The selection was made inside the palace. The young man history was to know as Thothmes II was one of many half-royal children sired by Hatshepsut's father by women other than his Great Wife Amose. He was Hatshepsut's half brother, and they were approximately the same age.

History gives us our first glimpse of him, with Hatshepsut, in the tomb of their mutual father in Western Thebes. He was her subject then, assisting his queen in the interment rites of Thothmes I, but he must have carried the aura of approaching majesty. It is our privilege to picture the imperial sister and half-royal brother, resembling one another in familial ways, wearing similar white robes of mourning, and performing in unison the final intricate ceremonies necessary to a royal interment. The Cairo Museum displays the lid of the sarcophagus of Thothmes I. It is a notable example of Eighteenth Dynasty funereal art, resplendent in gold and faience. Brother and sister shed their last tears over that lowered lid before leaving the mummified body of their king father in his long-prepared and carefully sealed tomb.

They returned to Thebes together. He resumed life in the palace.

With joyful assurance, Hatshepsut, defying convention,

launched upon her solo flight as the first sole woman regent of Egypt.

Records that have escaped the hammer round out events following her father's death.

She had inherited a kingdom, which, freed by her father and forefathers from the "long humiliation" under the Hyksos, had swollen its territories in Asia and other tributaries to vast properties. Loot taken in victory, also slaves, added to the increment of victory. Prosperity had loosened the iron regulations of more ancient regimes and in her father's time a new spirit had stimulated Egypt into an explosion of creativity.

Hatshepsut was a child of that movement. She had rejoiced as her father built to the glory of his name; she had developed dreams of her own. Now she possessed total power. She had the support of the priesthood and the military. She had labor power unlimited, gold virtually so, and the resources of the richest of kingdoms. The great architects and sculptors waited her command.

Now she could fulfill the dreams born at Saqqara and Giza and Heliopolis. (That my beauty be remembered!)

She had Ineni, who had built for her father and his father. But she began the search for a super-architect who would be another Imhotep, and build only for her.

For a time she ruled alone. She began her greatest building alone. The memorial temple at Deir el-Bahari was started, but work on it was postponed.

There was a more immediate obligation.

All the Egyptian queens, down to Cleopatra, the last one, were trained in the tradition of service. Hatshepsut was no spoiled, capricious beauty. She was of heavenly birth, but her slender feet were firmly planted on Egyptian earth and she knew that while Egypt was hers, she owed much to Egypt. Over her kingdom, Amon, the all-powerful patron of Thebes, kept a jealous eye, and to him she paid tribute and homage. To all humans she was Maat—the law.

And the law determined that an heiress to the throne had to marry.

Another practical reason may have contributed to her decision to accept a consort. When a king died, rebellion always broke out in various parts of Egypt. Rumors of incipient trouble started after the death of strong old Thothmes I. Hatshepsut had inherited woe. A powerful male presence had dominated the palace and the land. A man was needed to help her represent the throne. The young son selected by her father was young enough and royal enough to serve as Hatshepsut's consort and to father future heirs to the throne. He had been carefully chosen; he was approved by her supporters. As the son of a secondary wife or concubine, the younger Thothmes II was only half divine, but marriage to his fully royal half sister would annul the common strain.

The year of his ascension to the throne is given as 1512 B.C. Since the coronation would have synchronized with his marriage, this can be accepted as the year Hatshepsut relinquished her role of sole monarch and accepted the title and position her mother held before her, that of Great Royal Wife.

Once more there were the complicated rites of marriage in the Great Temple. Once more the streets of Thebes rang to the loyal shouts of "Long life to our new king, Thothmes II, living forever."

The ancient records describe his coronation:

> The Falcon in the Nest has appeared as King of the Black Land and the Red, of Upper and Lower Egypt.

Hatshepsut knew what was expected of her as a royal wife. She had been trained in court etiquette and in womanly ways. She pledged herself, as did all queens when they married, to be "feminine to a divine degree, to exude fragrance as she walked, and speak in tones that filled the palace with music." She must tend her lord with love and accept his affection. Her most important duty was "to make herself loved."

These rules Hatshepsut promised to follow during the ceremony of the great temple: promised Amon, the god of gods, and Hathor, goddess of the home. Her young husband returned with her to the palace, no longer one of the many well-cared-for illegitimate children of their late father, but the new Pharaoh of Egypt.

We may see the mummy of King Thothmes II in Room Fifty-two in the Cairo Museum. One seems to know the man, looking down at that calm form. Here is no Petruchio, determined to break the spirit of the girl he married. The second Thothmes appears in death much as he must have in life, as an easygoing man desirous of the good things of life, and who could marry, and be happiest with, a dominant woman.

There is a persistent rumor that Hatshepsut's husband was a weakling, even effeminate. This started after the discovery of the mummies and is based on the fact that the "falcon in the nest" was evidently addicted to fine feathers. Toenails and fingernails, as viewed in the glass case, are shown to be neatly trimmed, which is not true of the other royal bodies. It seems strange that in a period that placed so much stress on bathing facilities and body care, these famous royal forms show little attention paid to the pedicure. Or, is this apparent neglect due to after-death shrinkage around the nails and long interment underground?

Unlike most male Thothmes kings, he is only partially bald, and the long, dark, curly locks framing the narrow features are curled, not by nature, but by one of the hairdressers so esteemed in early Egypt. One wonders how the hair was curled then—with an iron?

Thothmes II, then, was fastidious in person, perhaps in an effort to please his beautiful young wife.

Folds in the mummified skin of Thothmes show him to have been a fat young man. Clearly, Hatshepsut had chosen a man who liked comfort, and marriage placed him in a position to indulge it to the full.

He was five feet five inches tall, which was five inches taller than their father, but in every other way he was definitely the lesser man. Maspero, who unwrapped the body, reported that Thothmes II appeared to lack vigor and muscular power. His shoulders were narrow, and with the gross body he must have failed in masculine standards. But the balding head, protruding teeth, and narrow features are Thothmesid.

He and Hatshepsut at this time were approximately twenty years old. They had been brought up together in the palace and knew each other well. Hatshepsut would have known her new mother-in-law all her life. Mutnefert was one of the women of her father's harem, or at best a secondary wife. We can only vaguely guess at the conniving that went on in royal harems as favorites sought to have a son elevated to the throne. Mutnefert was one of the successful mothers.

She saw her son elevated to the throne and evidently outlived him, for her mummy in the Cairo Museum is that of an old woman, wrinkled and bald, and less than five feet tall. But she must have had charm in her youth to have won the attention of Thothmes I, the Great Bull of Maat.

As his father had honored his own non-royal mother, so the new king paid tribute to his. A statue of Mutnefert raised by Thothmes II is inscribed, "Wife of the king, mother of the king." Hatshepsut would have concurred in granting her husband's mother the title she had never been given by Thothmes I.

Breasted observed that it is feasible to think that Thothmes II followed Thothmes I and that Hatshepsut's father forced him to share the throne. It is equally feasible, considering the power Hatshepsut held, and her iron will, to think that it was she who made the decision to share the throne with her half brother.

Either way, the choice was good. Thothmes II served as she could not, as the awe-inspiring male figure on the throne. He upheld the family standards while he lived. He would father her children.

She could have married a stronger man, had she chosen, one who would rule with an iron hand as her father had ruled Egypt. Did she believe her father's strength was in her doublefold, and that she was strong enough for two? The demoniac energy of the full-blooded Thothmesid was evidently intensified in her, and there is reason to believe that she was of far stronger stuff than the man she married.

Theirs was not a romantic marriage, but it would not have been loveless, for the deepest love known in Egypt then was family love. And she and Thothmes were "family," many times over.

Records reveal that marriage and even motherhood did not absorb her tremendous energy. She had been trained in leadership. Her upbringing was different from that of any other queen. She did not relinquish her ambitions to create and to build, and the young man she had married was not one to stand in her way.

Her first allegiance remained to the gods. Before Amon she humbled herself, forehead to altar, and offered tribute to him and to all the other gods. Then, rising, she dedicated herself to the task of making Egypt more beautiful in their honor.

She was no longer alone, in ambitions or in domestic life. She had married, as was required of her. For the other, the long search had ended. She had found at last the one who could express her most daring dreams in immortal stone, one she could love, it has been said, above all men with the exception of her father.

She had found Sennemut.

There is no reason to doubt that she was a beautiful woman gifted not only with every feminine charm but also with an extraordinary intellect and a powerful personality and will . . .

In addition to these qualities, she had the unusual good fortune to possess in the person of the official Sennemut an advisor and chancellor who was able both to encourage her thirst for power and to carry out her plans.

—Steindorff and Seele

Where Sennemut was born, of what family, and how he met Queen Hatshepsut, history does not say. His is one of the success stories that illustrate Egypt's early claim that any energetic and ambitious young man could attain any chosen goal. Sennemut was a man of genius. He set impossible goals for himself. He reached them all.

We study the stone faces of men and women dead for thousands of years and wonder, what did they mean to themselves and to others? Magnificent statues remain of Sennemut. They were authorized by Hatshepsut. There are exceptionally fine statues in the Cairo and Berlin Museums. The eyes arrest us with the coldness achieved only by black granite. Could they have held that icy appraisal in life? They must have warmed for Hatshepsut. She loved him—how, we are not sure.

His face is that of a man of iron determination. Björnstjerne Bjornson once described a character in fiction as having a face that came to a point and flew straight at you. Sennemut's expression does that. As for his features, they are blunt and strong, the cheekbones high, the mouth hard-set but sensual, the eyes wide-set and challenging under heavy brows. He has the look of a strong man whose authority no other could dare oppose; a man that a young queen trained in pride and suspicion could trust and defer to in matters that lay closest to her heart.

We know him first as a novitiate in the Great Temple of Amon. Bright young men from poor families were accepted and educated there, and many became successful, and wealthy, priests. Sennemut was intelligent and humbly born. In the temple he studied a variety of subjects and rose rapidly in the priestly ranks. He would be many things to Hatshepsut, but his first services to her were that of the architect she had hoped to find, who would be another Imhotep to her.

She entrusted the powerful young priest with her greatest dream. We know it as her memorial temple Deir el-Bahari.

They planned it together.

Can we not see them, standing on the western bank, as they must have so often during the building, looking up at the stone façade of the cliff towering four hundred feet above their heads? Hatshepsut's eyes were great with vision, shadowed by the parasol held over her by slaves to protect her from the merciless sun of middle Egypt. She had studied the architecture of all the great temples of Egypt. Hers must be the most beautiful.

And the man, quickening to her dream, pledged himself and his genius to build for her with a magnificence never seen before in Egypt, on the gigantic scale set by her antecedents, but with added grace and beauty that would express Hatshepsut—strong, delicate of line, imperishable.

He would build for her.

His architect's eye studied the cliff rising like a cathedral against the cloudless sky. A man trained in many sciences could sight the potential hidden in that natural edifice. Sennemut would master it, refine the outline, shape it into a shrine worthy of the lovely young regent who stood at his side, sharing with him her greatest dream.

There was a strangeness about the site. Deir el-Bahari held, and still holds, the aura of ancient temples and places of burial. Toward the base of the cliff the stone façade slanted into the ruins of the chapel that had been built there a thousand years before by King Mentuhotep, whose story impressed Hatshepsut because she had so admired this temple's design and because he had sent a ship to Punt. His temple was an architectural rarity. It was terraced into the side of a cliff, and it also contained a pyramid which was almost unknown in the Theban region, although Hatshepsut had seen many in the North. Royalty always destroyed or built over the buildings of their predecessors.

Every new reign called for the destruction, rebuilding, and refurnishing of previous temples and tombs. Hatshepsut knew what she wanted and was as ruthless as any. It did not matter that she could read the name and claims of the builder of the first mortuary temple on its pillars and colonnades. King Mentuhotep was worshiped as a god, but he had been dead for a thousand years.

She gave her new architect orders to destroy as he chose, that he might build. Architects built to a traditional order "by royal favor of the king." She placed at Sennemut's disposal the inexhaustible labor supply and the inexhaustible coffers of the kingdom. Build to last forever, she told him. That my beauty be remembered . . .

From this side of the Nile she could look back over the river to the gates and colonnades of Thebes, the gigantic ancestral statues, and the towering stone mass that was Karnak.

Her thoughts were fierce as the sun staining her cheeks under the slave-held plumes. "Mine will be more beautiful . . . supreme forever . . . that all who see may marvel at my name, Hatshepsut. . . ."

Sennemut put reed pen to papyrus and began the designing of the funerary temple that would be a memorial to his genius, and to her.

The architect Ineni, who had served her father and grandfather, was not discarded. Hatshepsut found work for his hands. She had many plans to carry out during these, her powerful years. Ineni was growing old, but he continued to design and to build to please Hatshepsut.

The building of a tomb or a memorial temple that was sacred to Amon had to meet with the approval of the priesthood in the Great Temple. The architects worked hand-in-hand with the priests. Mathematics, astronomy, and magic had to be given careful consideration before a stone could be placed. Every pyramid and sanctuary Hatshepsut had visited had been oriented after astral observations by the astronomer priests. Sennemut's carefully drawn plans were studied by the high priests; the placing of the shrines must please Amon and all the gods.

The artists hired by Sennemut to decorate the future temple had to submit their preliminary sketches to the priests. Each memorial temple or tomb painting had a special religious symbolism, to be used by the remembered one after his death.

It has been pointed out that modern nations put all their genius and knowledge into industry. The old Egyptians gave theirs to their monuments.

Sennemut started work with a destruction crew. Ruthlessly, as his queen had ordered, he cleared away much of the ancient building at Deir el-Bahari. He destroyed a small mud chapel built by her grandfather, Amonhotep I. Over its ruins, and those of the old Mentuhotep temple, he would build to his own plan. To make greater space, he leveled the slant of the tor. His plan was daring, and new. He would use the mountain itself for her temple, as a sculptor carves a shape out of stone. Nothing like this had been attempted before in Egypt, nor, as far as is known, in the world.

The approval of the priests was won, and Sennemut had permission to build. Again the stars were studied for an auspicious date for the preliminary ceremony known as the Stretching of the Cord (in modern parlance, the laying of the cornerstone).

Hatshepsut, "Daughter of the Sun God," was present, surrounded by her court and the Amon priesthood, and with her was her husband Thothmes II. But closer to her in understanding on this day at Deir el-Bahari was the stalwart young architect Sennemut.

He oversaw the ceremony of the cord, which, soaked in white paint and pulled straight over the leveled ground, set foundation lines so exact that Egypt's ancient buildings hold the admiration of architects to this day. The *Encyclopedia of Egyptian Civilization* comments upon such architects as Imhotep, Ineni, and Sennemut:

> It is impossible to imagine how they could build so much and so well without tools comparable to our own. . . . The monuments are there as a witness that these people, with only a plumb-bob, square, cubit, measuring line, leveling staff, and a kind of primitive theodolite, knew how to make constructional plans and elevations, simple but workable sketches, and to produce large and magnificent buildings.

An ox was sacrificed, and game birds. Four trenches were dug at the four corners where the white lines met. Into them went offerings, in the same way that builders still place mementos under cornerstones. These consisted of incense, fruits, barley cakes and bread, jars of oil and wine, celery and dates and a quail. With them were placed small images and idols and magic-working amulets, and small wooden and clay models of the building tools, and even a sieve for sifting sand (all to be uncovered by investigators in this century).

Hatshepsut watched the laying of the first stone.

Tribute and prayers were offered to the chief god of Thebes. This was his abiding place. Deir el-Bahari was named by Hatshepsut, "the sacred place of Amon," and the temple was known as Zeser-zesru-Amon (Holy of Holies of Amon).

She must have crossed the river many times to watch Sennemut directing its building. First, he excavated deep into the stony side of the mountain. Over the ruins of the Amonhotep chapel and the old Mentuhotep temple he raised the great Black Wall of the Hathor Terrace, which was unlike any wall the Egyptians had seen. It was five feet wide and constructed of sandstone blocks, some of them six feet long. The blocks were placed in alternating lengths, tightly joined, and sealed with mortar.

Hatshepsut had the ground floor of her temple copied from that dedicated to the god Min in Southern Thebes. It was known as the Sanctuary of the South, and was supposed to be the oldest of the sacred Theban buildings. But the temple built by Sennemut over this base was unique. Here was no ordinary funereal monument, dark and mysterious within as were so many of the mortuary temples. Sennemut built around the personality of his queen. Hatshepsut was a daughter of the sun and her memorial was open to the light.

So they planned it, she and Sennemut, her faithful one.

In approaching Deir el-Bahari on the western bank, one has the impression of viewing at a distance an antique Greek temple. The pillared colonnades rising tier upon tier against the mountain form what is surely the first "Greek" building in the world. The pillars, square or sixteen-sided, are the "Proto-Doric" columns later adopted by the Greeks.

Two of the sanctuaries were Speos, cut from the solid rock of the mountain. The first of these vaulted shrines was the southern Speos, dedicated to Hathor, the beloved cow-headed goddess of beauty and love. Another was devoted to the worship of Anubis, the protector-god of the dead.

The Speos of Hathor was the most revered of the shrines. A roofed colonnade led into it, columned with pillar-mounted heads of Hathor. The inner sanctuary was small, and in it would have been a shrine containing the gold image of the mother-goddess. The priestesses in charge were all princesses.

Around the sanctuary were storage rooms for the vestments of the priests and priestesses, the vessels of worship, the temple furnishings, and the gifts brought to the cow-goddess by her worshipers. These last soon filled the rooms to overflowing, and the priests, from time to time, had to clear out the overflow. A quarry near the temple was the disposal site, and to it the archaeologists owe much of their knowledge of churchly offerings in Hatshepsut's time.

Religious processions came to worship in Hatshepsut's temple. They crossed the Nile and climbed the sandy slopes to Deir el-Bahari. Vendors lined the dusty road with the religious offerings. The faithful bought, and placed under the cow statue of Hathor, miniature pottery cows in the shape of the goddess, other pottery idols, platters of blue and white faience filled with fresh fruit, and bowls and bouquets of flowers. They brought bronze plaques inscribed with cow images, pottery ears, eyes, and limbs that were curative amulets, vases and bowls of blue pottery painted with cows and flowers and stars, and strings of blue faience scarabs. Thousands of these beaded strings were thrown out by the priests. Among them were small personal treasures left by the women—hair nets, combs, necklaces and rings, ear rings, and bracelets.

The temple was dedicated to Amon with shrines for Hathor and Anubis, but it was Hatshepsut who was the true goddess of the temple. There was a court with an altar to Re, the sun her ancestor, and a hall where Hatshepsut was worshiped. Was she not divine, the daughter of Amon-Re? On an ebony shrine in the temple there is written three times:

> . . . he [Hatshepsut] made a monument for his father, Amon-Re, that she might live and abide for him, like Re, forever.

Her name is gone and the names of her father and husband-brother, Thothmes I and II, are on the carving. But the feminine pronoun was overlooked by the despoilers, and by that it is known as hers.

She presented her temple with more than one hundred of her statues, portraying her as a Sphinx, in red granite. Paintings show the sculptors at work. Many of the Egyptian treasures in the museums are from Deir el-Bahari. The Sphinx in the Metropolitan Museum was one of these.

She could look up through the avenue of sphinxes, each lion-bodied, couchant, with her face, to the wide steps of the ramp with its circular flower beds on either side, and T-shaped papyrus-fringed pools (papyrus stalks are still found there, brittle with centuries), to the wide terraces, colonnades, halls, pillars, and portico. Deir el-Bahari is beautiful today, but how much more beautiful it must have been as Hatshepsut saw it, completed, the white stone temple set against the rose-tinted cliffs, the white walls with the paintings and blue and yellow hieroglyphs with which Hatshepsut told the story of her life.

On the walls of Deir el-Bahari she placed other words.

"I am God, the beginning of Existence."

With her, life began. It would end with her.

In such moments, rejoicing with her in the perfection of their shared dream, was Sennemut. His genius was to outlast the centuries. He had drawn the plans, leveled the slant of the tor, raised what was certainly the most beautiful building in the world, to stand forever in the names of Amon and Hatshepsut, the god and goddess of the temple that bore, as one of its many names, "the Supreme of the Supremes."

Sennemut was a genius. He had built for her as he would not build again.

Did she, or Sennemut, conceive this style of architecture that was completely new? The Speos, a temple cut out of the rock, was first seen at Deir el-Bahari. Kings who followed Hatshepsut, notably Rameses II, would build shrines using its design, but hers is the first known.

Naville comments:

> To judge from remaining monuments, Hatshepsut was the first to conceive the idea of applying the subterranean architecture hitherto confined to tombs to the requirements of divine worship; with her, or with her architect, originated the rock-cut temple of Egypt.

Mariette describes Deir el-Bahari as "an exception and an accident in the architectural life of Egypt.

Viewed from any angle, Deir el-Bahari is a temple of love.

It is impossible to pinpoint the years in which Hatshepsut was building Deir el-Bahari. One believes the temple was built around 1480 B.C. Another states that her greatest works were accomplished during the lifetime of her husband Thothmes II. His son, Thothmes III, was to cover so many of her claims with his own, and obscure her name by substituting his own, or his father's, that inscriptions referring to "she" and "her" often bear the names of Thothmes I, II, and III. Still the records are decipherable and the accounts of events are clear, if confusing in their time element. Hatshepsut's enemies would not be able to rob her of a shred of her well-deserved glory.

There is no reason to suspect that her husband Thothmes II resented her activities. The "Thothmesid feud" would be developed in his name after his death by his son. Hatshepsut seems to have regarded her spouse in an amiable light. His name was associated with hers at Deir el-Bahari and other monuments. It is interesting to note that in paintings of royal functions Hatshepsut's consort is shown as a small figure in the background. This was indeed a reversal of tradition, for Egyptian wives had always been portrayed as small, doll-like figures, standing a little behind their mates.

Naville states that Thothmes II "played clearly a very subservient part in the state." We remember that the king's mummy in Cairo left us with the impression of a comfort-loving, overweight, and probably good-natured man. Little else remains of Hatshepsut's husband, but a shadow clock that was his is now in the Berlin Museum.

This timepiece, three and a half thousand years old, is an ingenious invention. It consists of three pieces of wood. Placed on the ground, it could be so adjusted that the morning sun cast the shadow of the shortest piece on the longest, which was marked in six sections. This accounted for the six hours of morning. The wood shape was turned at noon to accommodate the afternoon sun. It is to Egypt that we owe our twenty-four-hour day.

Hatshepsut would have marked her hours by it or by a similar clock.

She was a mother. She and Thothmes II had two little daughters, Merit-Re-Hatshepset and Nefrure. Hatshepset, her namesake, was the younger. (The spelling of their names is slightly different, and the meaning slightly so, but the general context is that of a noble woman leader of noble women.)

Hatshepsut had no reason to regret not having produced a son. Her husband could attend to that, as her father (and his) had before him. Thothmes II had his concubines and subsidiary wives in royal tradition. One of his harem-produced sons could in time marry one of his fully royal daughters. Hatshepsut had played her role in royal tradition. She had insured the continued possession of the throne for the great Thothmesid line—destined to survive forever!

In other ways Thothmes II was also doing his best to carry on in the footsteps of their father. As had happened in his father's time, rumors of active rebellion in Nubia reached the palace in Thebes shortly after Hatshepsut had made him king through marriage. Inscriptions describe her husband as growing "furious as a leopard" at this news, and setting off overnight for the south at the head of his army. "Let not one male rebel live," is reported to have been his war cry.

There have been critics who asserted that Hatshepsut's husband conducted his wars from his comfortable throne in the audience hall of their luxurious palace in Thebes, and sent his army out to fight without him. And why not? Egypt's tremendous military force had been developed by his and Hatshepsut's father, and Thothmes I had also trained the world's most skillful generals. There was no need for a royal consort to risk the discomforts, and dangers, of war.

This criticism may be due to an illustration on stone which Thothmes had made after his army had be-set the enemy and left "none of the barbarians alive," except one of the sons of the Chief, and returned in triumph to Thebes. Thothmes II is shown as the conqueror, seated on his throne with his sandaled feet resting on the necks of the captives. The text explains, "His Majesty had appeared upon the throne when the living prisoners were brought in."

On the other hand, it has been suggested that Thothmes actually did take part in some of the punitive expeditions, and that it was during his absences that Hatshepsut carried out such large-scale plans as the building of Deir el-Bahari.

He claimed to have led counterraids against the raiding Bedouin in Sinai and Syria, crushed an uprising in southern Palestine, and "conducted a successful campaign against the

Shasu." During a second campaign into Nubia he ordered a fort built at Kummeh, above the Second Cataract.

Hatshepsut's young husband evidently shared her Thothmesid passion for architecture. He was evidently associated with her during the building of Deir el-Bahari. On his own, he added large additions to the Great Temple at Karnak, and raised two obelisks there.

There was in neither of them the need to conquer. As King Thothmes was the figurehead of power, his very maleness could maintain peace in Egypt. Peace was also what Hatshepsut wanted. She was more like Victoria than Joan of Arc. She might have sent out armies in her own name to conquer other countries. She did not see conquest in such terms.

Was it her femininity, the innate female urge toward hearth and home, that caused Hatshepsut to set in Egypt the pattern of isolation that still exists? During her years on the throne she showed no interest in extending her kingdom, only in holding it safe from within.

During the reign she shared with Thothmes II, the garrisons built by their ancestors in Asia were permitted to become obsolete. But the army and navy assembled by their ancestors and brought to their peak strength by their father Thothmes I were maintained in full.

So the comfort-loving husband-brother served Egypt well as king. Much that Hatshepsut was doing obscured his career, but Thothmes II did present the warrior image to Egypt and upheld the military strength that had existed since the reign of Amose I.

Hatshepsut was content. Let her husband carry on the soldier-creed of their mutual father. She had inherited another interest from Thothmes I. She would be a builder of monuments, and of peace.

These were the radiant years. She was still young, in her

twenties, and virtual regent of the world's outstanding country. She had produced two children; the dynasty was safe. She had a husband who approved, or did not interfere, with all she was doing. And she was building as no women had ever built before.

She had her supporters well in hand. The political machine built so carefully and cautiously over the years, first by her father, then by Hatshepsut herself, was operating smoothly for her.

She was protected against the evil of two worlds. Professional sorcerers helped keep her safe from the power of curses. While she was the supreme being, she was still human, and vulnerable. Criticism of the ruling monarch, political unrest, and the protests of discontents, were not unknown. In reprisal she as monarch had the power held in "execration texts," which were curses written on pottery vases or human images of red clay. These were prepared by the priest-sorcerers, and, when smashed, with spoken curses, they could destroy the plans and even the lives of those plotting treason.

Was there a cloud on her horizon, even then? Was she aware of a woman of the harem, a concubine, or perhaps a lesser wife of Thothmes II, who was living in the palace and observing her from the shadows, plotting a future in which Hatshepsut had no share?

Did Hatshepsut smash red jars, the serene features we know convulsed with rage, while she pronounced with curses the name Isis?

Isis was a power name of ominous portent. It's meaning is "the throne."

And Isis was no helpless harem beauty. She had one strong advantage. During the same period that Hatshepsut was bearing her two small daughters, Isis gave birth to a son. The child would shortly be a pawn on the political field. He was born with the dual advantage of having an ambitious mother and a father who was Thothmes II, the consort and brother-spouse of Queen Hatshepsut.

Sennemut had become more than her chief architect. He was her right hand and her favorite. She placed complete trust in him and granted him every possible honor. Had he not shaped her greatest dream in stone by building Deir el-Bahari?

In his turn, Sennemut recorded his queen as being "the greatest of the great in all the land." He turned his genius, his energies, and his life over to her.

He built to his own glory as well. Imhotep's sponsoring king had permitted the architect to sign the memorials he built. Was it with Hatshepsut's permission that Sennemut inserted his own signed portraits into her Deir el-Bahari temple, skillfully hiding them behind the doors of the inner sanctuary dedicated to Amon? It has been suggested that she did not know they were there. They show the architect at prayer, and could only have been seen by one who, entering the shrine, closed the door, revealing the paintings in relief on a strip of the otherwise concealed wall. Still, others would have known of these paintings and Hatshepsut must have known.

In that narrow space, Sennemut insured his deathless fame.

She listed his honors, or permitted him to list them, elsewhere. They show the tremendous extent of his gathering power, which she needed for her own support.

She named him her Chief Steward (Steward of the King and Overseer of the Royal Residence). This put him in charge of the palace, the royal estates, and all her revenue.

He was a master administrator. He managed the holdings of the tremendously wealthy Amon priesthood. His title in that role was Steward of Amon; Overseer of the Fields, the Garden, the Herds, the Serfs, the Peasant-Farmers, and the Granaries of Amon: Prophet of Amon and Prophet of Amon's Sacred Barge

(Amon-Userhet); and Chief of the Amon Weavers. These responsibilities placed him directly inside the Great Temple and insured for Hatshepsut the continued loyalty of the politically powerful Amon priests.

He had titles for his other offices, which were the highest in the land. He described himself, "Hereditary Prince and Count, Sealbearer of the King of Lower Egypt, Sole Companion; Chief Prophet of Montu in Hermonthis; Spokesman of the Shrine of Geb, Headman in the House of the White Crown; Controller of the Broad Hall in the House of the Official; Controller of every Divine Craft and Controller of All Construction Work of the King [Hatshepsut] in Karnak, Hermonthis, Deir el-Bahari, the Temple of Mut and Karnak, and Luxor," and, as "a superior of superiors, overseer of all overseers of construction works."

The title of Controller put Sennemut in charge of all the buildings constructed during Hatshepsut's reign.

But the supreme honor she paid her favorite, and the one that showed her utter trust in Sennemut, was the strange title of "Great Nurse."

A queen could not tend her own child. When her first little daughter Nefrure was born, Hatshepsut placed her in charge of Amose-Pen-Nekhbet, the war correspondent and historian of her family since the time of King Amose, who was permitted to inscribe in his personal records: "The Divine Consort, the Great King's Wife, Makere [Hatshepsut] triumphant, repeated honors to me. I reared her eldest daughter, the Royal Daughter, Nefrure, triumphant, while she was a child upon the breast." He shared the responsibilites with Sennemut.

According to Hatshepsut's own account, she placed her first-born daughter in Sennemut's arms when the child was born, giving him the titles of Steward and Great Father-Nurse to the infant heiress. In time she added to her favorite's duties by making him administrator to the child's immense fortune. He tutored the little girl by way of preparing her for her sacred duties as the future occupant of the throne. So Hatshepsut had been prepared, as a child.

Sennemut was a very busy man.

He found time to pose for statues ordered by Hatshepsut showing him in protective custody of the little princess. These statues were set up in the temple at Karnak, to find their way centuries later into the Berlin and Cairo museums. They are the black stone statues of the great architect that hold our attention with their cold, arresting eyes under the heavy brows. His gaze challenges ours over the head of the child. He is holding Nefrure, protecting her with his robe.

The tiny figure in his arms is that of a child of two or possibly three years of age. Her eyes meet ours with his hauteur. She wears the youth lock on her right temple, a damaged cobra coronet on her forehead, and the disfiguring royal beard on her small chin. This is Hatshepsut in miniature, as she must have looked as a child. No similar statues remain of Hatshepsut at this age, only pictures.

And these pictures were to form part of the illustrations for Hatshepsut's own life story, including the scenes of her birth and coronation, which Sennemut recorded for her on the white walls of her memorial temple of Deir el-Bahari, and which both she and her architect intended to last forever.

CHAPTER 12

> Go, to make her, together with her ka, from these limbs which are in me; go, to fashion her better than all gods; shape for me, this my daughter, whom I have begotten. I have given to her all life and satisfaction, all stability, all joy of heart from me, all offerings, and all bread, like Re, forever.
> —Utterance of the god Amon.
> *Ancient Records*

Even in as rich and well-organized a country as Egypt there was dissension. There must have been veiled protest against a young and beautiful woman, who, while bearing the title of Great Royal Wife, was evidently in control of Egypt. The child born to the king's woman Isis was an incipient threat. He was one of the preferred palace children born to his royal father, and it is obvious that he held the attention of the king from his earliest years. Judging from his adult mummy in the Cairo Museum, the child who was to become Thothmes III was a sturdy throwback to his Thothmesid forefathers. He would resemble his grandfather Thothmes I in physique and aggressiveness. His stocky build and protruding teeth was Thothmesid. In every other way he was totally unlike his luxury-loving and easygoing father.

There was nothing about this small boy to endear him to

Hatshepsut. He was being reared as her enemy. His mother Isis must have instilled in him from infancy a resentment against the queen she hated and envied.

But his father was drawn to the boy. And his father was king.

History was to name the relationship of Hatshepsut to this Thothmes as that of his aunt, his sister, his half sister, his mother-in-law, and even his wife. She was actually the stepmother of the harem-born child and his aunt, since he was her half brother-husband's son.

Plottings in the harem were traditional. Mothers of likely sons besought their preferment from the king-father in intimate moments.

The semi-royal lads were given every opportunity to advance. They had priestly tutors and a chancellor who attended to their welfare. They were also likely to have conniving mothers. As a result, the palace apartments where the "other women" lived with the children sired by their king was always a hotbed of intrigue.

Hatshepsut had to defend herself against attack, both within and outside the palace. Her strongest weapon was her royal lineage. She had been born to the throne; her husband had only achieved it through marrying her. His son born to Isis was a threat. He had his partisans while he was still small. They sponsored him because of the one indisputable factor Hatshepsut and her two small daughters did not possess—his maleness.

Hatshepsut had Sennemut and Deir el-Bahari as her defenders. The most beautiful temple in Egypt pleaded her cause. On its walls Sennemut's artists painted and carved the life story of Queen Hatshepsut. Sculptors helped illustrate the biography with statues of her. It stressed the point she had to impress upon her people if she was to hold her position on the throne, a fact no man or woman dared dispute, that she was queen by the choice of the gods, having been divinely born.

Dr. Murray has observed: "Her magnificent temple at Deir el-Bahari is renowned not merely for its beauty but for the interest of many of the inscriptions on its walls."

The illustrated biography is in two reliefs, both badly multilated, but the colorings are still lovely and the remaining hieroglyphs as clear as when the artists painted them under Sennemut's direction. The reliefs run from the southern wall of the temple to the north, and describe in rotation the great events of her life, her conception, birth, and coronation, and the works she was able to accomplish as queen. The saga of a great woman is told in magnificent relief on the walls of Deir el-Bahari.

As she tells it, it is a woman's claim to divinity. In a reversal of all tradition, Hatshepsut showed herself as having been divinely born, and not as a girl, but as a boy! She explained why the birth of a king was the birth of a god.

Had this theory been impressed upon her, or was the story her propaganda weapon against the growing threat of her father's semi-royal male heir?

We have no way of knowing how the early regents of Egypt conceived the idea that they were gods, nor how they were able to impress that concept upon an advanced and intelligent civilization. Certainly Hatshepsut, having been born royal, believed in her own divinity. She accepted adoration. Her ears had heard only praise, the music of her musicians and singers chanting her praises before her, the adulation of her nurses, governors, tutors, her courtiers and ministers and ladies-in-waiting, and her people, the great worshipful masses of Egypt. How could she fail to believe in her own divinity?

She had known from the beginning who she was and what was expected of her and the elements that had gone into her making. So she dictated her biography, so Sennemut saw it set down on the walls of Deir el-Bahari as the indisputable truth, illustrated and in exquisitely-drawn hieroglyphs, that all people might know the divinity of Hatshepsut, triumphant, living forever. Those who read would understand why she alone held the legitimate right to the throne and none would dare dispute her authority as the true leader of Egypt.

It translates, as Hatshepsut tells the story, with the god Amon taking the form of her father, Thothmes I.

The god, and Hatshepsut's mother, Amose II, are shown seated on a lion-footed bed facing one another. They are upheld by two goddesses. The god (Hatshepsut's father) speaks, describing the situation.

> Utterance of Amon-Re, Lord of Thebes, presided over Karnak. He made his form like the majesty of this husband, the King [Thothmes I] . . . He found her as she slept in the beauty of her palace. She waked at the fragrance of the god . . . she rejoiced in the sight of his beauty, his love passed into her limbs, which the fragrance of the god flooded; all his odors were of Punt.

(Punt, the mysterious land of myrrh, was obviously on Hatshepsut's mind.)

The queen, her daughter relates, was enraptured, she cried out "in the presence of the majesty of this august god, Amon, Lord of Thebes: 'How great is thy fame! . . . thy dew is in all my limbs.' After this, the majesty of this god did all that he desired with her."

The mother Amose is lovingly portrayed. She is smiling, as in all her pictures ordered by her daughter, and she receives the god with an expression of innocence and wonder.

In the exact moment of conception, the relief goes on to explain, the queen cried out a word that came to her lips, "Hatshepsut!" And the god-husband-king responded, "Khnemet-Amon-Hatshepsut shall be the name of this my daughter, whom I have placed in thy body, this saying which comes out of thy mouth. She shall exercise the excellent kingship in this whole land. My soul is hers, my will is hers, my crown is hers, that she may govern the Two Lands. . . ."

It is clear that Hatshepsut was leaving no loophole for her critics to use in contesting her right to rule.

Amon, having committed himself to Hatshepsut's cause, moves on in the relief to the next scene, that shows him in consultation with Khnum, the god creator of all life, who wore a ram's head with double horns and modeled on his potter's wheel the egg from which the new life would emerge.

Amon is giving orders to the creator of life.

> Go, to make her, together with her ka [duplicate self] from these limbs which are in me . . . fashion her better than all gods; shape for me, this my daughter, whom I have begotten.

And the potter-god-creator promises, "Her form shall be more exalted than the gods. . . ."

The next scene shows Khnum seated before his potter's wheel shaping two small, childish figures that are Hatshepsut and her ka. Kneeling before them holding out the ankh (symbol of life) is the frog-headed goddess Heket, deliverer at births. Khnum repeats the orders give him by Amon, which he has carried out "as thy father who loves thee has commanded."

Here, as in so many places in her records, Hatshepsut uses the feminine "thee," although the royal infant shaped by Khnum is a boy! The reliefs remain clear and strong, and as to the sex of Hatshepsut, artlessly inconsistent.

Amose is then shown being led to her confinement. Holding her by either hand are Khnum and Heket. They follow nine divinities in rows of three; all are led by Amon.

The scene showing the actual birth is striking. Many goddesses are present, among them Isis, Nephthys, and the all-important goddess of motherhood, Hathor. Directing the delivery is Meskhenet, the goddess of births.

Queen Amose is seated in a chair, while two goddesses hold her arms as mid-Eastern midwives still hold those of women during childbirth. Two other goddesses hold their arms out to take the child.

The child (and its ka) is born, and the attendant goddesses breathe life into the tiny form. It is obviously male. She (he) is then given by the goddess Hathor to her father, who is still in the guise of Amon, and who takes "him" in her arms and caresses "her whom he loves beyond all things." Forgetting the premise of masculinity, the god-king croons to the newly born, "Live in peace, daughter of my loins, whom I love."

The next scene shows the child being nursed by seven Hathors.

The relief moves on. The child is portrayed growing; through the rites of coronation; the presentation of Hatshepsut by her father to gods and men; Hatshepsut's elevation to the throne.

This is her story, as Hatshepsut has left it. According to her, she had fulfilled prophecies made for her before she was born. There was no privacy in royal marriage. The priest-seers cast the horoscope of a royal child in the hour of its conception. Their calculations were not made by the stars, but by dates. There were lucky and unlucky days. Hatshepsut had been conceived in an hour held fortunate to Amon. So the priests foretold, according to the records. Their prophecy promised her greatness. She believed in it; she lived by it.

Her biographical series on the walls of Deir el-Bahari impresses all who have studied it, in her time, and on into our own. The story of her divine origin would be plagiarized by Amonhotep III, grandson of Thothmes III and also by the father of Akhenaton, who would reproduce it in its entirety in his own name on the walls at Karnak. It would be used again, in a later dynasty, by Rameses II. Her Deir el-Bahari series would be twice defaced, first by her rival Thothmes III when he attained power, and later by Akhenaton, who ordered the name of Amon chiseled from her shrine and replaced with the name of his one-god, Aton. Fortunately, the copy at Karnak remained undamaged, and by it the missing places in Hatshepsut's beautifully illustrated life story can still be read.

Barring the divine birth scenes, we have no reason to doubt her statements. We can be fairly certain that Sennemut, who directed the inscriptions, believed every word to be true.

There was a great deal of grave-robbing going on in the necropolis. The graves of the Seventeenth Dynasty kings were systematically plundered. The robbers were men who had worked in the tombs and knew the locations of their treasures, or citizens of Thebes who were carrying on a trade handed down in their families. The employees in the workman's village, Deir el-Medineh, were often without work for months at a time, and during such periods they and their families knew hunger. And these men knew where the wealth of the dead was hidden; had they not helped to conceal it? Tunnels were dug, sometimes from the rear of the tombs, so that the sealed doorways with their mystic warnings need not be touched. Working by torchlight at night deep underground, the vandals ripped away at bandaged forms, hunting the jewels concealed within the bindings. If a finger, arm, hand, even a head, was torn off in the frantic search, the robbers did not care. Amulets and written curses did not terrify them. They knew the dead had no power. The robbers grew rich, they attained high posts in the government, until, long after Hatshepsut's time, there was reprisal. Among those found guilty was a mayor of Thebes.

The royal dead were frequently shuffled by the priests from one grave to another in a futile attempt to keep them safe from the despoilers. Hatshepsut saw the empty coffins, the despoiled bodies that were sacred to her. There were depredations in the graves of Gurn, near her Deir el-Bahari temple. She became anxious for the security of her father's mummy that she herself had seen buried as the first occupant of the Valley of the Kings. She had his sarcophagus moved to her own grave and held memorial services for the dead Thothmes I in the shrine of Anubis in her Temple.

She showed anxiety for her own future burial. Another grave was prepared for her, nearer her beautiful temple, where her "ka" would have no difficulty visiting her and she might be safe for all the millions and millions of years. She had earned the right to this dream, which she shared with all Egyptians.

Her husband shared it with her. Thothmes II built his own mortuary temple near hers at Deir el-Bahari, and his burial place near that of his and Hatshepsut's father, in the Valley of the Kings. He looked forward contentedly to these well-prepared places of rest.

He had not long to wait. Thothmes II died young; his mummy in Cairo, badly damaged by grave robbers, is estimated to be that of a man under thirty. His white skin is spotted by some cutaneous disease. It is suggested that Hatshepsut's husband died of smallpox. The death was recorded in the usual formula: "Thothmes II went to heaven and mingled with the gods."

But before his death, he succeeded in naming his successor, as was his right. His choice was the son born to him by the woman named Isis. To insure the lad's claim to the throne he must first be married to his half-sister, Nefrure, the first-born daughter of Hatshepsut and Thothmes II.

If Hatshepsut protested the move at the time, she did not put it into the record.

How long had Thothmes II served as king? Opinions vary; some authorities say eight, others thirteen years. It was a brief regency compared with Hatshepsut's reign. She was now in full swing, with all her powers well in hand. Her young rival, who would be known, after his marriage to the fully-royal Nefrure, as King Thothmes III, presented no challenge at first.

Her son-in-law is believed to have been between six and ten years old when his father died.

Hatshepsut had buried two kings and was once more in sole

possession of the throne. The boy was too young, his mother too unimportant, to contest her will. Once more Hatshepsut tasted the irresistible delights of supreme power, and, using it to the hilt, she launched upon the career that was to make her unique among the Pharaohs of Egypt.

CHAPTER 13

The king [Thothmes II] ascended to the Heavens and joined the company of the gods; his son [Thothmes III] took his place. . . . His sister, the divine woman Hatshepsut, adjusted the affairs of the two kingdoms according to her own mind. Egypt, bowing the head before her, cultivated the excellent seed divine, sprung from the god. She was the cable which drew the North, the stake to which was moored the South; she was the perfect tiller–rope of the North, the mistress who issues commands, whose wise plans bring peace upon the Two Lands. . . .

—*Ancient Records*

The above report on the activities of Hatshepsut after her husband's death is from the biography of Ineni, the architect who had worked for her father and grandfather and was now building for Hatshepsut. He believed in her infallibility and her divine origin—opinions he shared with Egypt. There were the customary few dissenters. Among them was certainly the growing boy whose inheritance of his father's titles and throne was an empty legacy due to his extreme youth and the common blood of his mother Isis.

There is a statue of Isis in the Cairo Museum. The stone

face is expressionless, and one wonders what Isis meant to Hatshepsut, and Hatshepsut to her. Whether lesser wife or concubine to the dead king, Isis was a rival of the queen who had been the Great Wife of Thothmes II. Isis wanted recognition for the son she had borne the king, and the boy was obviously being reared in fierce resentment of Hatshepsut for his mother's ignoble position and his own present helplessness.

He had been brought up in the palace with Hatshepsut's daughters. He was being given the best education the priest-professors could provide–one worthy of a king's son.

Was Isis plotting ahead when the lad was entered as an acolyte in the Great Temple? Was she pointing out even then to persons of influence the many ways in which the boy resembled other Thothmesid kings than his father–the sturdy physique, hard-driving look under a low forehead, the stubborn will that no one could cross?

These were characteristics that would accentuate as he grew.

Certain palace forces were already rallying around Isis in support of her son. They helped her encourage his innate will to command and to keep his fierce young eyes trained on the throne.

Hatshepsut had her informers. She would know of the growing opposition. She could discuss the matter with Sennemut and other trusted advisors. The boy was more than another palace male child sired by her husband. His personality was unformed, but the potential was pure Thothmesid. His father had evidently recognized that indomitable force before his own death when he chose the lad as his successor. Even the throne name was chosen. The small boy was to be King Thothmes III.

But Hatshepsut held every advantage over the boy. She was on the throne. Power is a heady possession. Her husband's death had left her in sole command of Egypt and his son's future. Hatshepsut had time to plan; she would not relinquish the throne.

Her decision was justified. For years she had carried the entire burden of state. She had assumed responsibilities that would have tested the strength and courage of a man in the years when her father was dying, and carried them on through the decade when a compliant spouse had served as the royal male image. She had handled ably all the duties of a king. She had the position and the power of the Pharaoh, but not the name.

As Great Queen she was entitled to wear the cobra coronet. Its weight was trifling compared to the heavy dual crown worn by the kings of Egypt. She had assumed every other kingly burden and the acolyte in the Great Temple would be growing up; she had to establish herself firmly in supreme command before it was too late.

It took her almost two years to make up her mind.

In the second year after her husband's death, Hatshepsut made the most extraordinary move ever made by an Egyptian, or any other woman.

She made herself a king.

The coup began with an announcement. Court and temple circles were informed that a miracle had taken place. Amon, king of the gods, had spoken to Queen Hatshepsut!

The miracle manifested itself in the great hall in the Temple of Amon that had been built by her father. Hatshepsut was paying her respects before the gold image of Amon when a voice issued from the lips of the idol.

It said, "Go, my daughter, King of Egypt!"

Not as Queen, the god addressed her, but as King!

Hatshepsut lost no time in spreading the news among her constituents. "He [Amon], greatest of all the gods, speaks to me as a father to his son!"

It was nothing new for a god to speak to a king. The Pharaohs often reported man-to-man conversations with the heavenly ones. But they had been men. It did no good for the Isis faction to protest, "Hatshepsut is a woman!"

Her answer could not be disputed. "I am not a woman. I am the king!"

The formal announcement was made, and the necessary procedures carried out in the palace and the southern temple. With ceremonial pomp Hatshepsut placed upon her proudly-held head the heavy double crown of the two Egypts—the crown that had only been worn by kings. She was the first woman to wear that crown. She also claimed all the other crowns belonging to the kings, and donned them for the various occasions they required. She continued to wear the male dress that was so becoming to her slender figure, and it was now that she assumed the gold beard. Attached to the royal headdress, the beard was the symbol of divine male power that only a king might wear.

She was now King Hatshepsut I of Egypt. The royal edict demanded that henceforward she was to be addressed only as "His Majesty."

She used all her dead father's royal titles and added that of Kamere as her throne name, while continuing to use her own personal name of Hatshepsut. Kamere was a male prenomen. One title used by her father she did not claim—that of the Great Bull of Maat.

Her new status was acclaimed, she recorded, "by the joyful people."

Murray has commented that Hatshepsut confused the records when she claimed to be the Pharaoh. Hatshepsut further confused them with her choice of words. Her inscriptions are filled with curious discrepancies, such as "King Hatshepsut, she whom the gods hath chosen. . . ." One sentence in her biography describes her as "King of Upper and Lower Egypt, Daughter of Re . . . Hatshepsut."

Her inner circle of followers might refer to her as their king in their own inscribed biographies, but they, too, invariably shift genders and write of "her" as they never would of a man.

They accepted her divinity and her kingship.

The Amon priesthood supported her move, which she could never have made without their approval. But then—had not their god spoken to her as to a king? Her strongest weapon politically was her royal (divine) birth. It was her strongest defense against the lad Thothmes, who, no matter what claims he might make to royalty, could not erase his non-royal mother from the public eye.

He would have been twelve by this time—old enough to serve during the ceremony.

Isis and her son had to watch helplessly in the southern temple while his father's widow raised to her shaven head the double crown of the two Egypts, and what their thoughts were during that triumphant ritual we shall never know. But the infamous "feud of the Thothmesid," which had started with the death of Hatshepsut's father, was to mount in intensity which would end only with the death of one of the antagonists. For, while Hatshepsut was older and wiser and possessed of total power, this newest "young falcon in the nest" was of formidable quality and he would not long be a child. The years were his allies. In time they would atone for the helpless fury of a lad forced to watch his stepmother-aunt take her place on his father's throne, wearing male ceremonial robes such as his father had worn, and his father's crown.

Hatshepsut could not have dared the move to kingship alone. She had the support of the elite corps of advisors started for her by her father, consolidated by Hatshepsut in her own wisdom, and headed by the indomitable Sennemut. It was composed of the most talented and influential men in Egypt. All were men of foresight, and able administrators. Together they made up a political machine that overrode opposition like a juggernaut.

Spies and traitors lurk at the base of every throne. Hatshepsut's sex made her vulnerable. At any moment a strong opposing voice might cry havoc. "A princely ruler, true! But still, a woman. . . ."

She silenced such threats when she firmed her legitimist power circle with Sennemut as its hub.

She had the rare gift of inspiring loyalty. Those close to her were willing to die for her, and it is believed that some of them did.

The Egyptian kings had always rewarded valor and loyalty with preferment, titles, lands, revenue, slaves, and incredible gifts of gold jewelry set with precious stones. New Year's was marked by the giving of smaller personal gifts, such as faience boxes, painted fans, jewels, and portraits of members of the royal family. Hatshepsut gave more than any other monarch. She "filled the homes" of those she loved with treasure, she raised their life stations together with those of their families, and she gave them words of loving praise with permission to engrave such words on the walls of their tombs. Much that these favored ones were allowed to record was chiseled away by her enemies, but, as with her own biographical inscriptions, an amazing amount can still be read.

Hatshepsut was a wily politician. In past reigns the court and the temple had often locked horns. Devoted Hatshepsut aides held key positions in both institutions. She had chosen and placed them there. By this means she consolidated the two strongest political factions. Her ministers and the Amon priesthood held together in the name of King Hatshepsut all the civil, military, and religious power in Egypt.

Her favorite Sennemut was the whip of her power party. His power was second only to hers, and he wielded it under the modest title of her Chief Steward. His brother Sennemon and another devotee, Amonophis, were also entitled stewards and given extraordinary authority.

Second to Sennemut in political strength was Hapuseneb. Like Sennemut, he was an architect, and it is indicative of Hatshepsut's devotion to architecture that so many men in her inner power circle were architects. She made him her Vizier for Upper Egypt. It was a position his grandfather had held before him. He was also her "chief of prophets of North and South," or High Priest of Amon, another hereditary position that had been held by his great-grandfather. This placed him at the head of the Amon priesthood for all Egypt, where he was able to detect and nip in the bud any rumors of impending treason against his King Hatshepsut.

He continued to build as one of her leading architects. She entrusted him with such important structures in Western Thebes as a second smaller temple and another cliffside grave for herself in the Valley of the Kings. Hapuseneb was permitted to list the building he did for Hatshepsut in the tomb he was building for himself near her Deir el-Bahari temple.

Another architect of exceptional ability in that and other ways was Thuty, her treasurer. He was an able administrator and one of her most loyal supporters. He was also a thoroughly honest man. As "head of the house of gold and silver," he had charge of Hatshepsut's fortune. He had succeeded Ineni in this office. The aging Ineni was now devoting himself entirely to building.

It was Thuty who provided Hatshepsut with the precious material needed to adorn her monuments, disbursing the silver and gold and jewels from her royal coffers and keeping meticulous account of the amounts taken in and given out. His records show a regard for the exact that was often lacking in other officials of his time.

Hatshepsut's enemies would not be able to obliterate all the achievements Thuty listed in his tomb. Inscriptions that paid homage to Hatshepsut and his master architect Sennemut are only partially obscured.

His surviving hieroglyphic records offer a glimpse into the glittering interior of Hatshepsut's temple at Deir el-Bahari in the days when Thuty was helping Sennemut make it the most beautiful temple on earth, under the close observance of their adored task-mistress Hatshepsut.

Thuty was artist, metal-crafter, and jeweler, as well as architect. He built with granite and alabaster as all her builders did, but he also used rare and costly woods and precious stones. He described the completed temple as being "a palace of the god, wrought with gold and silver, it illuminated the faces [of the worshipers] with its brightness." He described his own works in the temple, which he named "Most Splendid . . . its great doors [the outer ones?] fashioned of black copper, the inlaid figures of electrum [mixed silver and gold]." He told of his contributions inside the Amon shrine, "the god's enduring horizon of eternity in the West . . . with its [inner?] doors of cedar wrought with bronze, its floor wrought with gold and silver . . . its beauty was like the horizon of the sun."

Thuty's greatest contribution to the Deir el-Bahari temple was the famed ebony shrine of Nubia. He described the stairs leading up to the shrine as being "high and wide, of pure alabaster of Hatnub."

His artistry also contributed to Hatshepsut's additions to the Great Temple at Karnak. He lists these as the tall, wide temple doors, "made of copper and bronze and inlaid with electrum; an impressive gate made of a single sheet of copper and named the "Terror of Amon"; a granite shrine, "its durability like the pillars of Heaven . . ."; and, to add to the glitter inside the Great Temple, he created for the priests many sacred vessels and chests and necklaces and amulets "of copper and electrum and every precious stone."

Another architect elevated to high office by Hatshepsut was Puemre. She made him a member of her inner circle and Inspector of Monuments, an office still highly regarded in Egypt. In his tomb and on his statue, Puemre inscribed his pride in having inspected in the Deir el-Bahari temple the construction [by Thuty] of the great ebony shrine wrought with electrum "by the King of Upper and Lower Egypt, Makere [Hatshepsut]. . . ."

Hatshepsut had a number of Viceroys. Among the most important to her were those at Elephantine and Kush and Ethiopia. Inebny, her Viceroy for Ethiopia, had charge of all the gold mines of Nubia.

An official named Thothmes was her Vizier for Lower Egypt, while his son Ptahmes served as High Priest at Memphis.

Nihisi, her chancellor, was her chief treasurer and guardian of the royal seal.

With these men she held contact and control with every part of Egypt. They were the leaders of the land. As a team they held every branch of the country's vast complex of power radiating out of the palace at Thebes. They were invincible, they were loyal to Hatshepsut, and for a period of almost twenty years they were to keep her in a position of absolute power.

She regarded them as her closest friends. But none were as close to her as Sennemut, who had built for her the beautiful temple at Deir el-Bahari. He remained her favorite, a wielder of extraordinary power under protection most high. All others answered to him.

She confided her ambitions to Sennemut with the implicit trust she had shown when she put him in charge of the education and finances of her daughter Nefrure. It was due to his leadership in her power circle and its control of Egypt that Hatshepsut was able to launch and complete the series of stupendous undertakings that would make her unique among monarchs. The first had been the temple at Deir el-Bahari.

Sennemut evidently began the memorial for Hatshepsut while her father was still alive. The name of Thothmes I is inscribed on its walls as that of a living king. But this may be one of the defenses she threw up against any possible claims of a boy to the throne of Thothmes I. In one illustration in the temple, Hatshepsut is shown with her father. His hands are on her in a protective way, as if to shield her. This is obviously propaganda. Hatshepsut used the names of her royal father and her husband to bolster her claim to the throne. Deir el-Bahari's walls stress that right as due to her legitimacy. The temple has been described as her advocate. It spoke, it stills speaks, for her.

It was a long time in the building. The work was interrupted, perhaps during the time when she was relegated to the role of Great Queen and her orders lacked the authority of total royalty. If started in the time of Thothmes I, work was resumed on it during her marriage to Thothmes II, and now in her widowhood it was completed and consecrated with Thothmes III playing the reluctant role of admirer. For the names of all her three Thothmesid are written on its walls, and all three are pictured there. Only her father is shown as her life-sized equal. Her husband Thothmes II and his son Thothmes III are shown standing meekly to the rear of Hatshepsut, and smaller in size. This was the way women were usually pictured in Egypt—doll-sized, and posed behind the male.

The effect this must have had on a budding despot with the empty title of Thothmes III explains much that took place later.

For the present, the widowed Hatshepsut met with no opposition as she launched the greatest construction project Egypt had ever known. The aged Ineni continued to build for her, but he resigned from his position as "Chief of all the Royal Works." Sennemut added the title to the many others given him by Hatshepsut. It placed him in charge of all the building undertaken in Egypt while Hatshepsut lived.

He called himself her chief Steward of Amon, but the modest title concealed power second only to her own. He built for her at Deir el-Bahari, Karnak, Hermonthis, and Southern Thebes. She gave every opportunity to his genius. She made him many personal gifts. The two statues of Sennemut holding her Crown

9. Thothmes III, who began his career as a boy-king sharing the throne with his aunt, stepmother (and perhaps, later, his wife) Hatshepsut was to become her most formidable rival for the throne. The infamous "feud of the Thothmesid" could culminate only in the death of one of these two powerful rulers.

10. Isis was the mother of the boy who became Thothmes III. She was a concubine or perhaps a subsidiary wife of Hatshepsut's husband, Thothmes II. It is believed that she connived with the Amon priests in the effort to place her half-royal son on Hatshepsut's throne.

11. Sennemut, the "great in love," was Hatshepsut's defense against the plottings against Hatshepsut by Thothmes and his mother. He was the steward of all her affairs and the architect who designed and built her great monuments. She entrusted him with the upbringing of her first-born daughter, Nefrure, shown here in his arms, in one of the two statues of her favorite ordered by Hatshepsut. Nefrure was the heiress royal but she died young without reaching the throne.

12. The memorial temple of Queen Hatshepsut at Deir el-Bahari in western Thebes was designed and built for her during her lifetime by Sennemut. This reconstruction shows it as it was when completed by Sennemut. The mountain of Gurn at its back is honeycombed by the tombs of forgotten kings.

13. King Amonhotep III, later in the dynasty, revealed the vitality and zest for living characteristic of Hatshepsut's family. As warrior, statesman and builder, he upheld the Thothmesid traditions and the position of Egypt as a world power. His marriage to the non-royal Tye is considered one of the outstanding romances of antiquity.

Amonhotep and Tye were lently a healthy and happy ·, content with their rich king- n and one another. But the verful genes of the Thothmesid ·e weakening and they became parents of the strange mystic o is known to history as ıenaton.

15. Akhenaton married Nefertiti, a non-royal girl considered the most beautiful woman of her time. She was the last of the glamorous Eighteenth Dynasty queens. Shortly after her death the dynasty came to an end with the death of Tutankhamon, the last member of Hatshepsut's family line to rule over Egypt.

16. Brooding and mutilated, this portrait in red quartzite of King Akhenaton reveals the intensity of the man who built the now vanished city of Amarna and became known as "the first monotheist in history."

17. Hatshepsut's enemies were unable to destroy all her records and monuments. One of her remaining obelisks upon which she had proclaimed herself to be king of Egypt, still towers over the ruins of Thebes. It is the tallest monument in Egypt.

18. The ruined memorial temple Hatshepsut built for herself on the west bank of the Nile at Thebes is considered the most beautiful edifice in Egypt. From a distance it resembled a Greek temple but it was built long before Greek architecture began. In this as in many other ways she was an innovator; a woman who was far ahead of her time.

Princess daughter Nefrure were ordered by Hatshepsut as gifts to her favorite. She placed one in the Temple of Mut at Karnak, the other at Deir el-Bahari. Both were found in these places.

The statues reveal a square block of a man, symbolized by the cloak in which he conceals the child, which forms the body of the cube-shaped statue. The robe is covered with hieroglyphs, that list Sennemut's many titles. No man stood higher then in Egypt. It also reveals Hatshepsut's love for the man. The Berlin statue impresses with the message that it was a royal gift to Sennemut from Hatshepsut, "Given as a favor of the king's presence, the King of Upper and Lower Egypt, Makere [Hatshepsut]. . . ."

On the walls of his own tomb, Sennemut wrote of his position as Hatshepsut's favorite, in glowing words both he and she could read while both were still lusty with life. He wrote of himself as one dead, as was the custom of one inscribing his biography in his own tomb. He wrote of his accomplishments, as was also the custom of one who while living prepared his advance argument to the eternal gods. But there was this difference from other appeals from the grave: Sennemut's inscriptions dealt largely with a woman—the woman he had helped to be a king. In his writings he referred to her as a king. That was her choice, not his. In places he speaks of her as feminine. That may have been his choice.

Sennemut was privileged. He wrote with frankness.

> I was a noble, beloved of his lord [Hatshepsut], who entered upon the wonderful plans of the Mistress of the Two Lands. He exalted me . . . appointed me to be chief of his estate. . . . I was the superior of superiors, the chief of chiefs of works. . . .
>
> I was in life under the Mistress of the Two Lands, King of Upper and Lower Egypt, Makere [Hatshepsut], living forever.

And again:

> I was one, whose steps were known in the palace, a real confidant of the King [Hatshepsut] his beloved. . . .

And,

> I was the greatest of the great in the whole land; one who heard the hearing alone in the privy council.

Again,

> I was the real favorite of the king [Hatshepsut], acting as one praised by his lord every day.

In several places he showed his concern for her welfare:

> I conducted [rites?] . . . of the gods every day for the sake of the life, prosperity and health of the king [Hatshepsut].

Even more revealing was his inscribed cry of triumph:

> I was one who entered in love, and came forth in favor, making glad the heart of the king every day, the companion, and master of the palace, Sennemut.

Do the inscriptions suggest a deeper relationship? It was with Hatshepsut's consent that he described himself as her "beloved, sole companion, real favorite, one who entered in love."

Gossip has persisted through thousands of years. That they were lovers is an opinion many in Egypt still hold of Hatshepsut and her favored architect. The records do not corroborate the rumor, which was perhaps due to the tribute Hatshepsut paid Sennemut and his genius, not alone in practical ways, but in her praise of him on her most precious memorial, the temple at Deir el-Bahari he had designed and built in his devotion to her.

They may have loved, and without criticism. Adultery was frowned upon, but Hatshepsut was for many years a widow. Sex was frankly discussed. Birth control methods were known. The hieroglyphs give over in places to bare-faced pornography. Stories, jokes, poetry, and even hymns could be of the "blue" variety. The act of sex was described as "spending a merry day." The gods had sultry love affairs which were duly recorded. Paintings and statuettes of naked female dancers and favorite concubines were placed in the graves of men royal or rich. The kings and all other men of wealth had full harems and their choice of secondary wives.

Hatshepsut had taken on every other kingly privilege. But of this one we simply do not know.

She had another towering ambition which she confided to Sennemut. She was nearing the time of her Jubilee which would mark her first fifteen years on the throne. Fifteen years had passed since her father had placed her beside him as his queen. (As a rule, the kings celebrated this festival after thirty years; Hatshepsut may have shortened the time for propaganda reasons). All Egypt would celebrate with her, and she wanted to commemorate the festival in a way that would make it remembered forever. She gave much thought to the problem. She never lost sight of the fact that she owed her fifteen years of rule to the god Amon, and, as all we know of Hatshepsut shows, one of her dominant traits was that of gratitude.

She expressed her gratitude to Amon every day of her life, with special observances in his temple. She had dedicated her beautiful Deir el-Bahari temple to him and built him a sanctuary in his Great Temple at Karnak, as well as other shrines. These were not enough. What more could she offer the god who had chosen her to be his daughter on earth?

Let Hatshepsut give the answer in her own words, inscribed on stone. She wrote as if a king were speaking:

> I sat in the palace, I remembered him who fashioned me [Amon], my heart led me to make for him two obelisks of electrum, whose points mingled with heaven. . . . Then my

soul stirred, wondering what men would say who saw this monument after many years and spoke of what I had done. . . .

A pyramid was a series of stairs on which kings mounted to heaven; an obelisk pointed the way. Hatshepsut confided her "soul stirring" to Sennemut. Together they planned her most difficult undertaking, the raising of two obelisks to Amon that would be the tallest pillars in Egypt.

It was a prodigious task she set for her favorite. The obelisks must be in place in time for her festival, which was only a half-year away.

Sennemut upheld Hatshepsut's serene assurance that the obelisks would be completed in time. It could be done, he said, and she believed him; she believed nothing was impossible to Sennemut.

CHAPTER 14

Oh ye people, who shall see my monument after years, those who shall speak of that which I have made, beware [lest] ye say, "I know not, I know not why this was made . . . a mountain fashioned entirely from gold. . . ."

I swear as Re loves me, as my father Amon favors me, as my nostrils are filled with satisfying life, as I wear the white crown, as I appear in the red crown, as Horus and Set have united for me their halves, as I rule this land like the son of Isis, as I have become strong like the son of Nut, as Re sets in the evening barque, as he rises in the morning barque, as he joins his two mothers in the divine barque, as heaven abides, as that which he hath made endures, as I shall be unto Eternity like an "imperishable," as I shall go down in the west like Aton, so surely these two great obelisks which My Majesty hath wrought with electrum for my father, Amon, in order that my name may abide, enduring in this temple forever and ever . . . are made of one block of enduring granite without seam or joining. . . .

—Hatshepsut's "Oath to Posterity,"
at the time of the raising
of her obelisks at Karnak.
—*Ancient Records*

Even the intrepid soul of Sennemut must have quailed before the prodigious task Hatshepsut had set for him. If it were not for the evidence left towering over the ruins of Karnak, the feat would be considered as mythological as one of the seven labors later credited to Hercules. Equipped only with stone tools, he and his workmen were to wrest Hatshepsut's giant obelisks from the red granite quarries at the First Cataract, at Aswan on the border of Nubia, one hundred and fifty miles south on the Nile.

"Bring me the tallest monuments ever carved in Egypt," Hatshepsut commanded her favorite. "Higher than any king has raised before. . . ."

That was early in February, in this fifteenth year of her regency.

Sennemut faced an engineering problem that would dismay modern contractors. To carve the shafts from the stone mountainside was hazardous work, but bringing them downriver to Thebes and raising them at Karnak were problems that must have seemed insurmountable even to him. But Hatshepsut's request to her favorite was serenely made. The creation of the Deir el-Bahari temple had convinced her that Sennemut could do anything she might ask of him.

She gave him full-hearted support. Manpower was unlimited. Sennemut had his choice of engineers, carpenters, quarrymen, and slaves. Hatshepsut contributed barges and galleys, manned by soldiers and sailors, and oarsmen to row the ships. With high hopes she watched Sennemut direct his formidable labor fleet away from the wharf at Thebes and turn the ponderous ships upstream, in the direction of southern Egypt.

Standing with him on the foredeck of the lead galley was her steward Amonophis, who would be his co-director on the project. With the pair were other members of Hatshepsut's power party, her chancellor Nihisi, and Thuty her treasurer. Two scribes, Tetem-Re and Minmose, went along to record the historic undertaking.

The flotilla reached the red cliffs at Aswan and set up an immense labor camp. Work started at once in the quarry. Outlines of the proposed pillars were drawn, and stone hammers pounded the surrounding granite to dust. This was called "entering the mountain." When the forms of the shafts appeared, other workmen using stone chisels shaped them into crude four-sided pillars.

The first was one hundred and twenty-five feet long. As Sennemut was directing its removal from the granite trench, a crack appeared in its base.

There was no time to be lost in lamentation. Hatshepsut wanted her obelisks for her jubilee.

Work began on a second pillar, then another, until two unfinished obelisks were cut out of the rock and dragged down to the river's edge on sleds and rollers by hundreds of slaves.

Wheels had been used in Egypt since the Hyksos invasion, but only for chariots. This may have been because the horses that were also a legacy from the Hyksos were still too small to pull heavy loads.

Sennemut's brow furrowed as he contemplated two enormous shafts of rough granite, each a solid block of approximately one hundred and eighty cubic yards of stone, almost a hundred feet long, eight and a half feet through at the base, and weighing, it has been estimated, over eighty thousand pounds.

Somehow, he had to get the two monsters back to Thebes.

He had worked out every move of the operation in advance. Hatshepsut had provided the expedition with logs of costly sycamore collected throughout "the entire land" (lumber was always scarce in an almost treeless Egypt), and these were lashed together forming a barge that was not only three hundred feet long, but one hundred feet high! It was steered by four gigantic oars. A small observation cabin was mounted on the foredeck from which Sennemut and his aides could direct operations. If the barge tipped, Sennemut was prepared to go down with his ship.

Somehow, in broiling sunlight, Sennemut's work armies completed the heart-breaking labor of lifting the two obelisks from shore to barge, centering them there, base against base, as a two-hundred-foot shaft of solid stone, adjusting the balance to a hairsbreadth, and lashing the double shaft firmly onto the three hundred-foot-long raft. How can we estimate the physical suffering, even the deaths, that went into the procuring of Hatshepsut's obelisks?

The pillars were now ready for their precarious trip down the Nile.

But first, Sennemut had one more commission to carry out at Aswan for his lady.

On the red granite cliff he carved a memorial to the completion of his mission. On it he is shown in relief, offering homage to Hatshepsut.

His inscription portrays her:

> Hereditary princess, great in favor and kindness, great in love . . . the King's Daughter, the King's Sister, the Divine Consort, God's Wife and King's Great Wife, Hatshepsut. . . .

He described himself as "her companion, great in love . . . who satisfies the heart of the Divine Consort, who pleases the Mistress of the Two Lands, Chief Steward of the Princess Nefrure."

He had lived, Sennemut proclaimed on granite, to conduct for his queen the work of cutting the two great obelisks which would commemorate her Festival, known as the "Myriad of Years." He ended in triumph: "Every thing was done . . . because of the fame of Her Majesty."

He left this record and the broken obelisk behind at Aswan as the work fleet, moving slowly around the heavily burdened barge, turned northward in the direction of Thebes.

Runners carried reports of the obelisks' slow progress to Hatshepsut, waiting impatiently at Thebes. While waiting she ordered deep-set stone bases that could hold their weight prepared for her obelisks in the Great Temple.

Sennemut was bringing the monuments on a hazardous journey. It was now late summer, and the time of the high waters. Sennemut was taking advantage of the annual flood to help propel the heavy ships downstream. The barge was under constant danger of overturning. His engineers, who were trained in navigation and knew the river, directed the fleet from smaller, circling boats. The unwieldy barge, drawn by its tugs, threaded dangerous currents, skirted waterfalls, and avoided jutting rocks. Even with the floods to aid them, progress was slow down the papyrus-bordered, mud-swollen Nile.

Hatshepsut had word of their coming. She was on the wharf to await the arrival. Around her was all her court, and behind it was all Thebes. Present were hundreds of young men in military kilts. Hatshepsut had mustered out "all her army and navy, from the Delta to Upper Nubia, from all the Two Lands," to help Sennemut and his work army bring the obelisks ashore. All showed intense excitement, dancing and shouting as the flotilla neared, while on the approaching ships Hatshepsut would note with keen appraisal and report in her biography that the men on board were also "rejoicing, marines and crew, sailing downstream in gladness of heart, all rejoicing, in jubilee . . . in peace. . . ."

(She was stressing that word, peace, more often as Thothmes, the warrior born, was nearing manhood.)

A queen does not shout her joy. A queen does not dance in public from the gladness of her heart. Hatshepsut remained silent, unmoving, magnificent, as queens face their world. Only the great eyes moved, seeking, through the curious maze of ships, over their decks crowded with men returning from Aswan, one face. . . .

It was a strange water pageant she viewed, a work fleet *en fête*, flying the blue and white pennants that were hers and Imperial Egypt's. The conglomerate fleet was patrolled by engineers in small boats shouting directions as the ships neared the landing. There was a secular escort of three galleys where priests were carrying out religious ceremonies on the decks. The main mass of water craft was clustered around the slow moving barge which was being borne along deep under the water-line with its colossal burden. The ponderous craft was towed by thirty-two boats lined up in rows of ten and rowed by eight hundred and sixty-four oarsmen. Each row was guided by its own pilot boat.

Hatshepsut's serene expression did not change, but her glances moved rapidly from one boat to another, widened briefly in awe at the size of the two gigantic shafts balanced end-to-end on the great barge, and moved forward to the deck. Eyes met, and did not move again.

Sennemut was standing in the bow of the obelisk barge. With him were her other trusted ones, Thuty, Amonophis, Nihisi, but none as valued as Sennemut. And he, returning in triumph to a city thundering with acclaim, knew his true welcome at journey's end was a smile flickering briefly in the great calm eyes of his queen.

She did not lose her reportorial sense in the excitement of the landing. She dictated her account; it is saved on stone. Over an illustration of the leading galley is its name, "Landing of the West," and a word description of the arrival of the obelisks, "Landing in peace at Victorious Thebes."

> With joy of heart, the whole land is in rejoicing . . . they give praise, they celebrate the King, Lord of the Two Lands . . . Star of the Two Lands [Hatshepsut].

(Her names and cartouches in this account have been cut away and replaced by the name of Thothmes II.)

Still referring to herself as the King, Hatshepsut continues,

> . . . himself took the lead . . . priests and officials joining in processional, offering the gifts they had brought to Amon. . . . They rejoiced in their hearts when they saw the monument she had established for her father [Amon].

The Amon priests rejoiced with her, careless of gender. "Oh king, beautiful of monuments . . . as she is, so they are for eternity."

Her court surrounded her, offering praise. Dignitaries, officials, military men, paid honor to her triumph. "Happy is thy heart; this is thy desire, it has come to pass."

What Sennemut had to say to her, and she to him, was left unregistered.

Hatshepsut summed up his success in her recorded history of the obelisks:

> My Majesty [Hatshepsut herself] exacted work thereon from the year fifteen [of her reign] the first of Mechir [sixth month] until the year sixteen, the last of Mesore [twelfth month] making seven months of exaction in the mountains.

Only seven months before, Sennemut had left Thebes with his labor fleet. He had completed an incredible task for Hatshepsut, and in time to put the crowning touch on her jubilee.

Thebes was rejoicing, but Sennemut's work had not ended. The solid stone shafts had to be brought from the barge to the Great Temple and raised there—a feat that wins the respect of modern engineers. Once more, groaning hordes of naked men lifted the stone monsters from barge to shore. Once more, masses of slaves dragged the burdened sleds and rollers up the sloping banks and inside the stone complex of Karnak.

They did not toil alone.

Hatshepsut had tried to ease Sennemut's final effort. She had summoned "her entire army and navy" to aid in the grueling task of pulling the obelisks up to the temple. Her soldiers and sailors, added to those who had been at Aswan, added their manpower joyously to Sennemut's task forces, and all were assisted by men of Thebes who had waited the arrival of the fleet with Hatshepsut. Court dignitaries, courtiers, priests of Amon, and other priests joined in the progress of the stone shafts to the Karnak Temple, and all, in Hatshepsut's words, "rejoicing and acclaiming."

Hatshepsut led the way.

A feast celebrated the arrival of the obelisks. There was a feast for every occasion. This one had its own proud name. It was her jubilee feast, and was known as the "Myriad of Years." We may be certain that Sennemut did not leave her side.

Hatshepsut's life held much triumph. This was one of her proudest days.

The Great Temple of Amon was in readiness for the god's obelisks. It was Hatshepsut's spiritual home, and the largest building in all Egypt—in fact, in the world. Its vast colonnaded hall was and remains the largest ever constructed. It was the sacred core of the religious center of Egypt, where the gold statue of Amon presided over the golden throne.

Windows were set high under a roof upheld by columns. European churches and cathedrals were to reproduce the great hall of the Karnak Temple.

On the walls of the temple, kings after kings had recorded the histories of their lives. It was the record repository of the Empire. Hatshepsut made her contribution to permanent history when she brought her Aswan obelisks to the temple.

Obelisks were traditionally placed outside a religious building. Hatshepsut, always "different," would have hers within the sacred walls. Behind the great hall was another, a forecourt with columns of cedar which her father had built between two pylons. Relays of slaves dragged the giant stone shafts into the hall. Relays of stone polishers set to work with abrasive tools grinding the hard red granite to a crystalline smoothness. Sculptors waited to inscribe on the shafts the words Hatshepsut wished to leave behind her for the million million years.

That my beauty be remembered!

It is said that sounds never perish, but move on forever like wavelets on a sea that has no shores. Does every word ever spoken continue to echo soundlessly in space? May we stand back for a moment, then, from the cold stone of the obelisks and listen to a conversation that could have taken place three and a half thousand years ago?

The setting is the council chamber in the palace at Thebes. The speakers are Hatshepsut and her architect Sennemut. The man is a lusty personage in the prime of life. He is relaxing in her presence, as others would not dare relax, after his exhausting seven months in the granite quarry at Karnak. The two are alone save for a scribe crouching at their feet with waiting pen and scroll.

Hatshepsut is in her mid-thirties, and the aura of supreme assurance that makes for beauty has deepened. This is an important conference. The pair are choosing the words that will be engraved on the obelisks. Her titles and achievements are to be listed as a matter of course, but a personal description is needed.

Does an architect dare speak first? touch with work-stained hand, perhaps, the jeweled sandal of a woman who is both goddess and king? Sennemut is worker and builder, a brilliant man, but no poet. He struggles for words that will describe his mistress' beauty, words that will last "longer than the world."

That beauty has been lauded in every flattering Egyptian word. Superlatives have been dinned in Hatshepsut's ears since babyhood. She accepts the most extravagant praise as simple logic.

And Sennemut, who has accomplished so much for her, who has built Deir el-Bahari and created her monuments, and is privileged to inscribe in the tomb that he is building for himself that he is Hatshepsut's "dearly loved," can find no exalted words for this idolized being. He waits for her to speak.

The wide-set eyes darken. "These words you must carve for me. I, Hatshepsut, more beautiful. . . ." The smooth forehead acclaimed by the sculptors is marred by failure. Modesty is not a Thothmesid characteristic. But so many words have been spoken and sung and shouted, in so many arrangements. She has described her mother, at Deir el-Bahari, as having been "more beautiful than any woman."

He alone is privileged to follow her thoughts, perhaps even in a teasing way. "More beautiful than the flight of ibis against the moon? Than gazelles running into the sunset? Than—"

She interrupts him, coldly, dangerously. "More beautiful than anything!"

These are the words Sennemut inscribed for her. They remain, testimony to Hatshepsut's faith in herself, not as the divinely-born regent, but as a woman safe in the assurance of love.

She had first envisioned her two obelisks flashing over the Karnak walls like twin mountain peaks of pure gold. She had once considered having them cast in gold. Discretion, perhaps advised by Sennemut and her treasurer Thuty, had shown the fallacy of such a dream to the richest woman in the world. Hatshepsut agreed to compromise by gilding both shafts, now engraved and ready for raising, with the electrum mixture of silver and gold. This, too, would have been an extravagance beyond the richest Pharaoh's dreams, and once more Hatshepsut yielded, but with reluctance, and prepared to gild only the tips of the shafts. These alone required a fortune in the precious metals reluctantly provided by her cautious treasurer Thuty.

The day of the gilding of the finials was a memorable day,

duly registered by the triumphant Hatshepsut. It is also described by others who were privileged to be present with Hatshepsut in the Hall at Karnak. The concentrated power of Egypt was there. The list of "among those present" comprises a "Who's Who" of ancient Egypt.

Sennemut's was an outstanding presence, and Puemre was officious in his role of inspector of monuments. He described the event in his tomb. But the star of the occasion was Thuty, who, as Overseer of Gold and Silver, had dipped into Hatshepsut's royal coffers to provide her with the electrum for the gilding.

In his tomb, which would be badly damaged by Hatshepsut's enemies in reprisal for his loyalty to her, Thuty described his pride in doling out the twelve bushels of precious metal "for Amon in the presence of the whole land."

Hatshepsut laid claim to have carried out some of the measuring herself. It leaves a pleasant impression of her wielding the treasure-heaped sieve like one of Sennemut's workmen. Her words show her delight:

> Hear ye! I gave for them of the finest electrum, which I had measured by the hecket like sacks [of grain]. My Majesty appointed the numbers more than the entire Two Lands [hath] seen. The ignorant like the wise know it.

Then, on the base of one of the obelisks, she apologized to Amon for her failure to plate all the surface of his monuments with gold.

> Concerning the two great obelisks which my Majesty has covered with electrum for my father Amon, that my name may live forever in this temple, throughout the centuries; they are hewn from a single stone which is hard granite, with no joints. . . . I did it in my fidelity to Amon, as a king to every god.
>
> It was my wish to have them cast in electrum. I have at least placed a surface upon them.

With the tips engraved and gilded, Sennemut faced the most difficult part of his Herculean assignment, which was the raising of the monuments to their full height in the roofless hall. There have been many theories as to the way he carried out this seemingly impossible elevation. Charles Nims offers the most logical explanation.

Research at Karnak has led the archaeologist to believe that the pillars were pulled into the hall bases first, which were brought up on ramps over receiving bases sunk in the floor of the hall and covered by hillocks of sand. Each tilted shaft's base was adjusted over the site of its floor base, then the sand was dug away while slaves dragged on ropes, pulling the monstrous shaft erect. There were breathless moments as the colossal shafts rose slowly upright and settled firmly into slots in the bases. One considers the stress on sisal rope and straining muscles and bursting joints as each pillar rose, almost one hundred feet tall, to tower over the stone walls of Karnak and flash gilded tips in the sun. In her dedication speech, Hatshepsut eulogized their glow "seen on both sides of the river. . . . Their height pierces to heaven. . . . Their rays flood the Two Lands when the sun rises between them. . . . Never was done the like since the beginning. . . ."

One of the obelisks has fallen—destroyed, it is believed, by Thothmes III. Many of its broken parts have been carted away to serve as the millstones that camels turn along the Nile. A broken fragment left in the ruins shows Hatshepsut dedicating her obelisks to Amon. "I did it under his command . . . he it was who led me. . . . I entered upon the affairs of his heart. . . ."

Hatshepsut's second obelisk remains at Karnak. It towers over the broken walls—still the highest monument in Egypt. It is one more of her memorials, and we stand dwarfed and mute with wonder, looking up its inscribed sides that continue to speak Hatshepsut's own words to a cloudless Egyptian sky. The making, transporting, and raising of her obelisks remains one of the most incredible achievements ever conceived and carried out by a woman.

The sides of the obelisks pay tribute to four kings—Thothmes I, II, and III, and "King" Hatshepsut. For it was on the tip of the fallen obelisk, now in Cairo, that she ordered her title of male pharaoh engraved, perhaps for the first time. In another place on a shaft she referred to herself, no longer as a Daughter of the Sun, but as the sun's male heir.

Let us cast a look back to the granite quarry at Aswan where Sennemut, only a few weeks before, had engraved a memorial for Hatshepsut identifying her as the Great Wife of the Great King. Sennemut did not name the king. Could he have been referring back to her husband, Thothmes II, who had been dead five years? She had ruled under the title of Great Queen for several years after his death.

Sennemut had been seven months away from Thebes. Was it during his absence that Hatshepsut had taken the giant step of implying a change in sex and status by naming herself the king?

There is another theory.

Present at all the obelisk celebrations, portrayed and named by royal title on Hatshepsut's obelisks and her temple walls at Deir el-Bahari, was a glowering teen-ager, growing now, but still barred from the throne. Thothmes III was nearing manhood.

He saw the obelisks rise in the roofless hall built by his grandfather. Ambition burned in the narrow Thothmesid skull. Wait! He too would build, burying all memory of this usurper aunt-stepmother, this ruthless woman who showed him small-sized on her monuments, and who treated him, in their daily life, like an obstreperous child.

Is it indicative of the lad's state of mind as he watched Hatshepsut's triumph on that day that later, when he came to power, he had this hall "exorcised of evil?"

It has been many times written, and believed by many, that Hatshepsut and Thothmes III were married. The theory is that in this way he achieved his title and right to the throne. If the marriage took place, it is not mentioned in either of their records. In his own inscriptions Thothmes was to write of Hatshepsut as his "sister." This was inaccurate, but it was also a common term used to denote an affection which he evidently did not feel. In another place he describes himself as the father of her daughters! This too may have been a form of family recognition. Nefrure and the younger Hatshepset were his cousins and his half sisters. Breasted has remarked that any attempt to explain the situation is to pass from fact to the purely imaginative. According to the ancient statistics Hatshepsut was Thothmes' aunt, stepmother, and a most determined woman.

In time she added to his status by making him her son-in-law and co-regent through giving him Nefrure in marriage. The frail Crown Princess would never wear as an adult the male gold beard Hatshepsut had strapped to the infantile chin when Nefrure posed for the statues with Sennemut.

Thothmes III won little from this promotion. He continued to be registered as a participant in all major events, but always as a background figure. Hatshepsut, replete with the triumph of the obelisks and the success of her jubilee, continued to claim all the titles, trappings, and prerogatives due to King Hatshepsut I of Egypt. An embittered young contender for the throne continued in his minor role as fledgling priest in the Great Temple, while in the palace he was regarded as that young upstart who had married Hatshepsut's heiress daughter. He was kept firmly in both places by Hatshepsut, who was supported by Sennemut, her "companion great in love."

The talons of the young "falcon in the nest" were being readied to strike.

> There is no doubt that the queen's remarkable career as king in opposition to Thothmes III was in some measure due to him [Sennemut] and in great measure to the coterie of legitimists, of which he was the most powerful member.
>
> —Breasted

For the next few years Hatshepsut asked no more of Sennemut that would take her companion away from Thebes. She had need of his support in the temple and the government. Thothmes III was a boy no longer, but a grown man. He chafed under the restrictions limiting a co-regent's powers.

There is a statue of Thothmes that shows him with his fists clenched at his sides and his head thrown back. It is the image of a man caught in the gesture of challenge. In size and temperament he so resembled a later conqueror that Breasted named him "the Napoleon of Egypt." His mummy in the Cairo Museum shows him to have been in life five feet two inches tall, of compact build, with the arched Thothmesid nose and projecting teeth. But the rounded face is unlike those of other men in his family. Its shape is like Hatshepsut's.

In every other way he is the typical Eighteenth Dynasty male. It is not pleasant to contemplate the extent of his frustration as

"King" Hatshepsut continued to rule on the throne he considered his by inheritance.

She recognized his claims, on stone. Her inscriptions show them worshiping the gods together. He is shown somewhere in all the pictures of important events.

Among the Pharaoh's most important duties was that of reverence. Kings danced before altars, fell supine before images, offered bowls of milk and wine and the cherished "cool water," food and incense and flowers. Flattened to earth, with her face to the floor, Hatshepsut lifted armfuls of fragrant flowers that were often the loved blue lotus. She offered more worldly gifts, pouring out a large share of her income to the gods, but most of it to the insatiable Amon. She burned the rare and costly myrrh in their temples.

Thothmes shared her reverence. He would also give lavishly to the gods when his turn came. A relief at Deir el-Bahari shows them kneeling, offering liquid refreshment to Amon. In appearance, they might be brother and sister. But he is placed a little to the rear, and Nefrure is shown kneeling even farther back in the place usually given to even a royal woman.

There may have been an uncertain moment in Thothmes' career when Nefrure died. She was still very young. She was buried close to the Deir el-Bahari temple, and Thothmes lost no time in marrying Hatshepsut's second and last daughter, Hatshepset. Hatshepset now was entitled the "Great Wife," but she would live to achieve distinction with Thothmes as Queen Hatshepsut II of Egypt.

Even in his limited position as Hatshepsut's co-regent, Thothmes had power which he used to its limits against her.

He was treading on her heels. Sennemut knew and she must have known how far his plans were reaching. Thothmes had served in the temple and would continue to serve there in high rank. He had great influence among the Amon priests. A growing number among them would have liked to see a real male king on the throne. He might have gone far as a high priest but his inclinations were not priestly. They were military.

He was a sportsman and warrior, a hunter of beasts and of men. He joined the army. It was a masterly move Hatshepsut could not protest. His kingly title placed him at once at the head of all her armed forces, under the title of "Commander of the Troops."

He won the admiration of his soldiers. One of his trophies was exhibited in the Temple of Amon. It was a copper target two inches thick with his arrow driven through. "It was shot without a phrase of boasting in the face of his entire army." The comment is his.

Hatshepsut had kept up the army she had inherited from her father as a show of strength. She had determined there would be no wars in her time. In modern parlance, she was a dove. She was well informed of enemies slavering beyond the boundaries of her rich and orderly Egypt. She would ignore them while they stayed outside.

But Thothmes was born to conquer. From his chariot he reviewed Hatshepsut's standing armies at Memphis and Thebes. From the Delta to Aswan there were garrisons manned by squadrons of foot soldiers and archers and charioteers assembled by Thothmes I. The lethal bow he had mastered, the horses and chariots he loved, the heavy bronze axes and spears, had been left behind by the Hyksos when his ancestors had driven them out of Egypt. The weapons, the chariots and horses, had been enlarged and improved upon under Hatshepsut, but only as threats to preserve the peace.

Thothmes did not want peace. He cast avid looks over the borders of Egypt where enemy lands waited to be plundered and added to the greatness of Egypt.

Hatshepsut agreed with him that invaders should be kept out of Egypt, but she did not sympathize with his need to pursue and conquer. Her armies were reserved against rebellion and invasion. She may have quoted to her son-in-law the words of a far-off king in their dynasty, Kamose, who had preceded their great warrior ancestor Amose. Kamose had protested rather peevishly to his nobles the demands being made by the invading Hyksos.

"Let me understand what this strength of mine is for. [One] prince is in Avaris, another is in Ethiopia, and [here] I sit associated with an Asiatic and a Negro! Each man has a slice of this Egypt, dividing up the land with me. . . . My wish is to save Egypt."

Her father had saved Egypt when he drove out the last of the Hyksos. Hatshepsut felt this had placed the obligation upon her to keep it insular, self-contained, and at peace.

This was directly opposed to everything Thothmes wanted. A growing clique of his admirers shared his hopes to enlarge Egypt through war. His soldiers were willing to follow where he led. The admiration and encouragement grew.

Writers of his day left words of praise for him on stone. "A young bull, ready with its horns, irresistible." And, "A circling comet which shoots out flames and gives forth its substance in fire."

Hatshepsut still had absolute power as Pharaoh over the army, navy, government, priesthood, and police. These were the links in her chain of power. The people of Egypt revered her as their protective goddess. Hatshepsut was no weakling. Pharaoh she called herself and Pharaoh she was, and one of Egypt's best.

Thothmes, driving his chariot through Thebes, had to pass under her banners flying from the tall fir poles before the Temple of Amon. They were a king's banners, but they did not fly for him.

On fire with ambition, he was off on campaigns unknown, leading divisions of his armies north and south to subdue disturbances and revolts inside Egypt. He returned from these sorties with wealth to add to the revenue he received as king. His more extensive plans were spiked by peace-loving Hatshepsut. His resentment grew, and in time he forgot that if it had not been for her willingness to let him marry her two daughters he could never have claimed the title of a king.

Hatshepsut went serenely on with her spectacular program for developing and beautifying Egypt. Sennemut, her architect, her love, her Minister of Public Works, in charge of all Egypt's construction, was building in her name as no king had ever built before. Thothmes and the partisans on both sides were building. Wealthy citizens joined in the wave of construction that swept Egypt.

Thebes and Western Thebes, Luxor and Karnak burgeoned with splendid new temples and other buildings, monuments, statuary, stelae, on a scale never attempted before.

Hatshepsut had launched a golden age for Egypt.

Thousands of architects, masons, bricklayers and brickmakers, carpenters and plasterers, were hard at work. The burst of activity brought Egypt to its highest prosperity level. Creativity rose like a bursting wave. Artists painted under lamplight in the temples and tombs. Art developed on a scale it would not reach again until the unparalleled advance at Amarna. Now the sculptors were active, providing the monuments and tombs with replicas of Hatshepsut and the other great ones of her day. On reliefs and stelae and as statuary she was portrayed hundreds of times as a sphinx, a *god*dess, a king, but never as mere woman. Sometimes she was shown in the skirted ceremonial robes of masculine royalty, but more often she posed wearing the kilt, with the ceremonial gold beard strapped to her chin and on her head a king's headcloth and one of the many male crowns. She installed at Deir el-Bahari the famous red granite series of herself as the Sphinx, and another row of herself as the bearded king.

She had herself carved in the shape of Osiris, the resurrected male of the Egyptian trinity, but with her face. In these she seems to be saying, "Like Osiris, I shall never die."

She was no longer shown as the boyish woman-king, but as the goddess-king.

She had herself portrayed as Sphinx and human in giant form. All the Eighteenth Dynasty regents regarded themselves as larger than life and many had themselves carved in stone as colossi. In this, as in other ways, she was imitated by Thothmes, who, possessed now of wealth, was also indulging in the Thothmesid passion for building and sculpture. His small stature developed heroic proportions in sandstone and granite in Hatshepsut's favorite Sphinx form.

He too was building. The adaptable Ineni built for Thothmes and so did her loved Sennemut, perhaps for political reasons. Sennemut, or Hapuseneb, prepared the grave for Thothmes near that of Hatshepsut's in the Valley of the Kings. Thothmes copied the ground plan of her Deir el-Bahari temple when he built his own memorial chapel at Medinet Habu.

He was not alone in this plagiarism. During the period of their co-regency ninety memorial chapels were built at Western Thebes, and more than half of them copied the architecture of Hatshepsut's temple.

Thothmes could not as yet match Hatshepsut's extensive building. But he could make promises. Given total power, he must have assured his followers, he would outdistance anything a woman had done.

Hatshepsut boasted on stone of all she had built for Amon, who in return had "established her great like the heavens."

With the comment that she had "made excellent her records," Hatshepsut listed her matchless temple at Deir el-Bahari and smaller temples elsewhere in Western, Eastern, and Southern Thebes. She had raised Amon temples at Medinet Habu, on a cliff at Pakht, and in Nubia. The small, exquisite temple at

Buhen in Nubia had been built near the fortress protecting her southern gold mines.

She added lavishly to the Great Temple at Karnak, building courts and halls and two new pylons (gates in pyramid form), the Sixth and Eighth. She added another sanctuary there to the god.

She had topped all these marvels by the feat of bringing the two obelisks from Aswan and setting them up in the Great Temple.

She told of the many feasts she gave honoring Amon.

Hatshepsut stressed the claim that she had been the first to restore temples and chapels left in ruins by the Hyksos. "The altars are opened . . . the sanctuaries are enlarged . . . every one [of the gods] is in possession of the dwelling which he has loved . . . every statue is overlaid on its body with electrum. . . ."

Her fierce pride showed in her summation:

"Hear ye, all persons! Ye people as many as ye are! I have done this according to the design of my heart . . . I have restored that which was in ruins, I have raised up that which was unfinished since the Asiatics [the Hyksos] . . . were in the midst of Avaris in the Northland, and the barbarians were in the midst of them. . . ."

And Thothmes III, treading on her heels, would in time reset her words into his famous Hymn of Victory.

I have restored that which was in ruins,
I have raised up that which was unfinished,
Since the Asiatics were in the midst of Avaris of the Northland
And the barbarians were in the midst of them.

Thothmes continued to advance in power and demands. Hatshepsut retained her alliance with the gods, held there by her two strongest advisers, Sennemut and Hapuseneb. She parried all Thothmes' efforts to push his way to the throne by pointing to an affluent and secure Egypt and beyond all else, to her divine birth. The beautifully inscribed conception scene on the Deir el-Bahari walls was one hurdle the young co-regent could not leap. His grandfather, father, and Thothmes himself had attained the divine status through marriage, but he would be stretching a point too well known if he claimed to be divinely born.

He gave a great deal of thought to this barrier. So did his advisory priests.

Hatshepsut continued to rule in total power.

There could have been no busier woman in Egypt. A Great Queen had duties, but a king had more. Hatshepsut, through her ministers, kept control of every activity in the kingdom.

Throne business took much of her time. Each day brought documents and deeds and petitions to be read to her by the scribes and be considered and stamped, if approved, with one of her cartouches.

Each day demanded audiences with her two Viziers, one of the North (Heliopolis, now Cairo), and one of the South (Thebes).

There were audiences to be given governmental heads and the Viziers who came from foreign lands to bring assurances of loyalty and costly gifts to the woman Pharaoh of Egypt.

There were consultations to be had with Hapuseneb and others of the trusted few and always time to be made for secret conferences with Sennemut.

A certain time each morning was set aside for her chief treasurer, the cautious appraiser, Thuty. It was Thuty's duty to report to her all tribute and taxes paid and to estimate the value of the treasure pouring into the palace from every corner of Egypt and its tributaries.

Once a wide-eyed child Hatshepsut had watched in this audience hall while treasure rose in heaps under the throne chair of her father the king. Now it was Thothmes III who watched from the sidelines as the mounds of tribute rose under the sandaled feet of His Majesty Hatshepsut I. Revenue flowed into Thebes in a stream wider than the Nile. From warehouses and factories and farms came every taxable product grown or manufactured in Egypt. Flax, cotton, wool, timber, charcoal, oil, honey, wine, hides, metals, grains, vegetables, fruit–every hen's egg must be duplicated for Hatshepsut. Lowing herds and cackling fowl came to the palace gates as once they had for her father.

The artistry of the land came to her–woven textiles, baskets, sandals, papyrus mats and scrolls, weapons, tools, jewelry, ivory –all brought as tax payments from every corner of the Two Egypts.

Gold and silver without end was poured into her coffers to be guarded zealously by soldiers pledged to die in defense of the treasure of His Majesty, their beloved queen.

From the mouths of the Nile in the Delta, over the deserts, came the tax payments in silver and gold (there was no money then but a system of exchange by weight was used), and foreign taxes arrived from all merchandise using the waterways in and out of Egypt.

The production of beautiful articles encouraged by Hatshepsut stimulated commerce. Egyptian-made goods crossed the deserts by caravan, moved down the Delta on slow barges, crossed the Mediterranean on larger seaworthy ships for trade in Crete and western Asia.

She had set the country into glorious motion. Donkey and camel trains followed the river paths to the Sudan to return with ostrich feathers for her ceremonial fans, ebony and ivory for her furniture, essences to make fragrant her body. Her caravans came and went from Thebes, to Nubia, to Sinai, to the Delta. In Nubia men mined for gold. In Sinai men mined for gold and cut the treasured blue rock in its turquoise mines.

Her explorers and traders ventured farther north and south and eastward in the direction of Asia.

And Thothmes, watching, saw a woman for whom the Nile rose and fell, and broad fields were sown and shorn, and herds grew fat and trees bore fruit and long trains of camels and donkeys bore burdens of treasure, and boats laden with tribute were rowed up and down the Nile by oarsmen chanting her name.

For her, coppersmiths melted ore for weapons and tools, goldsmiths wrought silver and gold into exquisite designs, jewelers fashioned ornaments and vases and boxes of the precious metals inlaid with rare stones.

Lapidaries polished bowls and vases of alabaster, potters spun jars and vases and urns on their wheels, glass blowers handled boiling glass to shape lovely dishes and vases and bottles and jars for Hatshepsut.

Women wove linen threads on hand looms into material as soft as her own anointed skin, to make her clothing, or hangings for her painted walls, and curtains for her windows, or, of harsher weave, the awnings that shielded her balconies from the sun.

Thousands toiled each day for her.

In her honor armies marched (but not to war), brandishing their spears and war clubs and leathern shields and chanting the glory of Hatshepsut, King of Egypt.

A glowering young man who was king in name only watched and waited, biding his time.

She was pleasant to Thothmes in many ways. She registered on her walls the social and religious affairs he attended with her. In these inscriptions she registered his name and titles and the illustrations show him as a lusty, regal young man. Apparently Hatshepsut would do anything for Thothmes except permit him to rule.

He was shown assisting her in her many religious duties. Much of a Pharaoh's time was given to the gods. Almost every day there was a religious ceremony to be observed. As "His Majesty" Hatshepsut was required to play the leading role in endless rites, ceremonies, feasts, and festivals. There were so many gods, each with its special needs for pomp and protocol, but not one could be overlooked.

Special deference went to Amon. The gold idol in the Great Temple was bathed, fed, and dressed in fresh clothing every day by the priests. Offerings rose at his golden feet. Incense favored his golden nose and the unceasing hymns and rattling of sistrums enchanted his golden ears. There was no more pampered, richer, or feared god in history. Even Hatshepsut feared Amon, and with reason.

When the god made one of his rare public appearances it was her duty to be beside him, sharing in the adulation given him, and giving hers to him. She took part in every great public Amon festival. On these duly inscribed and important occasions, Thothmes was shown with her.

She continued to boast on stone of all she was doing for Amon. Could this have been due to fear of the god, or of the followers of Thothmes? At the time of her jubilee she had built a splendid new sacred boat at Karnak for the god's water pilgrimages. She also built a magnificent new black granite and red quartz chapel in the temple to house the barge. There were fifty-four festivals each year when the barque was on view to the public.

Several times each year the god's image was taken from the shrine in the temple by chanting priests and placed aboard the sacred boat. (Only priests were permitted to carry the heavy gold image to and from the barge.) Priests drew the boat to the waterfront where with the god aboard it was launched on the Nile waters. These water journeys were connected with special festivals, the most important being the Feast of Opet.

For this the god, accompanied by the reigning monarch, made its journey up the river to Southern Opet (now Luxor). In the ancient temple there known as the "Sanctuary of the South," another of those remarkable changes took place that astonished no pious Egyptian; for the next two weeks Amon became the lettuce-eating god of sensuality, Min. During the next fifteen days, while all Thebes celebrated wildly, mystic rituals were carried out in the temple by Amon, Hatshepsut, and the Min priests, many of them in secret. Little is known of the ceremonies, which were based on ancient fertility rites, but according to the inscriptions there was a great deal of feasting and music, while religious dances were performed by young girl acrobatic dancers. The celebration ended with the elevation of a giant phallus carried in priestly procession while men prayed for continued virility and women for fruitful wombs.

Hatshepsut claimed that it was during the Opet feast in this temple during the year of her jubilee that she took the irrevocable step of crowning herself king. Her illustrations show Thothmes as being present, still in a subsidiary role.

An Amon festival of much significance to Hatshepsut was the annual "Feast of the Valley." This also entailed a brief water journey on the part of the god and the king. On the morning of a full moon the Amon idol was rowed across the river on its sacred barge. On the cliffs at Western Thebes Amon priests stood watching the slow progress of the barque across the Nile and the forming of the long procession of worshipers behind the litter-borne idol carried by the priests. Hatshepsut led the faithful over the harsh sands and up the wide ramps leading to her beautiful temple, glowing like a pearl in the light of morning. If the god grew heavy along the way and the priests had to rest, rites were held.

Pausing on the esplanade of the glorious temple she had built for Amon, Hatshepsut could look directly across the river and see the gold tips of the obelisks she had raised to Amon flashing over the walls of Karnak "like the sun itself rising on the horizon of heaven."

In his Deir el-Bahari shrine the god accepted tribute and prayers from Hatshepsut and its priests. That night the idol spent the night resting in the shrine his divine daughter Hatshepsut had built for him in the temple, while she and her fellow celebrants relaxed over groaning tables at the great annual "Feast of the Valley."

Amon and his daughter had still another yearly appointment with the river itself. This was "the Festival of the Nile." The reigning king opened it with offerings of fruit and flowers and milk and wine to Osiris. Then the Amon god in his sacred decorated barge was rowed slowly along the river's rim. Thebans swarmed along the shore, hailing the golden beauty of the god and praying that the Nile rise once again and re-enrich the arid valley of the Nile.

The Nile almost always did rise in answer to their prayers and to the rich offerings made on this day by the king. Its dark and angry waters might sweep away much that the people valued, including herds and plantings and human lives, still there was always rejoicing as the floods rushed again into the valley.

Herodotus would write long after this that Egypt was the gift of the Nile.

All that Hatshepsut was doing and giving to Amon was not enough to satisfy her (nor Amon, as she would learn in time). She sought a new way to express her love and gratitude to the god and to gratify her own Thothmesid passion to accomplish great deeds. She may have felt a need for greater achievements that would help bolster her position on the throne.

She might have been content with all she had done. Not even Thothmes could find fault with her dedication to the god and to Egypt. She had kept intact and increased the inheritance handed down by generations of conqueror kings. She had perfected in Egypt good government, trade expansion, domestic advancement, and despite Thothmes' efforts she was keeping the country at peace.

Egypt had reached its most glorious period in its entire history under her guidance.

Her only flaw as regent was that she was still a woman. She was the domestic lover of home and of peace. Thothmes was the warrior. His was the all-consuming military mind. He was determined to force her from the throne.

Whose side was little Queen Hatshepset taking? Was Isis still living, still plotting in behalf of her son? Which among Hatshepsut's clique was beginning to waver, wondering, If a man ruled . . . ?

They saw no advantage to be gained by such a change, and did nothing. Thothmes fumed alone. Hatshepsut retained her glamorous position on the throne.

She has been called "the world's first suffragette." Certainly she was staging history's first struggle for woman's rights. The mysterious "feud of the Thothmesid" was at its smoldering peak.

In the meantime she and Thothmes and others close to them were cheerfully, expensively, and reverently continuing the preparation of their "beautiful tombs."

CHAPTER 16

As one comes to have understanding of them [the ancient Thebans], of why they erected temples to their gods and their chapels and tombs for their dead, they will appear as a people of great achievement, of great hope, and as the creators of one of the great civilizations which underlie our own.

—Charles F. Nims

Dark and deep under the western cliffs lay the tombs, each glittering within with piled treasure for the dead. How much wealth was hidden in the Valley of the Kings and in the vicinity of Deir el-Bahari can never be estimated. The memorial chapels, set apart from the graves, were also treasure-filled.

Why, it has been asked, did the kings and queens keep on pouring untold wealth into hidden burial chambers, knowing that the grave-robbers would eventually get it all?

And the answer is, they did not know. They trusted their priests who were adept in concealing the mummies with their fortunes. The priests used every artifice calculated to keep the graves secret. Each royal body was buried in the hope that it would never be found. Aye was to bury Tutankhamon a hundred years after Hatshepsut, with such cleverness that the grave was not discovered until this present century. He had it dug under another's. It was the only grave to be found unlooted in the Valley of the Kings.

Hatshepsut and her friends built theirs in the hope that this time the robbers would not know.

Her friends, the leaders of the country and of her party, were sinking their costly tombs near her Deir el-Bahari temple. Sennemut and Sennemen and Amonophis and Puemre were among the first. Sennemut's was the most interesting, and the most magnificent. He sank the shaft on the plain level under the Deir el-Bahari temple as if even in death he would lie at the feet of his queen. He could not have taken over so important a site without her consent. The inner chamber holding the sarcophagus lay directly under the temple's inner shrine.

It was actually an underground mansion worthy of the architect who had designed and built the Deir el-Bahari temple. The artists he directed in its wall paintings and stelae were the same he had directed in the decorating of Hatshepsut's temple. The tomb, although vandalized, retains perfect examples of Eighteenth Dynastic art.

In one beautifully decorated room, Sennemut is shown offering homage to the cartouches of Hatshepsut that are painted on the wall. In another an astrological ceiling is covered with paintings of the constellations that are visible from middle Egypt.

The future occupant of each grave wrote his biography therein, and an argument to insure leniency from the gods of the underworld after death. All Egyptians made the plea in various forms. Thuty, Hatshepsut's loyal treasurer and friend, showed his devotion to her in his tomb biography, which was badly scarred later by vandals. Thuty's plea remains as typical:

"All these things happened in truth; no deceitful argument came from my mouth . . . I was vigilant, my heart was excellent for my lord [Hatshepsut]; that I might rest in the highland of the blessed who are in the necropolis; that my memory might abide on earth; that my soul might live with the lord of eternity. . . .

"May I go in and out like the glorious ones, who do that which their gods praise; may my name be goodly among the people who shall come after years; may they give me praise at the two seasons. . . ."

Each man who built pleaded for recognition after death.

Another of those who wished to lie near Hatshepsut and remained faithful to her in life was her architect Ineni, who had been the first to build for her. He had built for her father Thothmes I, her husband Thothmes II, and her grandfather, Amonhotep I. He had outlived three kings and lived to be very old.

There are men who are able to ride the tides of political change and retain the love and respect of everyone. Ineni was such a man. He was carrying out the construction of works for Thothmes III while continuing to serve as one of Hatshepsut's architects. His version of the Hatshepsut-Thothmes III co-regency, inscribed in his tomb at a time when both were sharing the throne, might have brought the usual reprisal on the old architect. But his words remain unscarred, which indicates the respect given him even by the third Thothmes. As for Hatshepsut, only with her permission could Ineni have set down the following words:

"Her majesty praised me, she loved me, she recognized my worth at the court, she presented me with things, she magnified me, she lifted my house with silver and gold, with all beautiful stuffs of the royal house."

"The revered dignitary, triumphant," as Ineni called himself, made the customary appraisal of his own spotless character.

"I will tell you, ye people; hear ye, do ye the good that I did, do ye likewise. I continued powerful in peace, I met no misfortune, my years were [passed] in gladness of heart, I showed no treachery, I did not inform against, I did no evil, I did no wrong. . . . My heart was not deceitful toward the great ones of the palace. I did that which the god of the city loved. I was devoid of blasphemy toward sacred things."

His good name, he added, would remain in the mouths of the living; his memory and excellence would last forever.

Ineni died during the joint regency of Hatshepsut and Thothmes III. He had earned the devotion of both regents and a goodly burial. Sennemut inscribed words of praise to Ineni, his teacher-architect, in his own beautiful tomb.

Not all were to remain faithful to Hatshepsut, who had given free rein to their genius and made them great. The defectors are apparently those whose tombs escaped major vandalism. Did Puemre, the architect Hatshepsut had made her inspector of monuments, eventually turn against her? Among the inscriptions in his tomb are scenes showing him as inspector at a historic raising in the Karnak temple of "the two great and excellent obelisks which the King of Upper and Lower Egypt" made for his father Amon . . . in Karnak, of silver and gold and every precious costly stone. . . ."

But the obelisks are not Hatshepsut's, although Puemre had also been present at their raising, and in the same important capacity. These obelisks are the pair raised by Thothmes, in imitation of hers, and the name of the lauded king is that of Thothmes III.

That the adaptable Puemre gained by a change in masters is shown by a relief in his tomb. He is holding the staff and baton of high office, and inspecting piles of royal tribute being listed for him by a scribe. The caption reads: "Tribute brought to his king by chiefs from the marshes of Asia, of Watet-Hor, the southern and northern oases," and a fragmented account of the weighing of "great heaps of myrrh . . . ivory, ebony, electrum, all sweet woods . . . living captives, which his majesty brought from his victories. . . . Menkheperre [Thothmes III]."

Puemre had shifted his allegiance. An architect had to live.

The joy-loving Egyptians who could afford the time and the treasure gave a great deal of thought to their deaths. Hatshepsut was deeply religious and believed the future life would be even more desirable than her glorious present. Had she not built Deir el-Bahari as the future refuge of her ka? All she planned was contributing to that future.

The dead kings buried in Western Thebes were known as "the Lords of the West." She intended to join them there eventually. Life was temporary, although desirable, and the genius of architects and artisans and sculptors and artists was devoted not to the palace, but to the preparation of her future home.

She could contemplate with satisfaction the vision of herself, living again as she was now, although even more perfect in body and beauty and happiness, and ruling eternally in an after-kingdom that was even lovelier than her present Egypt.

To reach that desirable state care must be taken to preserve the body that was "more beautiful than anything."

Hatshepsut prepared for herself while living three granite coffins and two graves in the Valley of the Kings.

One marvels as to the construction of the first grave, which was reached by a tunnel sunk hundreds of feet above the valley floor, south of the Deir el-Bahari temple, in the almost sheer stone façade of the cliff. It would have served her well if she had died as Crown Prince, or even as Great Queen. It was not fine enough for a ruler with supreme power. It was left empty with its stone sarcophagus therein, while Sennemut, or perhaps Hapuseneb, built her a second cliffside tomb worthy of a king. This was sunk on the opposite side of the mountain from Deir el-Bahari, close to the temple, but in the Valley of the Kings.

In imagination, Hatshepsut surveyed herself there in death, wrapped in fine linen, beautiful in the fragrance of myrrh, surrounded by the heaped treasure amassed in life. Her repeated prayer was that all Egyptians made, for "a venerable old age, a goodly burial."

The new tomb was built with every known security measure. Its entrance was hidden in the side of the cliff. Four hundred feet of stairs led down into the mountain, craftily turning to reach the burial rooms which lay about two hundred feet below the surface. Viewing this secret underground crypt by the light of torches, Hatshepsut must have expressed her satisfaction, for how could vandals ever find her there?

Thothmes was also building his own grave, not far from hers, using the same Thothmesid security pattern of deep passages leading to the secret burial room. He had built his own memorial temple, using her Deir el-Bahari floor plan, near Hatshepsut's. It lacked the exquisite grace of hers. It was evidently a stocky, unimaginative temple, built of mud and stone.

The inscriptions within reveal increasing activity on the part of Hatshepsut's nephew, son-in-law and stepson. Thothmes III was striking out in his own behalf and Hatshepsut could no longer hold him back. There is added word of his progress in the tomb of his Vizier, Rekhmire, at Western Thebes, which is considered the finest of all the Eighteenth Dynasty graves.

Rekhmire was to Thothmes what Sennemut was to Hatshepsut. His office of Vizier of Upper Egypt had been held before him by his grandfather and a paternal uncle. He was chief magistrate of Egypt in charge of taxes and tribute for Thothmes, and the remarkable wall paintings in the large chapel of his tomb detail the duties of a man trusted by his king. One painting shows the dark and slender people of Crete bringing tribute to Thothmes III. The caption reads: "It was the confidante of the sovereign, the mayor and Vizier Rekhmire, who received this tribute."

Rekhmire was only one of the growing political party determined to place Thothmes in total control of Egypt. Thothmes was developing the army. He was a warrior with an army who was determined to go to war. Rekhmire wrote in his tomb his appraisal of Thothmes.

"There was nothing he did not know . . . there was no affair which he did not complete."

Thothmes had his advisers in the temple and in the garrisons.

A propaganda campaign was launched against the pacifist Hatshepsut. He was being presented to Egypt as the noble conqueror who would make Egypt greater and richer than ever before. She was the peace-loving woman in his way.

All his efforts were nullified by the inscriptions at Deir el-Bahari. Hatshepsut was registered there as of divine birth. How dared an upstart king try to thrust a divinity from the throne?

There was only one solution. Thothmes had to establish himself firmly under the aegis of Amon, who had served Hatshepsut so long and well. He would be her rival with Amon as he was her rival on the throne. Let the god choose for Egypt!

It was a clever attack worked out, it is suspected, by his mother Isis in connivance with friendly priests in the Amon temple.

Hatshepsut's story of her divine birth was propaganda. Thothmes would use counterpropaganda to discredit her.

He now claimed to have been chosen as king by Amon while serving as an acolyte in the temple. If not divinely born, he was at least a divine appointee!

He affirmed this took place in the god's presence, in the same hall where Hatshepsut claimed the god had spoken to her and named her king. No one had disputed her then. No one would dare dispute Thothmes when he announced that he had been chosen as the true king, in words as fanciful as Hatshepsut's own account of her divine birth.

As Thothmes described the miracle, he was carrying out his duties as acolyte during a great festival in the Amon temple. As he approached the niche containing the golden idol and offered Amon "a great oblation of oxen, calves, and mountain goats," the god left his throne and paced up and down before the altar, peering into faces, seeking his. Then, in Thothmes' own words, "He caused me to stand in front of him, and lo, I was put in the place of the King! I saw the glorious form of the god . . . Re himself consecrated me. . . ."

This description Thothmes III had inscribed on stone as the clinching argument favoring his position over Hatshepsut's. But she had inscribed almost the same argument at Deir el-Bahari, long before his claim was made, and she was still the heiress born. She kept her title as the "female Re," the double cartouche and the fourfold names and the throne of the king.

His warning signals were set everywhere for Hatshepsut to see. She had frequent word of Thothmes. "He lets his beard grow. [He was going to war.]" She could not halt the rising tide of criticism, against her, in his favor. "He wears what you cannot—the codpiece of a soldier."

Her lips may have curled over the golden beard. "His followers swarm like bats in a cave. . . ."

She had asked help of Sennemut, and of Amon.

Until this time, no one had stood in her way. Her enemy was the man she had made her co-regent, her alter ego, her living ka. She could point to the two great obelisks, to the fortune she had given, the building, for Amon. It was not enough. Thothmes had been and was a priest of Amon. War would bring riches to Egypt; Thothmes too would build. He would re-write the history of Egypt in blood.

Her inscriptions registered no battles, no victories, only the magnificent buildings, Deir el-Bahari and the obelisks, the economic and commercial rise in Egypt, her love for her people, and a country enriched and at peace. Her record with the proof of her divine birth was inscribed on the walls of Deir el-Bahari. Why were these not enough?

She was fighting for her life.

Eight years had gone by since Sennemut had brought her obelisks to Karnak. Another tremendous achievement was needed to turn attention from Thothmes and keep her firmly on the throne. The inspiration she asked of Amon came to her. She confided it to Sennemut, setting for him one last labor which, if it succeeded, Hatshepsut believed would be the greatest achievement of her life.

She would duplicate the incredible achievement carried out by King Mentuhotep back in the Eleventh Dynasty. She would send an expedition to the fabulous country of Punt.

CHAPTER 17

I have made bright the truth . . . I eat of its brightness . . . My fame makes the great ones of the countries to bow down . . .

Punt is mine, and the fields of sycamore bearing fresh myrrh, the highways which were closed up, and the two ways. . . .

—Hatshepsut,
Ancient Records

She had known of Punt since her childhood. It was the land of fable, known as "God's Land, Hathor's Land, the Land of Incense." It was the country of the myrrh-terraces where grew the fragrant myrrh beloved by gods and men. The amber-colored resin exuded an aromatic oil used by the Egyptians in many ways, for embalming, anointing, medicines and perfumes. (It is still used in the manufacture of perfumes.) The priests anointed the golden limbs of the gods with myrrh and burned myrrh before the altars. Men and women were rubbed with its oil after bathing and cones of myrrh mixed with fats were worn atop the heads of diners to melt and scent their bodies as they feasted.

"His body had the fragrance of Punt," Hatshepsut had written of the god Amon.

Punt was mentioned in the love songs. It was the El Dorado

of the ancient world. Hatshepsut's thoughts were often on Punt, where the myrrh trees grew.

She wanted myrrh to anoint the golden limbs of Amon, and her own; to delight the sensitive golden nostrils of Amon's, and hers. And also, legend held, all the wealth in the world was centered in fabulous Punt.

Thothmes was clamoring to make wars that would add to the glory and wealth of Egypt. If she, a woman, could bring these to her country without violence, it would be a strong argument in favor of her stand for peace.

But where was Punt? It was the land everyone knew about and nobody knew. In the past various lands have been suggested —Somaliland, South Arabia, Zanzibar. It is now believed to have been on the Somali Coast of East Africa on the Red Sea.

But no one knew the location of Punt when she confided to her companion Sennemut her dream of bringing to life the ancient legends of kings who had sent expeditions to Punt, that had returned with fabulous treasure and fabulous tales.

Sennemut listened and approved. Hatshepsut consulted Amon. She has described her conference with the god.

We may picture her as a tiny supine figure on the floor of the Great Temple, in that vast stone cavern glittering with silver and gold and bronze and jewels, much of them out of the yearly tribute sent to Hatshepsut each year by the kings of Syria-Palestine, Canaan and even Crete. Face to earth under the altar, arms upstretched in supplication, Hatshepsut describes herself:

> The king himself, the King of Upper and Lower Egypt, the Majesty of the palace, Makere (Hatshepsut) . . . made petition at the stairs of the Lord of the Gods.

Amon listened. Amon answered! The Lord of Thebes spoke to her in words she recorded on the walls at Deir el-Bahari.

> Welcome! my sweet daughter, my favorite, the King of Upper and Lower Egypt, Makere, who makes my beautiful monuments. I have given thee all lands and all countries, wherein thy heart is glad. I have long intended them (the myrrh terraces) for thee, and the aeons shall behold them. . . .

Amon described to his daughter how little was known of Punt, and how the expedition she suggested would dispel that ignorance forever.

> No one trod the myrrh-terraces, which the people knew not (said Amon). It was heard from mouth to mouth by hearsay of the ancestors . . . the marvels brought thence under thy fathers, the Kings of Lower Egypt, were brought from one to another, and since the time of the ancestors of the Kings of Upper Egypt, who were of old. . . .

Then the god assured Hatshepsut that her emissaries would reach Punt.

> I will cause thy army to tread them (the myrrh-terraces) . . . I will lead the army on water and on land, to bring marvels from God's Land for this god, for the fashioner of her beauty . . .

Sennemut, appointed commander, prepared to carry out the most dramatic project of Hatshepsut's career. Nihisi and Thuty who had been with him when the obelisks were brought from Aswan, would serve as his co-commanders. His brother Sennemen had charge of organizing the expedition. Months of strenuous effort brought together at the Theban wharf a fleet of five ships, equipped with oars and sail, well provisioned and heavily manned with soldiers, sailors, engineers, and oarsmen.

Since this was to be a trading expedition Egyptian-made products were carried aboard together with articles intended as gifts from Hatshepsut to the King of Punt. Nihisi, who had charge of the Amon storehouses, would supervise the trading, while Thuty the treasurer would appraise the value of any precious objects the Puntites might offer in exchange.

And Sennemut? Hatshepsut's right hand was leaving her. In private farewell she may have wished him godspeed with the term of blessing then in use, "May the soles of your feet be firm!" She could not have spoken so at the wharf for every soul in Thebes was out to see the departure of the fleet. Amon in person was drawn down to the shore in his sacred barge by the priests who had chosen this day of the sailing as an auspicious one fortunate to Amon. Hatshepsut stood close to the god wearing her ceremonial dress (male). She was surrounded by her nobles and priests. Thothmes was present to offer myrrh to the sacred boat. Offerings were made to Hathor that she might send winds to speed the ships to Punt.

Hathor heard! As sails and anchors lifted a strong wind swept down the Nile and swelled the sails. The heavily burdened ships moved slowly northward to the Delta. Hatshepsut watched their going, glimpsing to the last between the palm trunks the stalwart figure of Sennemut in the prow of the foremost ship.

The progress of the fleet can be followed on the relief scenes at Deir el-Bahari. The ships in full sail are shown moving first over waters that are plainly those of the Nile as fish shown swimming below the ships exist in the river today. The ships entered the Delta by the branch of the Nile farthest east, threading it and a canal that at that time linked the Delta to the Gulf of Suez (a pioneer canal cut at tremendous cost by the Egyptians). They reached the Red Sea as is shown by the paintings of different varieties of fish, still found there.

Here Nihisi evidently turned back to Thebes to report to Hatshepsut that at this point, all was well.

No word came after that. Hatshepsut waited, and the months and years went by, and her costly ships and the three men she most depended upon for her very life did not return.

Hatshepsut was never idle. It was while she was waiting the return of the fleet from Punt that she sent labor armies to reopen the gold mines on the Sinai peninsula that had been closed since the time of the Hyksos. A rock inscription at Wadi Maghara marks the reopening of the mines. Thothmes III is shown standing with her but it is Hatshepsut who is entitled "Makere, the Son of Re, beloved of Amon, Hatshepsut."

Thothmes had all of the terrifying Thothmesid energy and no outlet for it. He was possessed of an iron will and a brilliant mind and his disposition is described as being unhappy and restless. And no wonder, for his conqueror's soul was subject to the whims of a woman. He was a king. He wore a crown. His four titles were included by Hatshepsut in her inscriptions. His helplessness must have maddened a man who was described as "a fierce young bull with lowered horns."

He unleashed some of his energies in sports. He was a master archer and huntsman and a hunter of savage game. A scarab inscription describes him as "the harpooner of the hippopotamus, powerful of arm when he takes the spear." Once during a hunt in Asia he was charged by a mad elephant. One of his generals rushed between Thothmes and the beast and cut off its trunk. This is the only time on record when Thothmes needed another's help.

He led his army driving his own chariot. It was his army but he was not permitted to take it outside the borders. He charged up and down the Nile with it, pursuing malefactors, uncovering corruption and tax evasion and plots against the government. He was a man without softness and he alleviated frustration by meting out violent justice.

His palace in Thebes was magnificently furnished, but Hatshepsut's was grander, and it was in hers that the powerful gathered to exchange the gossip of the day.

There was a new familial link between Thothmes and Hatshepsut. He had a son, the first-born fully royal future Amonhotep II, born to him by his queen, Hatshepset, the second daughter of Hatshepsut. The intensified relationship did not ease the situation between them.

It is difficult to picture Hatshepsut as a grandmother. The portraits continued to show her glamorous in her thigh-high kilts, still supreme in control over a man whose will to rule was as strong as her own, but far more ruthless.

That ruthlessness reactivated years later in his son Amonhotep II who brought his battle barge back to Thebes after a victory with seven princes, captured in battle, hanging head down from the prow. All the Thothmesid rulers were violent, but in Hatshepsut the violence had become energy devoted to the development of her country's beauty, progress, and lasting peace.

The prowess of Thothmes III was winning the admiration of the Egyptians but she continued to hold their love.

Dr. Bakry has written that the rivalry between them was profound and well authenticated but that she remained feminine and nonaggressive.

Her writings hold no hint of injustice or cruelty and the affection given by those close to her was apparently constant and well-deserved.

Antagonisms faded in a burst of excitement. Word reached Hatshepsut from the Delta. Sennemut had brought the fleet back to Egypt!

Once more the volatile city of Thebes prepared for celebration. The Punt expeditionary forces were heading upriver. Hatshepsut's fleet was on its way home.

It had been gone two years!

The loveliest and most informative of the Deir el-Bahari reliefs describe the expedition to Punt. The paintings were made by someone who went to Punt or was capable of describing the journey and the country to the artist. This could only have been Sennemut.

The series covers the southern wall of the colonnade and are the least damaged by Hatshepsut's enemies. The words and choice of illustrations are her own.

We can follow along the wall the progress of her five ships after leaving the Gulf of Suez. They pushed on, down the eastern shoreline of the Red Sea, under the incandescent red cliffs that give the inland water its name. They reached the Somali coast and the primitive settlement that was the home of the Puntite kings.

The village is shown in detail. The domed grass huts are set on stilts over what is obviously marshland. The trees are recognizable. They are ebony and sycamore and palm and the myrrh trees that inspired the long and difficult journey. Animals ranging under the trees are long- and short-horned cattle and a variety of non-domestic beasts.

The Puntites are shown as resembling the Egyptians and, in fact, they were a related ethnic group. They were long-haired, small-boned, and slender, except for the queen and her daughter. The queen, Ati by name, is shown as being so monstrously fat that for a long time archaeologists believed her to have been the victim of some disease. A more recent theory suggests that since obesity is regarded as beautiful by many primitive peoples, Ati in her own domain may have been regarded as a beauty without peer.

A small inadequate-appearing donkey is captioned, "The ass that carries the queen."

Parihu, the prince of Punt, is a thin man with a hooked nose and a beard, holding a boomerang in his hand. A dagger is in his belt. His right leg is encircled to the thigh with what are apparently gold rings.

Both men and women wear kilts and are naked from the waist up.

Behind the royal pair Puntite slaves are bringing gifts to the strangers.

At first the Puntites were afraid of the Egyptian soldiers, who carried axes and spears. When they were reassured that no harm was intended they expressed amazement. "How have you reached this country unknown to men? Have you descended from the pathways of the sky?"

Sennemut is a dominant figure in the scene. He stands beside a table under the trees where goods brought from the ship are on display. The inscription reads, "All good things are brought by order of Her Majesty to Hathor, Lady of Punt."

The articles make a poor showing in contrast to the treasure Sennemut intends to take from Punt. On the table lies an axe, a sheathed dagger, tools, leg bangles, necklaces, rings and strings of beads. The beads were probably similar to the thousands of blue faience scarab strings dug up by the thousands at Deir el-Bahari. The rings were probably glass, which was new in the Eighteenth Dynasty and often used for making jewelry. Gold jewelry would not have been taken to a Punt that was reputedly rich in gold.

Whatever Sennemut thought of the display nothing interfered with the briskness of his actions. A tent was raised at once, and his next move was to erect on the shore a statue of Hatshepsut with Amon. It may still be there, hidden under sand on the eastern coast of the Red Sea and if found will put an end to the question, Where was Punt?

Seven Puntite chiefs joined the Egyptian in paying homage to Hatshepsut's statue. Parihu was among them. Then the seven were invited to a feast in the tent where they were given beer, wine, fruits and vegetables "all good things of Egypt, which the queen has commanded."

Queen Hatshepsut's royal gifts to the King of Punt were foods brought from Egypt, a few weapons and tools, a showing of beads.

In return her soldiers and sailors and slaves were filling her ships with bounty being pressed on them by the Puntites. The Deir el-Bahari relief shows the burdened men marching up the gangplanks of two of the ships, over the caption:

> The loading of the ships very heavily with marvels of the country of Punt; all goodly fragrant woods of God's Land, heaps of myrrh-resin, with fresh myrrh trees, with ebony and pure ivory, with green gold of Emu, with cinnamon wood, khesyt wood, with two kinds of incense, eye-cosmetic, with apes, monkeys, dogs, and the skins of the southern panther, with natives and their children. Never was brought the like of this for any king. . . .

The lumps of resin gum were carried in sacks and living trees were dug up and set in earth-filled baskets. Five ships sank perceptively lower as the Egyptians "took myrrh as they wished, they loaded the vessels to their hearts content, with fresh myrrh trees, every good gift of this country. . . ."

The good gifts are listed. They include thirty-one myrrh trees, a live panther, panther skins, leopard skins (used by the Amon priests for ceremonial robes), gold in nuggets and dust and rings, baskets "of the Negro land," and more than three thousand small cattle. Also aboard the ships went seven men of Punt—Hatshepsut refers to them as chiefs—with their wives and children. Whether they were going to Egypt with or without their consent, and what became of them later, history does not say.

Among the Punt gifts for Hatshepsut was a cheetah, or hunting leopard, which could only have come from India. There are indications that Indian trade seeped into Egypt in Hatshepsut's time. The barnyard hen that appeared in Egypt during her dynasty is supposed to have come from India. Thothmes III kept hens that provided him with two freshly laid eggs a day. The cobra and lotus motifs, so popular in Egypt, are believed to have originated in India.

The Egyptian ships were stuffed at last with every ounce of bounty they could hold and anchors and sails lifted again for the long journey home. We can imagine messengers watching along the Nile, ready to mount their small swift horses and carry word to Hatshepsut in her palace in Thebes. "The ships have passed Heliopolis; the ships are on their way."

Two years is a long time for men to be gone from home.

Once more Hatshepsut is shown standing on the Theban wharf surrounded by her court and the Amon priests and all Thebes that had been set free on holiday to watch the arrival of the fleet. Three of the ships are shown moving along the river under full sail, "Sailing, striving in peace, journeying to Thebes with joy of heart, by the army of the Lord of the Two Lands (Hatshepsut), with the chiefs of the country behind them. They have brought that, the like of which was not brought for other kings, being marvels of Punt . . ."

Sennemut and Nihisi are then shown with Hatshepsut. They are reporting to her on their triumphant return from Punt. It is an odd situation, for instead of her praising them for the success of the expedition, they are congratulating her!

The presentation of the Punt tribute to the queen evidently takes place in the audience room of the palace. Sennemut and Sennemen are seated at her feet. The Puntite chieftains and other dignitaries from Red Sea countries are kneeling before her cartouches. Behind them rows of Puntites and Egyptians are carrying the myrrh trees and other Puntite treasure to Hatshepsut "who hath set all the lands beneath her feet."

Over her mounds of treasure Hatshepsut announces, "Punt has been transferred to Thebes." She shares with Amon, listing every article presented to the waiting priests, but retaining for a special purpose "the thirty-one fresh myrrh trees, brought as marvels of Punt for the majesty of this god Amon."

The southern chiefs who have brought the tribute pray for peace. Peace is a word often mentioned by Hatshepsut. It was one of her most fervid hopes. In this instance it may have been stressed to impress Thothmes III, glowering among his coterie of war-hungry friends.

But he remains helpless, for all the people of Thebes are rejoicing "because of the greatness of the marvels. . . . Never did the like happen under any gods who were before, since the beginning."

Hatshepsut lost no time in carrying out Amon's order to build for him "a Punt in Egypt." The thirty-one living myrrh trees were hurried across the river to Deir el-Bahari. They were planted against the walls in the temple enclosure in stone pots that had drainage holes in their bases. Now the god could walk with delight in his "garden of Punt" and Hatshepsut too could walk there with Sennemut and other courtiers, drinking in the fragrance of the perfume-dripping resin. Sycamore trees were also planted and acacia and persea (the laurel).

There are impressive scenes that show the weighing of the myrrh and the silver and gold. Thuty has charge of the scales and accounts. The priests are waiting for Amon's share. Hatshepsut's role is enthusiastic. She is helping with the weighing. Equipped with a scoop made of electrum she is shown bending over the heaps of fresh resin. "Her majesty herself is acting with her two hands. . . ."

Her hands also assist Thuty in the weighing of the mixed silver and gold. Four aides are scooping the dust and nuggets from four treasure-filled chests.

The aromatic oil of myrrh has saturated Hatshepsut's hands and arms and the gold dust clings to her. Fragrance envelopes her. There is a description as she is scooping up the precious elements.

> She exhaled the odors of the divine dew, her fragrance reached as far as Punt, it mingled with the odors of Punt, her skin was like kneaded gold, and her face shone like stars in a festal hall. . . .

(The last reference is probably to the type of painted ceiling popular then in Egypt where gilded stars looked down from a field of blue.)

Thuty is shown keeping the record of the queen's share of metals and myrrh. Thoth, god of scribes, is pictured as present and listing the share intended for Amon. Thuty is speaking.

> Behold, all the marvels and all the tribute of all countries, the best of the marvels of Punt, were offered to Amon, Lord of Karnak, for the sake of the life, prosperity and happiness of the King, Makere (Hatshepsut) . . .

It was honest Thuty who had dipped into Hatshepsut's coffers to provide her with the precious electrum that tipped her obelisks. Hatshepsut comments that while the metal is being weighed "he is recording in writing, reckoning the numbers, summing up in millions, hundreds of thousands, tens of thousands, thousands, and hundreds . . . for Amon . . ."

In his tomb Thuty corroborates Hatshepsut's account of the weighing. His version can still be read on walls brutally scarred by her enemies. He describes the trust Hatshepsut has placed in him, while the gold is being measured.

> Now, I was one who counted them, because I was so excellent in my heart . . . my integrity of heart for him (Hatshepsut). He recognized me, as one doing that which is spoken, concealing my speech concerning the affairs of his palace. He appointed me to be the leader of the palace . . . the double silver-house; every splendid costly stone in the temple of Amon in Karnak, filled with his tribute to their roof. The like has not happened since the time of the ancestors.

Now Hatshepsut could formally announce to Amon that the Punt expedition had succeeded. She is shown in the Great Temple, standing, staff in hand, before the enthroned image of Amon.

Behind her the god's sacred barge is upheld by priests. Thothmes is offering myrrh to the boat. This is a poor role the mighty warrior is playing.

Hatshepsut's report to Amon has been defaced but it can be deciphered.

> I will cause you to know that which is commanded me, I have harkened to my father (Amon) . . . commanding me to establish for him a Punt in his name in Egypt . . . to plant the trees of God's-land beside his temple, in his garden . . .
>
> I was not neglectful of that which he needed . . . He hath desired me as his favorite, I know all that he loveth . . . I have made for him a Punt in his garden, just as he commanded me . . .

She explained to the god the way the myrrh-terraces had been transferred to Deir el-Bahari.

> Trees were taken up in God's-land, and set in the ground (in Egypt) for the king of the gods. They were brought bearing myrrh within, for expressing ointment for the divine limbs, which I owed to the Lord of Gods.

She told of all else the expedition had brought from Punt for Amon, and then she sternly charged posterity to note what she had given and ordered it to continue in the pattern of her generosity to Amon.

> Ye shall fulfill according to that which I have exacted. Your lifetime is the life in my mouth . . . I have given a command of my majesty that the offerings of him who begat me should be made splendid.

Amon, in amiable mood, accepted her tribute with a brief speech made through the media of the hidden oracle. The god accepted credit for the success of the Punt expedition and thanked his "daughter Hatshepsut, King of Egypt," for her kindness to him. He reminded her, "I have given thee all of Punt!"

The success of the expedition was celebrated with the customary feast.

If we linger over the scenes in the Deir el-Bahari temple it is because Hatshepsut herself lingered over their making. She thought of the Punt expedition as the crowning achievement of her life. Her pride still glows through the colorful records at Deir el-Bahari.

She had much else to stimulate pride. For seventeen years she had ruled a prosperous Egypt. She had rebalanced its economy, expanded its trade, stabilized its government, developed architecture and art. She had built the Deir el-Bahari temple and raised the two obelisks at Karnak. Now the Punt expedition showed her to be a hard-headed business woman as well as the most charming woman in her world.

Above all, she had kept peace in Egypt.

Once only does Thothmes III appear in the Punt murals, in the scene where he is shown offering myrrh to the barque of Amon.

She was the pacifist, he the militarist. She wanted to preserve her safe and orderly kingdom. Thothmes wanted war and its winnings for himself and for Egypt. For seventeen years since the death of his father he had struggled against this hated female relative who had refused to yield the throne. His attempts to oust her had been thwarted by that stalwart defender of her power circle, Sennemut, whose grip on the government had been stronger than any forces Thothmes could rally.

In this year, the seventeeth of her reign, his name and her's were linked together on a stele at Serabut. Then for the next five years a shadow lay over Hatshepsut's Egypt that would never lift for her. During that interim strange things happened in Thebes and the history of the country changed.

Which way, now, would list the loyalty of the powerful Amon priests?

CHAPTER 18

> My command stands firm like the mountains, and the sun's disk shines and spreads rays over the titulary of my august person, and my falcons rise high above the kindly banners to all eternity.
>
> —Hatshepsut
> *Ancient Records*

For the next several years no records exist to let us know what was happening between Thothmes and Hatshepsut. In the twentieth year of their joint regency their names were linked on stone for the last time. After that, there was silence.

That silence was to envelop Hatshepsut for more than three thousand years.

She had shared the throne with three kings, Thothmes I, II, and III. She had ruled alone as a king. Still history lost trace of her. Her name is not to be found in the official lists at Karnak and Abydos. Thothmes III saw to that. She is referred to briefly in the state archives as his co-regent. Thothmes recorded himself as having assumed the monarchy directly upon his father's death in 1490 B.C. The official records and his own remarkable Annals at Karnak state that he was given the crown at that time and that his regency started then.

Hatshepsut had made the same claim in reverse. She would admit to the co-regency but claimed to have been the king.

Her claims would be lost until her biography on the Deir el-Bahari walls was deciphered. They offer a running commentary on her life from her birth until the seventeenth year of her reign. She was probably in her forties when the last portrait was made. It shows her as still lovely and lithe.

Unfortunately for those who would like to know exact dates the Egyptian monarchs only recorded the years of their regency until her reign was over. Dates were set accurately in Egypt after Thothmes III became the sole occupant of the throne.

Her biography is therefore confused as to dates, but it ends on the triumphant note of her happiest achievement, the expedition to Punt.

We lift our eyes from the exquisite recordings on the Deir el-Bahari wall and are confronted with darkness. From the seventeenth year of her reign until the twenty-second no figures move in that shadow; no chisel or brush leave their marks on stone. Only by studying subsequent events can we determine what was taking place during those years as the Thothmesid feud entered into its final intense struggle between a man and a woman. Thothmes fought to rule; Hatshepsut to survive.

Somehow, during those years, and certainly without her consent, Thothmes succeeded in building Hatshepsut's defensive army into a tremendous instrument of war.

Conscription was mandatory in Egypt. He enlarged upon it, and urged enlistment upon Egyptian youth by making the military life a promising career. Thothmes promised lavish rewards. Young Egyptians rushed to join up, fired by the hope of war and of booty. (We can have no idea how much he promised to Amon.) Officers and soldiers were promised large shares in the loot of victory in the event of war and were awarded "Gold of Praise" for acts of courage. Officers who had seen service were placed in lucrative positions in the Great Temple.

Thothmes started the custom of appointing royal princes as army commanders. His son Amonhotep, the Crown Prince, was given the majestic title of "Commander in Chief of the Army." Thothmes kept sole power and the title given with his crown, that of "Sole Commander of the Troops."

His troops were legion. He enlarged the ranks to an army of 700,000 men. Axemen, spearsmen and archers were being trained to the quick at Thebes and Memphis. He developed an immense cavalry which consisted of a chariot corps with the lead chariot driven by the First Charioteer.

He led his forces driving his own chariot.

He enlarged the ranger troops that patrolled the desert and guarded the cemeteries and the frontiers. Every city and hamlet in Egypt had its commandant and military force, all answerable to Thothmes III.

He created his own elite corps. They were known as "the Braves of the King" and were the most admired and dreaded body of men in Egypt.

All this Thothmes developed during the lost five years while he was growing in arrogance and power. By the end of that time, in the year Thothmes lists as the twenty-second of his co-regency with Hatshepsut, he and his war-mongering cohorts had won control in the Great Temple and forced their way into the government.

Amon was a fickle god with a sound political sense. He had switched favorites. Hatshepsut had given without stint to her father-god, but Thothmes held out richer promise. Eventually all the Amon priests had come to see the advantage of having one of their brotherhood in the position of all-out power.

Thothmes could never have taken the throne without the protection of Amon. It is believed that his mother Isis connived with the priests to support his claim and that his "divine appointment" in the Temple was staged by them.

Amon had picked a winner.

The Egyptians were bored by being prosperous and at peace. They wanted the excitement of war and the booty promised by Thothmes if it came. Thothmes was the new hero of Egypt, and he would fully justify the trust placed in him by the Lord of Thebes. He was ruthless both as conqueror and king, and he overthrew Hatshepsut, his sister and his love, with the help of the Amon priests.

The tombs at Western Thebes hold evidence that was not being written during that period of time when Hatshepsut's power circle was being broken and death and destruction put an end to her brilliant world. The woman who had been king was stripped of influence and pride and the strong men who had supported her were either dead or had fled the country.

We may judge those who remained faithful to her by the condition of their tombs. Those of the men closest to Hatshepsut were viciously vandalized. One by one her friends were punished for their loyalty, either before, or after, their deaths.

The tombs of Sennemut, Sennemen, Amonophis, Nihisi, Thuty, and Hapuseneb were found with scarred walls where their names and hers and all praise of her had been erased.

Sennemut's tomb suffered most. It is believed that he was the first of the group to die. He had sustained Hatshepsut in the position of supreme power for seventeen years. She feared no living man, while he lived.

Thothmes obviously hated Sennemut. The queen's favorite had blocked his every thrust toward greater power. Sennemut's death followed soon after the success of the Punt expedition and Hatshepsut's listing of her greatest achievements, all of them due to him. Certain authorities state flatly that he was murdered.

That may be true. Thothmes was soon to reveal himself as a violent and ruthless king who would let no man stand in his way.

Sennemut was never to occupy the tomb he had constructed and lavishly furnished at Deir el-Bahari, directly under the temple he had built for Hatshepsut. Its gaping entrance opens on one more of the mysteries surrounding Hatshepsut and her friends. For that magnificent underground mansion was never used by anyone. When found, in this century, its furnishings had been stolen and its beautifully decorated walls were defaced. The handsome sarcophagus stood empty. It had never been used.

Even more strange—the entrance to the grave had been filled in.

The mutilated hieroglyphs in that tomb still attest to the continual prayers sent up in life "for the life, prosperity and health of Hatshepsut, by her Steward Sennemut."

In her temple, directly over his grave, his names and portraits have been hacked out of the Punt reliefs, along with those of his fellow expeditionaries, Nihisi and Thuty. By this means three who were faithful to Hatshepsut were erased from eternal life.

Sennemut's drawings of Hatshepsut and of himself were also chiseled out by the partisans of Thothmes III.

It has been suggested that Hatshepsut quarreled with Sennemut and that it was she who sealed his tomb against him. Why then did she not erase his portraits from their secret places in the Deir el-Bahari temple? They remain in her inner shrine, the holy of holies, with the colors pure and clear; the pose arrogant.

His name was chiseled out on the two magnificent statues Hatshepsut had ordered made of Sennemut holding her little daughter Nefrure. Otherwise the pair are undamaged. They were works of great art and the name of Amon is prominent on the box-shaped robe that conceals the steward and the child. When Hatshepsut ordered those statues made by one of the finest of Egypt's sculptors (name unknown) she loved her chief steward. The robe testifies for Sennemut after thirty-five hundred years. "I was one who entered into love . . . the greatest of the great in the whole land."

Sennemen's tomb was entered and vandalized and Hapuseneb

was also punished harshly for his loyalty. He was her strongest supporter after Sennemut. As her Prime Minister and High Priest in the Great Temple he had succeeded for two decades in keeping the priests at bay. It has been suggested that he sided at last with Isis and her priestly plotters in behalf of the young male king. The damage done to his tomb at Deir el-Bahari should disqualify that charge.

On its walls the great architect-administrator recorded his construction works for Hatshepsut. It is an impressive list and viciously defaced.

The tomb of her treasurer Thuty was entered and his records of his services to Hatshepsut were chiseled away. Inscriptions still readable attest to his achievements, his exceptional honesty, and his personal loyalty to her.

The chisels of the destroyers did not go deep enough. Theban hands may have held back before the magic implied by her still august name and those of the men who had held her safe in their circle of power. Faint and scarred, replaced in places by the names of still later kings, the records of Hatshepsut can still be read.

The Egyptians believed that a person's name held their essence. To erase it was a form of murder. In ordering the removal of the names of Hatshepsut and her supporters from their tombs at Deir el-Bahari Thothmes was making himself responsible for their second deaths as he may have been for their first. For at the end of the twenty-second year of his co-regency with her Thothmes placed himself on records as the sole ruler of Egypt.

By this we know that Hatshepsut was dead.

The year was 1468 B.C.

Now Thothmes could show himself worthy of the trust placed in him by Amon. He placed himself at the head of the dead Hatshepsut's armies and started out on the career that would make him the greatest conqueror and the strongest king that Egypt would ever know.

Hatshepsut had left the indestructible record of her life on the Deir el-Bahari walls. Thothmes tried to lay claim to it, but he also wrote his own on the inner walls of the Great Temple at Karnak. Hers stress a lifelong involvement with the peaceful, the exotic and beautiful. His are all of war.

Peace in Egypt ended with Hatshepsut. For the next thirty-four years Thothmes kept the country in a constant state of war. Two generations of young male Egyptians enriched their families with booty won in his battles, and other young men died. Living and dead added to the glory of Thothmes III.

Within three months of Hatshepsut's death, as marked by his move into full monarchy, Thothmes was leading his tremendous army over the Egyptian border and into Palestine-Syria. There followed the historic battle of Megiddo in Palestine.

The town and fortress of Megiddo overlooked the waterway entrance from Palestine into Syria. The mighty armies massed there were under the three kings of Palestine, Syria, and Kadesh. The King of Kadesh alone had brought to Megiddo three hundred and thirty Asian princes, each with his own army.

Thothmes defeated them all. It was months before the fortress fell. Magiddo was his greatest victory.

He led his army on to capture Kadesh, the city on the Orontes river that was the key to North Syria, and then on into the Kingdom of Mitanni.

Seventeen times within the next thirty-four years Thothmes mounted his chariot and led his troops into Asia to defeat Asian armies. Campaign was followed by campaign. He took his soldiers twice across the Euphrates. He marched them south to subdue Nubia. Egyptian authority stretched north and east.

Thothmes had founded a new empire. Wherever he marched he built garrisons, raised monuments, set up puppet rulers and returned to Thebes after every foray with vast treasure and the sons of defeated kings to be held as hostages in his palace where they were reared on the same social level as his own sons.

He developed a formidable battle fleet that prowled the Aegean shorelines and the west Asian coasts, invading in places and leaving the interior a wasteland. He captured three hundred and sixty-seven cities. He was named the greatest of the conquerors, the ruler of Africa and Asia; "his world bowed down to him."

His winters were spent profitably making war. In summer when the river was high he and his elite cohorts sailed up and down the Nile terrorizing Egypt into its best behavior. No hamlet administrator escaped his questioning. No fortress roll or farm report, tax statement and armament list, could escape the falcon eye of Thothmes III.

The fine tomb of Rekhmire, his Grand Vizier, in Western Thebes, records a list of tribute received by Thothmes. Emissaries from conquered lands are shown carrying treasure into the king's palace in Thebes. These diplomatic "gifts" from the puppet kings were actually bribes offered in the hope that the conqueror would cease paying return visits. Tribute, battle plunder and taxes continued to pour into the Thothmes coffers and storehouses. Gold and silver, jewels, richly ornamented chariots, horses, ivory—every conceivable form of wealth came in continual tribute from kings in Asia and Africa, from Assyrians and Hittites, from Tunip and Nubia. Even "wretched Kush" bled its coffers for Thothmes III.

He divided his plunder with his soldiers and Amon. The god was being richly awarded for its defection from Hatshepsut. Thothmes enlarged the Karnak temple. New furnishings for the great hall of worship were supposed to have been designed by him. New temples and chapels rose to Amon "giver of victories." New festivals and feasts were held in the god's name.

Thothmes was covering Egypt with his own statues and memorials and detailed accounts of his victories and good works. Pylons, portals, doors, gates, chapels, shrines, monuments, buildings and restorations were raised in the Thothmes name, more, he claimed, "than any king has done since the beginning." Religious and government buildings were built to a larger scale. Construction zoomed as never before. Imperial Egypt was larger and richer than it had ever been, or would be again.

All Thothmes was building was intended, as Hatshepsut had before him, to last through eternity.

Among his works is the seventh pylon at the Karnak temple. The pyramid gate shows Thothmes the triumphant conqueror with captives kneeling at his feet. Prayers for mercy are apparent on their stone lips. He shows them none. With efficient dispatch, Thothmes is lopping off their heads.

His Annals, inscribed on the inner walls of the Karnak temple, is the longest and most complete account of the exploits of any Egyptian king and the most important historical inscription in Egypt. Thothmes listed all his victories. He recorded his own version of his divine appointment to the throne. He recorded his famous Hymn of Victory in which he quoted words spoken to him by Amon-Re, Lord of the Thrones of the Two Lands.

I give thee valor and victory over all foreign countries,
I set the glory and the fear of thee in all lands,
The terror of thee is as far as the four supports of heaven . . .

Hatshepsut must have sensed that terror before dying.

Thothmes had made himself the strongest, richest and most feared monarch in the world, but he had not sated his thirst for vengeance. How else can we explain the outburst of anger that came to him after twenty years of uninterrupted successes? For Hatshepsut had been dead twenty years when he finally unleashed his hatred against her.

The nature of his revenge is more appalling when we recall more laudable acts on the part of this greatest of kings.

The long humiliation, the boyish frustrations, the relegation in manhood to second place, the refusal of equal powers, were appeased in his attack on a woman long dead. Hatshepsut had been his queen, his father's wife, his "sister," his aunt, the grandmother of his children, his co-regent, and, many authorities believe, his wife. (The Encyclopedia of Egyptian Civilization describes her as his "aunt-wife.")

The evidence of his hatred is in the ruins at Deir el-Bahari.

Thothmes launched his belated attack with the same fury he showed the enemies of the Empire. He determined to erase her name and all references to her from the face of Egypt. Only then would she be truly dead to him and the scars on his ego could fade.

He sent squads of soldiers armed with axes and chisels to Western Thebes. They had their orders; all must be as if a woman named Hatshepsut had never lived. It may have been at this time that the graves of Sennemut and her other friends were entered and vandalized.

The destroyers marched into the exquisite Deir el-Bahari temple. They chiseled out her cartouches and portraits and names and inscriptions. They took axes to her rows of statues of herself and of all the hundreds she had raised to perpetuate her personality in Egypt, not one statue was left whole. Hatshepsut as king, goddess or Sphinx was smashed into fragments that were hurled into a quarry nearby where the priests of her temple had tossed the surplus of small offerings left in the shrines by worshipers, such as thousands of strings of scarab beads.

The places that held her name were carved over with the names of Thothmes III, II, or I. Her name was left in a few places, perhaps by accident.

The Punt series received little damage, probably because she had not taken an active part in the expedition.

Her beautiful temple was left standing. They dared not demolish a building dedicated to Amon!

We can imagine the satisfaction Thothmes knew as he looked down into the gravel pit onto thousands of granite fragments that had once been the statues of Hatshepsut. At last he had washed his hands of that woman!

Thousands of years later experts from the Metropolitan Museum's Department of Antiquities were to fit together these stone fragments with painstaking care, so that we may see again her statues ordered by Hatshepsut, including that of the large Sphinx that guards the museum entrance in New York.

When the orgy of destruction ended, all her images were broken and her name had been chiseled from all monuments. Even her beloved myrrh trees in the Deir el-Bahari colonnade were uprooted and burned.

Her obelisks in the Karnak temple baffled the wreckers. They stood tall and defiant against the sky. Thothmes the mighty conqueror could look far up overhead and read the boasting of King Hatshepsut, who had raised these pillars "to her father Amon, Lord of Karnak, that her name might remain enduring in this temple forever and ever."

Hatshepsut had been dead twenty years but her obelisks still spoke for her.

They still speak for her. Thothmes gave up his attempt to destroy them and had them sealed in behind a wall of solid stone masonry. It has been called the first spite fence in history. He did not take the precaution of having her inscriptions erased before their concealment and to this we owe their preservation. In this present century, when the wall was taken down, all Hatshepsut had wished to say on that glorious occasion when the pillars were raised were revealed, enduring in the Great Temple of Karnak forever and ever.

Thothmes concluded his vicious attack against the dead Hatshepsut with the certainty that he had destroyed her memory forever.

He was a great man who was capable of the pettiest meanness. The Thothmesid feud was not over. He continued to show his hatred of the dead woman who had made him a king by laying claim to all she had done.

He took credit for the building of her beautiful Deir el-Bahari temple when he defaced her inscriptions and placed his name over hers on its walls.

He built his own chapel to Hathor there over her Hathor shrine.

He had a new coffin made of quartzite for his grandfather Thothmes I, and took the mummy from her tomb where she had it hidden.

He claimed to have built the sixth and eighth pylons at Karnak. Both had been built by Hatshepsut.

He defaced the quartzite chapel she had built at Karnak to house the sacred barque of Amon and built a red granite Amon chapel of his own.

He rebuilt and renamed the hall where her obelisks were hidden behind his concealing wall. He raised a pair of obelisks of his own before her hidden ones. The hall was used for his festivals and he feasted there aware that behind the thick masonry wall the boastings of Hatshepsut still promised that she would live forever.

Statues of King Thothmes as king or god or Sphinx rose by the hundreds where similiar statues of Hatshepsut once stood.

In much that Thothmes was doing he seemed to be gloating. "Anything you have done, I have done better."

All Eighteenth Dynasty kings portrayed themselves as colossi. Hatshepsut had followed in the family pattern and Thothmes followed her. They thought of themselves as giants and certainly not as ordinary folk. In this, both were right.

At one time during the years of Thothmes' reign a tremendous star blazed across the Egyptian sky. (It is supposed to have been Haley's comet.) All Egypt fell on its knees before the miracle. Did the people, awed by that flaming star, remember their beautiful Hatshepsut who had vanished over the horizon of history?

The pride Thothmes took in his deeds and victories showed in his carefully detailed inscriptions in the Great Temple. The military accounts are the product of an orderly mind that knew exactly what it wished to express. In one place the king serves as his own character witness. "My Majesty detests falsehood. It is not in me to weave tall stories."

Did he actually believe in his miraculous appointment by Amon in the Temple? And did Hatshepsut believe in her own divine birth? Each claimed to have talked with and been chosen by the god. We cannot know how much of this was due to hard-core ambition, and how much to religious ecstasy.

Hatshepsut had claimed to be a son of Amon. Thothmes called himself the son of Amon. He took on many of the epithets Hatshepsut had used, including the following of his own name with the flattering, "living forever" or "beautiful of years."

Both men and women in early Egypt thought of themselves as beautiful. They left prayers in their graves that their beauty be remembered. Kings boasted of their beauty. It was not a wholly feminine privilege.

Hatshepsut's complacent description of herself as being "more beautiful than anything," may have added fuel to Thothmes' rage against her, but he could not have considered it bad form. He had carved on a monument at Karnak, in an ode dedicated to Amon:

"I am his son who came forth from him . . . Thothmes, Beautiful of Form . . . princes of all lands do obeisance because of the fame of my majesty; my terror was in the hearts of the Nine Bows; all lands were under my sandals."

Hatshepsut had praised herself in almost the same words.

Thothmes added: "The monument is a work in the temple for

a memorial of my beauty in his house, and I shall endure . . . forever."

Thothmes grew old but his energy did not wither. He continued to lead his army on forays into Asia. He continued to build. On every return from a conquered land he brought more riches to expend on his flamboyant plans. He is on record as having placed two obelisks of solid gold in the Karnak temple! That had been Hatshepsut's dream, but only Thothmes was rich enough to raise pillars of gold. If they did exist they have long since been stolen and melted down.

Of his obelisks, one stands now in Istanbul and another is the obelisk in Central Park in New York, behind the Metropolitan Museum.

He had only one failure, after he had reduced the fame of Hatshepsut to rubble. He had an obelisk cut in honor of the sun. It was not raised when he died and lay neglected for many years outside the Karnak temple on the bank of the sacred lake. His son Amonhotep II ignored it and it was finally raised by his son Thothmes IV, who believed he owed his throne to a miraculous dream in which he saw and spoke to the sun-god. Visitors to Rome have seen this pillar in the piazza of St. John Lateran.

There is a place on the walls of the temple at Karnak where the personalities of Thothmes and Hatshepsut touch for the last time. Thothmes is shown paying devotion to her statue. Why he left this portrayal of them together, after all the damage done to her memory, is another small mystery in their curious relationship. His attitude in the picture shows a devotion it is not likely he ever paid Hatshepsut while she lived.

She had been dead for thirty-four years when a Theban mason raised chisel to stone and carefully engraved an important obituary.

> . . . Behold! The King ended his time of existence of many good years of victory, from the first year to the fifty-fourth . . . On the thirtieth of the third month of Proyet, the Maj-

esty of the King, Thothmes, true of voice, ascended to Heaven and joined the Sun's disk; the follower of God met his maker.

Thothmes III, Founder of the Empire, Conqueror of Asia, military commander, administrator, statesman and king, and the strongest Pharaoh ever to rule Egypt, was a ruthless despot and a great Egyptian. He was probably the murderer of Hatshepsut, still, much of the greatness of Egypt died with him.

"How greatly the gods loved him," was written of Thothmes III.

He tried to make her name anonymous and his own remembered. Within a few centuries his name was also forgotten. Even the names of the gods were lost underground.

His was the splendid interment he had planned, carried out by his son Amonhotep II. Thothmes was buried in his cliffside tomb in the Valley of the Kings near the graves of Hatshepsut and his father. Hatshepsut's daughter, his wife Queen Hatshepset, was buried with him.

And still, when found, his tomb had been looted and his mummy was found in another place. It was still in its wooden coffin inside the yellow quartzite sarcophagus, but the body had been torn into three parts and stripped of its linen wrappings by grave robbers. The arched Thothmesid nose was crushed.

The robbers had been as ruthless as Thothmes had been toward Hatshepsut.

The Annals Thothmes had registered on the Karnak walls with the promise that they would last forever was credited for many years to a later king.

Visitors linger over the mummy of the great Thothmes III in the Cairo Museum. All the Thothmesid pride that remains to this greatest of the Eighteenth Dynasty kings is in the way he is holding his left hand. It is clenched against his right shoulder as if it still gripped the royal sickle and flail.

Hatshepsut may have anointed in life that now broken body with myrrh, as queens did the limbs of those they loved. We study the dead mutilated face, sealed forever with its terrible secrets, and wonder what the despotic pair meant to one another and what bred between them such lasting enmity. Sibling rivalry? Sex antagonism? Love turned to hate, family resentments, the thrust for power?

No trace of the anger that reached its breaking point shows on the sunken features of Thothmes III. Egypt's strongest monarch lies in his narrow glass case, reduced for all his one time majesty to being "a shriveled leaf upon the stream of time."

And Hatshepsut? Where is she?

The sun-god Re cast a copper sheen over the Theban cliffs and the temple at Deir el-Bahari. Mohammed Selah, the inspector general of Western Thebes, and I, were relaxing over cokes at the base of Hatshepsut's temple. The opening to the empty tomb of Sennemut was a gaping gravel pit beneath Hatshepsut's magnificent ruined shrine.

We were resting after scrambling up a steep shale-sliding path to her hillside grave in the Valley of the Kings. Steel mesh barred the entrance and inside it clouds of bats were clinging to the wires. As we watched the creatures dropped one at a time to the mound of dead bats at the base of the door. They were being held captive in the tomb until all died of starvation and the place could be aired and studied.

I waived the privilege of entry. Not even to see what Hatshepsut had painted on the walls of her tomb would I follow my host through thousands of bats dead and alive. And Hatshepsut, who had planned and furnished this underground mansion of death, had not been permitted to rest there, near her father in the Valley of the Kings.

When Davis cleared the Hatshepsut grave in 1904, her two handsome sarcophagi were found empty. Her canopic box had been used to hold the viscera of a later queen.

Her father's mummy was found in a well at Deir el-Bahari. That of Hatshepsut has never been found.

She reigned with three kings and was "king" of Egypt for seventeen years. She lived five years after that and what happened then we do not know. She may have died in her own golden bed in her palace at Thebes. The army may have turned against her. The Amon priests could have fomented a rebellion.

It is more logical to believe that Thothmes had her poisoned. He was a king who brooked no opposition and poison was ever an occupational hazard for Egyptian royalty.

Across the river the broken walls of Karnak reflected the copper light. Once her obelisks flashed their gilded tips over those walls like the sun "lighting all the Two Lands." One still stands there, dominating the ancient Thebes that has become modern Luxor, representing all that civilization owes to Egypt, and Egypt to her.

It seems incredible that for centuries Thebes itself was a lost city and no one recognized the pillared ruins as fabled Karnak.

The Deir el-Bahari temple before us had vanished under landslide as all memory of Hatshepsut vanished.

Its now uncovered ruins rising terrace upon terrace on the hill of Gurn are her splendid cenotaph. No woman has had one more beautiful.

We talked, Mr. Selah and I, of the discoveries on this site that had brought together the life story of Hatshepsut after more than three thousand years. Fragment and hieroglyph had been fitted together, forming the mosaic whole. Only a few weeks before another chapel built by Thothmes over Hatshepsut's temple had been found under a landslide. A narrow stone walk covered with shale had led the archaeologists there.

Egyptian earth has been probed for centuries but it still yields surprises.

All praise goes to those who have dug and persevered in discomfort and actual danger, and to those who search through the defaced inscriptions to their original meanings. Hatshepsut's writings on her glorious temple have been mutilated by many kings, but Deir el-Bahari still speaks for her. Alexander Moret has written that she seemed to have had "all the qualities of a Pharaoh, and probably the only reproach that was brought against her was that she was a woman."

The portraits she has left of herself in the Deir el-Bahari temple are those of a woman small and delicate of form, touchingly brave in the short boyish kilts, in the proud stance of the first woman to rule alone a now-vanished world.

The sun warmed our shoulders and the terraced temple shimmered in the strong light. My thoughts hazed. I remembered Hatshepsut had built this temple that her beauty be remembered. What personal relics remained of her? There are the reconstructed statues, the sarcophagi, the pictures and words and a pretty ornamented box she had never used. Where are the jewels, the furniture, the incredible fortune that were hers?

I remembered how little is left of a later queen, Nefertiti, whose life I had written. Why has all that belonged to these two glamorous women disappeared when the museums hold articles that belonged to kings and queens who lived long before them? And neither of their bodies found. . . .

In the Nefertiti book I had hazarded a guess that had seemed wild even to me, that someday her grave might be found. It was sheer guesswork, based on nothing known then.

Now I remarked dreamily, "Perhaps some day Nefertiti will be found here in Western Thebes."

My host's emphatic response startled me.

"Not here! At Amarna!"

Four artifacts carrying the name of Tutankhamon led to that fabulous find in the Valley of the Kings. Now half a dozen artifacts have been dug up on the Amarna site with Nefertiti's name. On this day as we drank our cokes at Deir el-Bahari archaeologists were hard at work on that site that was long ago thought exhausted, in the hope of finding her tomb.

Our thoughts meshed and soared. If Nefertiti, why not Hatshepsut? And the tremendous treasure buried with Rameses II has never been found!

So much that we know once existed is still missing. There is much we do not know.

Egypt, and in fact all of our wonderful world, has not exhausted its yield of secrets. Men continue to dig, to discover, and slowly fit together the picture puzzle of our past. Until the last discovery is made, how can we possibly write *The End?*

BIBLIOGRAPHY

A Guide to the Egyptian Museum. Government Printing Offices, Cairo, Egypt, 1966.

Annales du Service des Antiquities de l'Egypte. Cairo, Egypt.

Anthes, Rudolf, *Bust of Nefertete.* The Berlin State Museum, Egyptian Department.

———, *Tutankhamun Treasures.* Circulated by the Smithsonian Institution, The University Museum, University of Pennsylvania, 1961–63.

Bakry, H. S. K., Ph.D., *A Brief Study of Mummies and Mummification.* Al-Takaddum Press, Cairo, Egypt, 1965.

Bezold, Charles, *Oriental Diplomacy.* Luzac and Company, London, 1893.

Bibby, Geoffrey, *Four Thousand Years Ago.* Alfred A. Knopf, Inc., 1961.

Borchardt, Ludwig, *Excavations at Tell el-Amarna.* Orientalia, 1915.

Breasted, James Henry, *Ancient Records of Thebes.* Edited by W. R. Harper, University Press, Chicago, 1906.

———, *The Conquest of Civilization.* Edited by Dr. Edith Williams Ware. New edition, Harper and Row, New York, Evanston and London.

———, *A History of Egypt.* Charles Scribner's Sons, reprint 1959.

———, *Ancient Records of Egypt.* University of Chicago Press, Chicago, 1929.

Carter, Howard, *The Tomb of Tutankhamon.* George H. Doran and Co., London, 1927.

CERAM, C. W., *Gods, Graves and Scholars.* Alfred A. Knopf, New York, 1956.

COTTRELL, LEONARD, *The Anvil of Civilization.* New American Library, 1960.

——, *Life Under the Pharaohs.* Holt, Rinehart and Winston, Inc., New York City, 1960.

DANIEL, GLYN E., *A Hundred Years of Archaeology.* Gerald Duckworth Company, Ltd., 1952.

DESROCHES-NOBLECOURT, CHRISTIANE, *Tutankhhamen.* New York Graphic Society, 1963.

DIA, ABOU-GHAZI, *The Mummies Room in the Cairo Museum (No. 52), or A Supplement to Engelbach and Derry's Article on Mummification.* Annales du Service, Archaeology, Cairo, Egypt, 1946 and 1961.

Egyptian Museum, published by Egyptian State Tourist Administration.

Encyclopaedia Brittanica.

FAIRSERVIS, WALTER A., JR., *The Ancient Kingdoms of the Nile.* Thomas Y. Crowell Co., New York, 1962.

FRANKFORT, HENRI, *The Birth of Civilization in the Near East.* Anchor Books, Doubleday and Company, Inc., Garden City, New York, 1956.

——, editor, *Mural Paintings at El-Amarneh.* Egypt Exploration Society, London, 1929.

FRAZER, SIR JAMES GEORGE, *The New Golden Bough.* Criterion Books, 1959.

FREEDMAN, DAVID NOEL, and WRIGHT, G. ERNEST, editors. *The Biblical Archaeologist Reader,* Anchor Books, Doubleday and Company, Inc., Garden City, New York, 1961.

GLANVILLE, S. R. K., M.A., *Daily Life in Ancient Egypt.* George Routledge and Sons, Ltd., London, 1930.

HALL, H. R., *The Ancient History of the Near East.* Tenth edition, Methuen and Co., Ltd., London, 1947.

HAYES, WILLIAM C., *The Scepter of Egypt.* Harper and Bros., in cooperation with the Museum of Art, New York, 1953.

HOLMES, WINIFRED, *She Was Queen of Egypt.* G. Bell and Sons, London, 1957.

HUXLEY, JULIAN, *From an Antique Land.* Crown Publishers, New York, 1955.

Journals of Egyptian Archaeology, The Egyptian Exploration Society, London.

KELLER, WERNER, *The Bible as History.* William Morrow and Company, New York, 1956.

LAUER, JEAN-PHILIPPE, *Les Pyramides de Sakkarah.* Imprimerie de l'Institut Graphique Egyptien, Cairo, Egypt, 1961.

LLOYD, SETON, *The Art of the Ancient Near East.* Frederick A. Praeger, New York, 1961.

MOHAMMED, DR. M. ABDUL-QUADER, *Two Theban Tombs,* 1963.

MORET, ALEXANDER, *Kings and Gods of Egypt.* G. P. Putnam's Sons, New York, 1912.

MURRAY, M. A., *The Splendour that Was Egypt.* First Four Square Edition, New English Library, Ltd., Barnard's Inn, Holborn, London, 1965.

MUSÉE DU CAIRE, *Description Sommaire des Principaux Monuments.* Imprimerie Nationale, Le Caire, 1956.

NAVILLE, EDOUARD, *Deir el-Bahari.* Four Volumes, Egyptian Exploration Fund, London, England.

NEWBERRY, PERCY E., *The Journal of Egyptian Archaeology,* May, 1932.

NIEBUHR, DR. CARL (pseudonym for Carl Krug), *The Ancient East II—The Tell El Amarna Period.* Translated by J. Hutchinson. David Nutt, London, 1903.

NIMS, CHARLES F., *Thebes of the Pharaohs.* Photo by William Swaan. Stein and Day, New York, 1965.

NORTH, LEIGH, *Predecessors of Cleopatra.* Broadway Publishing Company, New York, 1906.

PENDLEBURY, J. D. S., *The City of Akhenaten.* Egypt Exploration Society, Oxford University Press, Amen House, London, 1951.

———, *Tell-el Amarna.* Lovat Dickson and Thompson, Ltd., London, 1935.

PETRIE, FLINDERS, *Social Life in Ancient Egypt.* Constable, 1923.

POSENER, GEORGES, with the assistance of Serge Sauneron and Jean Yvotte, *Encyclopedia of Egyptian Civilization.* Tudor Publishing Company, New York.

PRITCHARD, JAMES B., editor, *Ancient Near Eastern Texts Relating to the Old Testament,* Princeton University Press, 1955.

ROEBUCK, CARL, *The World of Ancient Times.* Charles Scribner's Sons, New York, 1966.

SMITH, WILLIAM STEVENSON, *Ancient Egypt.* Published by Beacon Press with the Museum of Fine Arts, Boston, 1961.

STEINDORFF, GEORGE, and SEELE, KEITH C., *When Egypt Ruled the East.* University of Chicago Press, Chicago and London. Fourth Impression, 1965.

VELIKOVSKY, IMMANUEL, *Oedipus and Akhnaton.* Doubleday and Company, Inc., New York, 1960.

WEIGALL, ARTHUR, *History of the Pharaohs.* Thornton Butterworth, Ltd., London, 1952.

WHITE, J. E. MANCHIP (M. A. Contab), *Ancient Egypt,* Allan Wingate, London, 1952.

WILKINSON, SIR JOHN GARDNER, *Ancient Egyptians,* Volumes I and II. John Murray, England, 1871.

WILSON, JOHN A., *The Burden of Egypt.* University of Chicago Press, Chicago, 1951.

———, *The Culture of Ancient Egypt.* Phoenix Books, The University of Chicago Press, 1951.

WINLOCK, H. E., *Excavations at Deir el-Bahri, 1911–1931.* Macmillan Company, New York, 1942.

WOOLLEY, SIR LEONARD, *Digging Up the Past.* Penguin Books, Baltimore, Maryland, 1961.

INDEX